Eva

nish.

THE
ISLE OF WIGHT
BOOK
OF
DAYS

JAN TOMS

The
History
Press

First published 2014

The History Press
The Mill, Brimscombe Port
Stroud, Gloucestershire, GL5 2QG
www.thehistorypress.co.uk

British Library Cataloguing in Publication Data.
A catalogue record for this book is available from the British Library.

ISBN 978 0 7509 5354 2

Typesetting and origination by The History Press
Printed in India

~ January 1st ~

1900: On the first day of a new century, from her drawing room at Osborne House, Queen Victoria sat down to record her thoughts. 'I begin today a New Year and a new century, full of anxiety and fear of what may be before us! May all near and dear ones be protected. I pray that God may spare me yet a short while for my children, friends and dear country ...' The queen had reason to feel less than optimistic. As the year opened, Britain was caught up in the Boer Wars where upwards of 50,000 people perished, including her grandson Prince Christian Victor of Schleswig-Holstein who died of enteric fever. In the Far East, the Boxer Rebellion smouldered but, on a more positive note, Victoria made an historic visit to Dublin and an increasingly rare visit to London. Apart from these excursions she remained at Osborne House. The death from cancer of her second son Alfred, Duke of Edinburgh was a devastating blow. The queen, to date the longest reigning British monarch, now plagued with arthritis, was to survive for another year and three weeks. (*Queen Victoria's Journals*, January 1st 1900)

— JANUARY 2ND —

1792: Today's *Hampshire Chronicle* gave notice of the forthcoming sale to be held on Saturday 7th at the Green Dragon Inn, Newport. It was advertised in the following terms:

> All that complete, new-built and commodious WATER CORN-MILL known by the name of EAST MEDINA MILL, commonly called BOTANY BAY MILL, situate in the parish of Whippingham in the Isle of Wight. The building is 80 feet in length, 25 feet wide and five doors above each other with a flat roof for drying, and at present can grind 30 loads of wheat per week; and is so constructed that at a small expense it may be made capable of grinding 50 loads of wheat per week, or converted into two commodious mills ... No mill in the county of Hants can be better situated for business ... being in a plentiful corn county with the convenience of vessels of 70 tons burthen, lying close alongside the mill. For further particulars, apply Mr John Gilbert, Attorney, Newport, Isle of Wight.

The mill had been built in 1790 and possibly got its alternative name from supplying ship's biscuit to the convict ships that moored nearby. On several occasions it served as a barracks and it ceased trading as a mill in 1939. A fire later caused irreparable damage and it was demolished in 1950. The site is now a marina known as Island Harbour. (*Hampshire Chronicle*, January 2nd 1792)

~ January 3rd ~

1891: A ball planned on this day to celebrate the appointment of Prince Henry of Battenberg as Governor of the Isle of Wight and Keeper of Carisbrooke Castle was postponed because the banqueting hall at Osborne would not be ready for some time. The day was saved when the event was transferred instead to Northwood House at Cowes. The *Hampshire Telegraph* reported that by going to Cowes the old traditions of entertaining royalty would be revived. As it explained: 'The late owner, Mr Ward had had theological rather than social tastes, and when he came into the property, shortly after his secession to the Roman Church, his first act was to obliterate the frescoes on the drawing room walls as being too Pagan to be proper in the home of a Papist gentleman. Perhaps it was with some chagrin that he learned later that they were the copy of a set within the Vatican.' (*Hampshire Telegraph*, January 3rd 1891)

— JANUARY 4TH —

1853: Feelings ran high when Felix Cosgrove, a former private with the Connaught (88th) Rangers based at Parkhurst Barracks, was forcibly detained and forbidden to deliver a lecture at Ryde. Cosgrove had devoted much of his time to studying subjects of a 'scientific, historical and metaphysical nature' and by lecturing on these themes he had raised sufficient money to buy himself out of the army. His discharge date was December 31st 1852. Leaflets had been distributed announcing the lecture, the title being 'Popery, and the Idolatries Practised in the Church of Rome'. Cosgrove's regiment, the 88th Volunteers, was a Catholic unit and the day before the lecture two soldiers, armed with muskets and fixed bayonets, called at Cosgrove's lodgings and forcibly escorted him through Newport and to the orderly room at the barracks. He was ordered by his commanding officer not to give the lecture. When he questioned whose authority they acted on, he was told that a letter had been received from a 'Catholic in Ryde'. The officer refused to give the correspondent's name. An investigation was demanded into the forcible restraint of Felix Cosgrove, no longer a serving soldier, on the say-so of a priest. The army was apparently an unwilling instrument in carrying out this act. (*Isle of Wight Observer*, January 4th 1853)

~ JANUARY 5TH ~

1947: In good weather the Greek ship *Varvassi*, carrying nearly 25,000 boxes of mandarins, 438 casks of wine and various ores, ran aground on the submerged rocks about 100 yards from the Needles. The Yarmouth lifeboat immediately went to her assistance but she declined help, waiting instead for a tug to pull her free. Overnight the weather worsened; waves enveloped the ship and it was taking on water. Despite the efforts of the crew the only answer was to abandon ship. All thirty-five aboard were safely taken to Yarmouth in lifeboats. Here they received terrific kindness, being fed and clothed at the Kings Head. Mr Rupert Simpson and Mr Morris Dabell, members of local branches of the Shipwrecked Mariners' Society, managed to collect enough clothing for all thirty-five crewmembers. One of the rescued men presented the ship's mascot, a kitten, to the landlord of the pub. The following day some of the crew returned to the wreck to collect their belongings, including various pets. There was also concern for seven heifers on board, kept for meat during the journey. The captain refused to have them shot, and fed and watered them, returning at considerable risk on another occasion to do so, but unhappily the British authorities refused permission to bring them ashore so they were destroyed. On a happier note for local people, the boxes of fruit were brought ashore to be sold, some despatched for a knock-down price, others simply vanishing. A part of the cargo of wine (about eighty barrels) had broken free and over the next few days they were discovered floating in the sea to be picked up by local fishermen. Not all of it made its way to the customs! (*The Dundee Courier*, January 6th 1947)

← JANUARY 6TH →

1873: Today a report from Portsmouth detailed the sinking of the brig *Valid* that came to grief two days earlier off St Catherines with the loss of all hands. A heavy gale had blown from the south-west as the ship struggled to avoid the rocks known as 'Rocken–End-Race'. Finding herself among the breakers her crew of nine took to the longboat and hoisted a distress signal while struggling with the heavy surf. On shore, Mr A. Livesay from Sandrock Spring Cottage sent his servant on horseback to inform the members of the Brooke Lifeboat Station but, instead of launching the boat immediately, it was carried on a waggon along the military road towards Chale Bay where there was then no way to get it down the cliff. The longboat overturned and all nine crewmembers were drowned. Three of the bodies were washed ashore the following day and carried to the Clarendon at Chale for an inquest. The *Valid* was carrying spices and other foreign products that were claimed by the Receiver of Wrecks. (*Reynold's Newspaper*, January 12th 1873)

— January 7th —

1907: Less than two weeks after Christmas, the whole of Ryde turned out to mourn the deaths of lifeboatman Henry Heward and fisherman Frank Haynes. The occasion was the more poignant in that they had been called out to rescue a rower who turned out not to have been in difficulties. Having failed to find anyone, the lifeboat *Selina* turned back and was nearing Ryde Pier when a freak wave upturned it, throwing all nine crewmen into the sea. The men clung onto their upturned craft shouting to attract attention, but no one heard them. They drifted across the Solent and were finally rescued within a few yards of Southsea Castle. In spite of their efforts to help each other, Heward and Haynes succumbed to cold and exhaustion. At the inquest, one question was why the men had decided to take the *Selina* rather than a self-righting boat that was available to them, but it was concluded that no blame was attached to anyone and this had seemed a sensible choice at the time. Unsurprisingly, the entire town wished to salute the tragic pair, lining the route from the town to St James church and then to the cemetery, and flags throughout were flown at half mast. It was especially tragic for Elizabeth, Frank Haynes' widow, for a few days before her husband's death her 3-month-old daughter Edith had died; the little one's coffin accompanied her father to the graveyard. They had earlier lost another little girl of 4 months. Elizabeth was also pregnant and their last child, Harold Victor James, was born after his father's death. (Courtesy of the Ryde Social Heritage Group)

⚊ January 8th ⚊

1898: Gunner Charles Edwards of the 13th Co. Royal Artillery found himself in court on this day, charged with stealing a till and its contents. Mr Fred Merwood, the grocer at the sub-post office at Norton Green, said that he left the room at around 5 p.m. to get some change and when he came back the till, which contained about 17–18s, was gone. Unsurprisingly, inquiries were made at neighbouring Golden Hill Fort. According to a soldier named Patrick Casey, he, Edwards and others had been for a drink that morning at the Standard in Freshwater and then gone for a beer at the Red Lion before continuing to the New Inn at Norton Green. Edwards had not paid for any drink and later he borrowed 1½d to go towards the 4d for a quart of beer. At the barracks, Casey and Edwards had argued and had a fight so Edwards left and returned later when they all played cards. Casey noticed that Edwards had about 2s in change and had also paid for refreshments. Edwards was in receipt of 1s a week, soldiers' pay, some of it reduced as a penalty for an earlier attempt at till robbery. His jacket was searched and about 8s discovered. However, as no one had actually seen him at the shop, the case was dismissed to applause that was 'quickly repressed'. (*Isle of Wight County Press*, January 8th 1898)

— JANUARY 9TH —

1897: Before the bench today in Newport was James Davey, aged 11 of Barton Village, prosecuted by his father Henry Davey, a widower and a fish hawker by trade, for stealing various articles of clothing from home on the previous Thursday and selling them. The prosecutor said that while he was away from home on Thursday, the prisoner entered and stole two pairs of trousers, a cape and a coat, which he afterwards found had been sold to a Mrs Barber, a lodging-housekeeper in East Street as rags, for 3½d. The prisoner said that he sold the clothes to get food, but the father said that he had plenty. The bench ordered the prisoner to receive six strokes with the birch and warned Mrs Barber to be more careful about purchasing things from children. Mrs Barber said the case was a great warning to her. (*Portsmouth Evening News*, January 12th 1897)

~ January 10th ~

1760: A meeting took place at the Sun Inn, Newport, to agree on the rules for the newly formed Society of Gentlemen. The usual preliminaries were passed, 'to meet monthly on ye Tuesday preceding or on the full moon. No gentleman to be admitted against whom 3 Black Balls shall appear, No gentleman once rejected to be proposed again' and so forth. The membership was strictly limited to Islanders and other conditions seemed to lean heavily on the consumption of alcohol. For example, every member absenting himself from the meeting was to forfeit three bottles of port 'toties quoties'. Such was the importance of port wine to the proceedings that, 'having declared that the Drinking of port Wine is prejudicial to his Health it is proposed that Mr White should, till his health is re-established be indulged with the drinking of Brandy and Water or Punch'. On another occasion, 'The most infamous practise has prevailed in this club, of drinking Mixtures with water after dinner – it is resolved that for the future, each member shall drink Wine on the penalty of one dozen of port for each offence.' ('Rules for the Formation of a Society of Gentlemen', Isle of Wight Public Record Office)

~ JANUARY 11TH ~

1879: A lengthy warning was issued to local traders about the dangers of 'Clerical Co-operation'. It had come to the notice of the press that not only were the civil service and the military conspiring against the tradesmen, but now the clergy had been encouraged to join the 'Clergy Co-operative Association Limited'. Clearly they intended to reap the profits that currently went to the tradesmen. In high dudgeon the *Isle of Wight Observer* reported that the 'intent [was] to supply such incongruous articles as grocery, guns, coals, church furniture, "bacca", beer and books. These rev traders will deal in spirits – not the spirits of charity, but in whisky, gin and rum.' The project was to cost £100,000 with 50,000 £2 shares. The *Observer* visualised that the church would next branch out into hotels and even 'Banking and Life Insurance' and that the profits that had hitherto gone to the tradesmen would now be lost to them: 'the connection between the tradesmen and the rich will be severed almost entirely.' The paper warned that little notice might have been taken of this scheme had not the name of 'a certain, well known Chaplain to the Queen' been implicated. It ended with a passionate warning that if the clergy persisted in being traders, then they would entirely lose the 'old fashioned respect and affection with which they have been hitherto regarded'. (*The Isle of Wight Observer*, January 11th 1879)

∼ January 12th ∼

1867: A correspondent calling himself the 'Gloworm' passed on the following snippet in today's *Yorkshire Gazette*: 'The poet laureate is about to leave the Island to take up residence in the metropolis, solely on account of the manner in which he is disturbed by "lion hunters of the island".' Tennyson had an aversion to uninvited visitors, whom he called the 'cockneys', many of whom made day trips from London especially to catch a glimpse of him. Fans would climb over his walls, hide in his trees and generally invade his privacy. He built a bridge from the back of his garden so that he could escape onto the downs behind his house, but his solitary rambles across High Down were frequently disturbed by 'groupies'. Such was the nuisance that during the season he sought solitude on the mainland. (*Yorkshire Gazette*, January 12th 1867)

– January 13th –

1898: On this day at Osborne House, Queen Victoria presented medals to eight soldiers who had fought at the Battle of Omdurman. The men arrived at East Cowes barracks and marched to Osborne where they were provided with lunch in the servants' quarters. They then went to the Indian or Green Room to await the arrival of the queen. Her majesty, arriving with Princess Beatrice and various other ladies of the court, was seated in a wheeled chair. She entered leaning upon the arm of her Indian servant, Abdul Karim. Acknowledging the men's salute, when the queen was seated her secretary, Sir Henry Ponsonby, introduced them one by one. Each man then knelt before her while she pinned the medal that bore the inscription 'for distinguished service in the field' to his breast. Colour Sergeant McIver of the Seaforth Highlanders had his arm in a sling and the queen 'spoke to him tenderly and asked if he was getting better'. A ninth soldier, Sergeant Instructor Lewis, was unable to attend because of ill health. (*Isle of Wight Observer*, January 14th 1898)

~ January 14th ~

1854: The *Isle of Wight Observer* carried a news item bound to infuriate Queen Victoria; they reprinted various charges brought against Prince Albert for undue interference in Home and Foreign Politics. Originally printed in the *Morning Herald*, the *Observer*'s column had been received with the 'most profound sensation by all classes in the Isle of Wight. The general belief is that these charges are not without foundation and that every influence will be exerted to smother enquiry.' The editorship of the *Observer* had 'entertained a very unfavourable opinion of the prince', since he had been nominated as Chancellor of Cambridge University against another candidate and won only by a bare majority, a step considered 'undignified'. In a similar situation he had accepted the Colonelcy of the Guards on the death of the Duke of Wellington, contrary to the expressed understanding of both Parliament and the army. He was considered as showing 'a lust for power sufficient to induce a belief that the rumours to which we have alluded may be substantially correct'. The *Observer* expressed regret that this situation should have arisen and looked forward to a time when Parliament had cleared it up. (*Isle of Wight Observer*, January 14th 1854)

— January 15th —

1887: A meeting of the Guardians of the Poor at the workhouse was sidetracked when Mr J.R. Deacon asked the committee, 'Is skating allowed on Sunday on the workhouse pond?' The chairman replied that he was not aware of any order forbidding it, to which Mr Deacon responded: 'Then we ought to make an order forbidding skating on the pond on Sundays.' A heated discussion followed, during which trustee Mr Blake said that 'skating on the pond is an ancient custom and it would be difficult to interfere', but Mr Deacon insisted that 'it was all out of character to sanction such a thing'. He therefore moved that no Sunday skating should be allowed, the proposal being seconded by Mr Morris. The chairman responded that 'it had always been the custom and he thought it would be very undesirable to lay down such a hard and fast line. It would be far better to leave it to people's own sense of propriety.' This was greeted by calls of 'hear! hear!' Charging for the privilege was then suggested to which the chairman responded that, beyond two of the workhouse officers (the porter and the house clerk) skating one Sunday, he knew nothing of it. It was pointed out that some officers from the barracks had applied and been given permission to skate. Mr Estcourt thought it was not seemly or becoming for officers of the house to skate on Sunday. Mr Tucker, however, assumed that there was no harm in them stretching their legs by taking a walk, so 'where the harm is in exercising their legs in another way, I can't imagine'. Mr White Popham added that 'there is surely no more harm in moving along on skates than in shoe leather'. On that note, the guardians voted to leave things as they were, to more shouts of 'hear! hear!' (Meeting of the Isle of Wight Board of Guardians,. January 15th 1887)

∼ January 16th ∼

1858: Having failed to find sufficient magistrates on the preceding Saturday, the magistrates' court took place on Monday instead. Before the bench was Peter Footman, a navvy working on the bed of the River Medina, charged with ill-treating his wife and threatening to shoot the landlady of the Row Barge public house in Pyle Street. Having been arrested in a state of intoxication, the two women stated that he had not only threatened to blow their brains out but had actually pulled the trigger twice whilst pointing the gun at the head of his landlady, a Mrs Cotton. Fortunately it misfired on both occasions. On the barrel being examined in court, it was found to be heavily charged with powder and mixed shot. When it came to the court, however, neither of the women would give evidence and in consequence there was no choice but to release the prisoner with a dire warning. The prisoner said that he was too drunk to remember anything about it and denied all knowledge of the gun. The weapon was retained by the court. (*The Hampshire Telegraph*, January 23rd 1858)

~ JANUARY 17TH ~

1904: Today 'hundreds of visitors from all parts of the Island visited All Saints church in Godshill in order to view the ancient church which had been so seriously injured by lightning on Thursday morning. The sacred edifice was thrown open to the public at noon, and from then till dusk there was a never-ceasing flow of spectators. The church presents a remarkable appearance and gives one the impression that it has been in disuse for some time. The church services were held in the Parish Room.' During a violent storm on Thursday, serious damage had occurred with the pinnacles of the roof torn off, the clock face torn out, the font split in the middle and the roof ruined. (*Portsmouth Evening News*, January 18th 1904)

⤙ JANUARY 18TH ⤚

1947: A destroyer picked up a man found clinging to a buoy in the Solent. He was identified as Arthur James Anderson, 39, who had escaped from a working party at Parkhurst ten days earlier and had been clinging to the buoy for 17 hours after a boat he stole from Gurnard sank. His feet heavily bandaged, he then appeared in court where he made the following statement:

> With regard to the property I stole … I only took cash and one or two articles of jewellery, with a view to their practical use … I refrained from taking basic rations and confined myself to tinned food … I was forced by exigencies of circumstance. I should like to tender my sincere apologies to the people concerned. Originally it was my intention to swim instead of stealing a boat … thus obviating the annoyance that I caused.

At the time of his capture he had 14*s* 6½*d* on him. He was wearing a pinstriped suit stolen from the home of a Newport councillor. Anderson was sent for trial at Winchester. As he left the court he waved and smiled at the crowd outside. (*Derby Daily Telegraph*, January 18th 1947)

~ January 19th ~

1892: On this day two pauper inmates of the Isle of Wight Union were charged with stealing a quantity of bones valued at 2s, the property of the Isle of Wight Board of Guardians. James Barling and James (alias) Arthur Jeffery, both described as able-bodied, had left the workhouse at 9.45 p.m. on the 19th January. The bones were stored in a shed and had been there in the evening, but the next morning the hasp on the door was broken and about 1cwt of bones were missing. Charles Cooper, a miller at St Cross in Newport who ran a bone mill, said that the accused had come to him on the morning of the 20th offering to sell him 64lbs of bones, which he bought. He believed he had given the money to Jeffery. Having been picked up, the pair were taken to the mill where the miller identified them. They were both committed for trial at the next quarter sessions. (*Isle of Wight Observer*, January 30th 1892)

─ January 20th ─

1860: A gruesome case came before the magistrates at Newport today. In court were two Americans, Edmund Lane and Gordon Hires, first and second mates of the ship *Anna*. They were accused of killing John Turtle, William Johnson, David Pagins, James Armstrong, William Pomery and a man called Frank on the voyage to England. The victims were all men of colour. Lane had struck Armstrong over the right eye with a mallet and felled him from the forecastle to the deck below. He then knocked out his eye which left Armstrong unable to carry out his duties, so Hires threw him overboard and dragged him along the water. When another man went to his rescue, he ordered, 'Don't haul the nigger in, cut him loose and let him go.' Hires released his hold and Armstrong was lost. James Turtle was accused by Hires of stealing rum and as punishment he stamped on his head, leaving him unable to work. Hires announced, 'Tell him if he don't come out and get on the pump, I'll murder him.' He then repeatedly stamped on Turtle's head, who died later that night. Similar violent punishment resulting in death was meted out to the other crewmen. An objection was raised as to the jurisdiction of the court after which the magistrate confirmed that as the accused were American citizens and the crimes had occurred outside British waters, he had no option but to release them. They were therefore escorted to Cowes amidst 'the hooting of the mob gathered outside the court'. A week later the *Isle of Wight Observer* was pleased to report that the accused had been arrested and charged elsewhere. (*Middlesex Chronicle*, January 21st 1860)

─ January 21st ─

1828: Magistrates at Newport Quarter Sessions were working long hours and the *Hampshire Chronicle* reported that on this day:

> The number of cases on the calendar occupied the attention of the Court till a very late hour. John Kingswell and James Mason for breaking into the Catholic Chapel in the night of Thursday se'nnight [*sic*], and stealing a pair of plated candlesticks and two silver boxes, were each sentenced to seven years transportation. This is the first instance of transportation by our Court for many years, and it is hoped that it will operate as a check on the numerous depredations to which this neighbourhood has been so long subjected ... The prisoners are very bad characters, one of them, Kingswell, having lately returned from Transportation.

Other cases involved 'George Stephens, an idle lad, for stealing a pair of shoes, to be imprisoned till this day and then to be whipped. Isaac Vine, for assault – seven days hard labour. Joseph Waldron, Wm. Bartlett, and George Tuck, for obstructing constables in their duty – to be imprisoned for various terms. Henry Hayward, for stealing a pair of shoes – one month's imprisonment, and to be whipped. James Jolliffe, landlord of the Nag's Head, for keeping a disorderly house – one month's hard labour.' (*Hampshire Chronicle,* January 28th 1828)

~ January 22nd ~

1901: The press, having reassured the public as to the queen's improved health when she rode out from Osborne on January 16th, soon afterwards reported that her condition was 'serious'. Her grandson Wilhelm abandoned his duties in Germany to hurry to her side. Other family members soon followed and on this day it was announced that her Majesty had died at 6.30 p.m. When the news reached London, Hubert von Herkomer, a German artist employed as an illustrator for the *Graphic* was despatched to Osborne House with a commission to paint the queen on her deathbed. He was not alone, for artist Emil Fuchs had been granted similar permission and throughout the night, the two men worked in the queen's bedroom, she being laid out on the bed in her bridal gown and surrounded by lilies. On the bedhead was a portrait of Prince Albert, also painted in death. Herkomer only had time to do an outline sketch but the queen's physician Sir James Reid, who had a glimpse of it, pronounced it an ethereal and altogether flattering portrait of his royal patient. Herkomer and Fuchs travelled back together on the train but throughout the journey nobody spoke, which Fuchs later blamed on Herkomer because, being a Royal Academician, it was up to him to speak first. Herkomer's watercolour of the dead queen was entitled *Queen Victoria on her Deathbed, Osborne during the night of January 23 1901*, framed in ebony and hangs outside the bedroom at Osborne House. (J. Saxon Mills, MA, *The Life and Letters of Sir Hubert Herkomer*)

~ January 23rd ~

1881: 'Nothing is talked of here but the frost and the snow.' The Island had been more badly hit by the weather than the mainland and, since Saturday the 15th, 120 men had been employed cutting a way through the streets with the use of a hastily made snowplough. On Monday there had been a heavy fog and consequently no boats. And although there was no thaw on the Tuesday, the sun was shining. The Compassionate Fund had been put to good effect in assisting the old and infirm and the cold remained as intense as ever; fish, including eels were being picked up frozen hard on the beach. Meanwhile, on Sunday 23rd Queen Victoria drove from Osborne Cottage to East Cowes in a sleigh, then crossed the river and walked through the snow to the church while the Empress Eugenie, then a guest at Osborne, attended a service at the Catholic church. (*The Hampshire Advertiser*, January 28th 1881)

– January 24th –

1863: 'A bazaar and fancy fair has been held this week at Belgrave House, the residence of Dr and Mrs Martin in aid of the distressed Lancashire operatives: it commenced on Tuesday and was continued up to Friday. The articles for sale consisted of a large assortment of the useful and ornamental, together with some valuable paintings, several of which were presented by General Napier. There were also others, one a sketch in water colors [*sic*] of the beach, rocks, and cliffs at Highport near Ventnor by W. Player, esq., was much admired. There were also colored [*sic*] prints, books, ornaments, medieval printing, children's clothing, dolls and etc. Two dolls, 100 years old, dressed in the male and female costume of the last century, were exhibited for sale. The stalls were conducted as follows: – Mrs Martin assisted by Miss Kelly; Miss Martin assisted by Miss Nairn; Miss Macknees, Misses Cumberledge; Miss Kelly, and Miss Johnson.' There were also a handful of 'gentleman assistants'. Despite the bad weather, upwards of £75 had been raised by Wednesday night and the journalist reminded the readers that 'the distress still exists, and is likely to do so for some time'. Doing good works was a major occupation for the unmarried daughters of well-to-do families and this report illustrates that the welfare of the wider population was also of concern to Islanders. (*Isle of Wight Observer*, January 24th 1863)

— January 25th —

1842: Today being the christening of Albert Edward, the new Prince of Wales, at St George's Chapel Windsor, numerous celebrations took place across the Island. A 'much respected gentleman', l'Abbe de Grentlie who lived at Caesar's Cottage near Newport, fired a royal salute from his cannon and raised the colours that had been presented to him by Queen Victoria's father, the Duke of Kent who had patronised his late academy. At the Black Gang hotel a celebratory pigeon shoot took place by twelve crack shots, the winner being Mr Horlick of Dungewood. Mr Jacobs of the hotel then supplied a well-attended dinner. Across the Island the church bells rang and there were dinners at the Vine and Bugle inns, while gifts of coal was supplied for the poor. Meanwhile, business continued as usual and a meeting took place at the Grapes Tavern to appoint a deputation to meet up with other deputations at Southampton in order to consider what to do about the Corn Laws. The *Hampshire Telegraph* added that 'The Chartists interrupted the business of the meeting as usual, for about an hour.' (*Hampshire Telegraph*, January 29th 1842)

— January 26th —

1862: At an inquest on Newport printer Robert James Denyer, Samuel Goodwin, landlord of the Railway Tavern, gave evidence that Denyer, one of his regulars, had been worried about the health of his dog. He had called in briefly on the night in question (the 26th) then gone home to check on the dog, accompanied by another customer, Thomas Cheverton. They returned after about half an hour and Denyer drank a glass of rum then joined Cheverton in a pint of beer. He asked Goodwin to make up some gruel for the dog and at around 11.30 p.m. Denyer and Cheverton left together. Cheverton stated that at the house, where a fire was lit, Denyer declared his intention to sit up all night with the dog and Cheverton helped him administer a dose of castor oil. He left around 12.15 a.m. and Denyer locked the door behind him. When he returned the following morning he could rouse no one so when Denyer's apprentice (who was also his nephew) arrived, the boy entered through the fanlight. They found Denyer kneeling on the floor beside an old sofa, his arms resting on the sofa and his head in his hands. Both he and the dog were dead. Inspector Grapes of the local constabulary suspected poison but none could be found. Dr Tuttiett confirmed that there was no poison and in his opinion the death had been caused by excitement that had resulted in congestion of the brain or a rupture of the vessels of the heart. The jury returned a verdict of death from natural causes. (*Isle of Wight Observer*, February 2nd 1862)

~ JANUARY 27TH ~

1925: Sir Godfrey Baring, chairman of the management of the Royal National Lifeboat Institution, delivered a lecture to the prisoners at Camp Hill Prison. Shortly afterwards the RNLI received a cheque for 9s from the prison governor for contributions made by the prisoners to the charity. The men were able to earn up to 1s 6d a week as payment for hard work and good behaviour that they could then spend as they wished on certain permitted luxuries.

Camp Hill Prison opened in 1912, the ceremony attended by former Home Secretary, Winston Churchill. It was regarded as a luxury establishment and a soft option, allowing, amongst other things, smoking. It closed in 2013. (*Gloucester Citizen*, January 27th 1925)

~ JANUARY 28TH ~

1811: A sorry tale concerning a German soldier found its way into the press today:

> A soldier belonging to the King's German Legion, being detected in stealing stockings etc in a shop in Newport, was committed to the bridewell, where he hung himself, about two hours afterwards, with some worsted binding he had purchased at a shop; he fastened it to a nail in the partition, his knees nearly touching the ground. A coroner's inquest sat on the body, and after four hours deliberation, returned a verdict of Felo de se. He was accordingly buried in the high road within the borough of Newport, a circumstance never known before.

The King's German Legion was a battalion raised by the Duke of Brunswick, cousin and brother-in-law to the future King George IV. Following a defeat against the French, they were brought to the Island to be reformed and continue the fight against Napoleon. One can only feel pity for this poor man and his ignominious end. (*Hampshire Chronicle,* January 28th 2013)

– January 29th –

1875: On this day James Salter a 'burly young fellow' of Yafford found himself in court on three separate charges of assault. At the Five Bells inn, Shorwell, the landlord George Toghill stated that on the 29th Salter had come in asking for a pot of ale and then deliberately dropped it on the ground. When asked to pay 4*d* for the damage he set about first the landlord, then his wife and sister. It took two other customers to help evict him at which point he went to the back door and tried to force his way in. On this charge he was fined 10*s* plus 7*s* 6*d* costs for the assault on Mrs Toghill or fourteen days in gaol. Two further fines of 2*s* 6*d* plus 7*s* 6*d* costs were imposed for the attacks on Mr Toghill and his sister, plus a third amount for refusing to leave the pub. Failure to pay would mean seven days' imprisonment for each charge. Salter was next charged with assaulting a policeman, Police Constable Triggs who had been on duty at the blacksmith's shop on the same night. He had come across a horse and cart in a ditch and suggested to the driver (Salter) that he should attend to the horse, whereupon Salter knocked off his helmet, hit him on the breast and kicked him on the knee. When the constable rose, Salter kicked him so severely about the legs and lower body that he had been unable to work since. In view of the seriousness of the charge, the magistrates sentenced him to two months' imprisonment with hard labour, plus costs and in default, yet a further seven days in gaol. (*Hampshire Advertiser*, February 3rd 1875)

— January 30th —

1863: When Mr Charles Watts, an engineer at Parkhurst Prison, went out for a walk he took the two sons of Mr Strickland, a steward at the prison, with him. En route they called at the East Cowes Gasworks where Mr Billow, the manager:

> 'attended by a man holding a lighted candle, was in the meter-house explaining some defect in a small brass pinion.' A light was being held to it to enable [Mr Billow] rule in hand, to take its dimensions, when the meter exploded and Billow and [young] Strickland were instantly killed by the flying fragments of iron plate, the front of the skulls of each being torn away. At the time of the explosion, Mr Watts was holding the deceased boy by the hand. The man, Guy, holding the candle received some frightful injuries about the head. Mr Watts escaped with a deep cut on the cheek and a wound on the lips and loss of four teeth. Mr Strickland's other son, eight years old, received a deep gash in the neck and some other injuries, but no danger to his life is apprehended. Guy lies in a rather a precarious state …

At an inquest on the two bodies of Mr G. Billow, 45 years of age, and Travers Strickland, aged 7 years, the verdict was that of accidental death. (*Dorset County Chronicle*, February 5th 1863)

~ JANUARY 31ST ~

1846: Today's *Hampshire Telegraph* reported on the successful visit to the Island of the Revd Dr Wolff, the 'celebrated Eastern traveller', his mission being to raise funds for the Society for the Propagation of the Gospel in Foreign Parts, and the Curates' Aid Society. Having preached sermons in both St Thomas's church and the Church of the Holy Trinity in Ryde on the previous Sunday (January 25th), he then lectured on his travels to Bokhara at the town hall on Monday. His friends invited him to give a further lecture on Tuesday at which the sum of £22 was donated. The *Telegraph* reported that the excitement generated by the good doctor was so great that forty people put their names down for a copy of his *Travels to Bokhara*. (*Hampshire Telegraph*, January 31st 1846)

⟶ February 1st ⟵

1901: Following the death of Queen Victoria on January 22nd, her body was transported from the Island on the yacht *Victoria and Albert*. Today the *Portsmouth Telegraph* explained that:

> It was her Majesty's favourite yacht, endeared to her by many associations. Built early in her reign it was in this vessel that her beloved husband and the Queen made many delightful trips around the British Isles. All the fittings of the yacht were designed by Prince Albert even to the silk tapestry with which the royal cabins are draped and faithfully adhered to ever since in the re-decoration of the craft for on no account would the Queen allow any more modern fittings to be introduced. Even the piano that Prince Albert was accustomed to play remains in the saloon. The Royal Apartments always had sweet memories of some of the happiest memories of Her Majesty's wedded life. It is in this beautiful craft with its old fashioned paddle wheels that the body of Victoria the Good is to be borne to Portsmouth Dockyard for conveyance to its last resting-place in the magnificent Mausoleum at Frogmore.

Prince Albert had died in 1861 and it was forty years before the queen finally joined him. (*Portsmouth Telegraph*, February 1st 1901)

~ February 2nd ~

1839: In their section 'Isle of Wight February 2nd' the *Hampshire Telegraph* forwarded the following unlikely tale. Headed 'Isle of Wight Cheese in America' it announced that two men had been killed in a shocking accident. When arriving from England, Captain White of the Potomac presented a valuable Isle of Wight Cheese to his old friend Mr John Adams of Vermont. It seemed that in order to protect the cheese from rats ('with which the Island is so much troubled') a hard coating or rind was applied, so hard in fact that it couldn't be cut. Mr Adams therefore resorted to placing it edge-ways on his breast and pressed with all his might on a stout Dowey knife in his right hand. Unhappily the knife slipped and John cut not only himself in half, but also his son who had been standing behind him. (From the *Vermont US Gazette*, *Hampshire Telegraph*, February 4th 1839)

— February 3rd —

1912: A spirited account of what was to be expected by the new inmates at Camp Hill Prison was forecast today:

Taxpayers will be gratified to learn that everything is being done for their comfort. They will take their meals together and although a warder will be on hand he will be in an adjoining room. We suppose this is arranged lest his presence should put a restraint on conversation. There will be a large reception apartment where inmates will see their visitors … One wonders whether 'guests' at Camphill will be properly supplied with papers and magazines, and whether a gramophone or pianola will be provided. The worst of it is that in order to enter Camphill, you must be one of the army of 'habituals.' Readers who imagine that they may qualify for a holiday at Camphill for some petty offence such as breaking a shop window or using violent language … will find themselves mistaken. They must practice crime for a number of years before being promoted to the habitual class. The fact is, crime is decreasing so rapidly that we are in danger of treating the criminal as a kind of pet. The day will come when he will be so rare that when a criminal is captured, he will be put in a museum.

(*The Cheltenham Looker On*, February 3rd 1912)

— February 4th —

1854: Today's *Isle of Wight Observer* announced that the ship *Carrysjoot* was about to be sent to the Island to replace the hulk *Talbot*, moored at Sconce Point near Yarmouth. Thirty years earlier the *Talbot* had seen active service at the Battle of Navarino but had lately been called into service to provide accommodation for the engineers working on Sconce Fort – latterly known as Fort Victoria. The men were referred to as 'navvies' and life on-board was described as a 'very hell'. On October 22nd the year before, an inquest had been held at the Nelson inn, Freshwater on John Penfold, a bricklayer's labourer who had been working on the construction of the fort. Penfold had been sleeping aboard the hulk and witnesses confirmed that he had been very drunk and must have fallen into the water. William Lane, a fisherman at Weston, deposed seeing the body floating in the water while fishing and towing it to Freshwater Bay. Doctor Charles Wise Hollis, having examined the body, reported that 'he saw no marks that led him to suppose that the death was occasioned by violence and that he had no doubt it was caused by drowning'. The verdict was that he was found drowned. On October 18th the following year, Maria Kennedy, also living in the hulk, was buried at Freshwater. Her role at the fort is not recorded. (*Isle of Wight Observer*, February 4th 1854)

~ February 5th ~

1853: The *Hampshire Telegraph* reported today on a lecture given at the Atheneum and Mechanics Institute Newport on Thursday night (the 3rd) by Mr William Wells Brown. The talk was entitled 'Uncle Tom's Cabin, a Fugitive American Slave', and there was a packed audience. The *Telegraph* reported that 'Mr Wells Brown had visited the Island on previous occasions and his reputation was such that on this occasion the hall was overflowing. All present were deeply affected by his talk which was received with unmistakable tokens of applause.' On an earlier visit, the *Telegraph* seems to have been surprised that the lecturer was 'well informed, with a free and good delivery and an excellent choice of words'. Brown was born into slavery and managed to escape. By dint of self-education he made his way to Europe and lectured on the evils of slavery, also writing works of fiction, non-fiction and plays. As an escaped slave he could not return to the United States until a British family purchased his freedom. Meanwhile in Britain his lectures took him as far afield and Glasgow and Edinburgh, Cheltenham and Tunbridge Wells. As his reputation grew, he was referred to as a mulatto, an escaped slave, a gentleman of colour, then as a doctor. Following his talk at the Mechanics Institute, he returned on February 26th to lecture at the Queen's Rooms with 'pictorial illustrations'. (*Hampshire Telegraph*, February 5th 1853)

— FEBRUARY 6TH —

1886: On this day, complaining of fatigue, Edward Edwards, founder member of the Library Movement providing free libraries for everyone, retired early to bed. The next morning he was found to have died in his sleep. He was aged 73 and lived at Niton. He was a surprising champion of books, his father being a London bricklayer who had taken his son on as an apprentice. Perhaps fortuitously the firm became bankrupt and through Thomas Binney, a Nonconformist minister, Edward was introduced to books. In 1838, he secured a temporary assistant's post, preparing a catalogue at the British Library. Five years later, still there, he met and married Margaretta Hayward and, despite family disapproval on both sides, it was a happy union. During this time Edward supported the campaign to get a national system of free libraries, an idea opposed by the Conservatives on the ground that the rich would be paying for something that they would not use. When the bill was passed, Edward became the first librarian of the Manchester Free Library, the opening attended by Charles Dickens and William Thackeray. Edwards' radical views sat uncomfortably with the management however and in 1858, he was dismissed. Thereafter, he and Margaretta travelled the country and on her death, he settled in Niton. He was not a good tenant, rarely paying his rent and on one occasion he returned to his lodging to find his belongings on the lawn – all except his books, held in lieu of rent. Taken in by the Niton Baptist minister, he remained a not entirely welcome guest until his death. In 1902, Thomas Greenwood, 'an apostle of the library movement', placed a red marble monument on his grave in Niton churchyard. (*Gloucester Citizen*, February 8th 1902)

— February 7th —

1861: During the night the barque *Victor Emmanuel*, bound from Alexandria to London, came to grief near Blackgang Chine. The Islanders were alerted when four seamen managed to get ashore in thick fog and, not knowing where they were, stumbled upon a cottage and raised the alarm. The fog had come down suddenly and the *Victor Emmanuel* had virtually nil visibility. The man on watch, Robert Burns, gave evidence at the inquest two days later. Leaving Portland Bill, the captain had set his course by navigating in the dark and, when Burns informed him that he could see what he thought was St Catherine's lighthouse, the captain insisted that they were nowhere near St Catherine's and did not take any significant action. When the gravity of the situation was realised, the lifeboats were launched but each suffered serious damage and the men left on board found their craft breaking up. One by one they were washed overboard and drowned, including the captain. Burns was wearing a life belt and had been able to get to the land. Thomas White, who had been steering the ship, confirmed that the captain had admonished Burns for making false reports and had not significantly changed course. The captain also countermanded him when Burns had called out to drop the anchor. In White's view, had they done so the ship might have been saved. Summing up, the coroner said there was no doubt they owed their death to the determined obstinacy of the captain, but he had shared their fate. The finding was that they had been accidentally drowned. (*Isle of Wight Observer*, February 9th 1861)

─ February 8th ─

1841: On this day a tragic accident occurred at Cowes when 'Mr Slade, a butcher of this town, having overcharged an old gun barrel, placed it in Mursell's field in order to prove it by putting a squib to the touch-hole and firing the same with a red-hot iron bar. The barrel immediately burst and some of the pieces knocked him senseless to the ground. One piece lodged in his head.' All was not lost, however, for the *Hampshire Advertiser* of February 13th added: 'We are happy to hear that he is fast recovering.' (*Hampshire Advertiser*, February 13th 1841)

~ February 9th ~

1853: On this day a Ryde resident signing himself 'A Tick' felt compelled to write to the *Isle of Wight Observer* to complain about the inadequacies of Ryde's town clocks. The church clock at St Thomas's for the last year and a half had been misleading the town by showing the wrong time – to his great personal inconvenience. He therefore recommended that it should be either abolished or kept correct. The church at St James's, however, kept good time, but the bell that told the hours was too small and therefore could not be heard. He recommended that the commissioners should provide a good striking clock, marking the hours, halves and quarters to be placed on an iron bracket with faces towards the high street, Lind Street and Cross Street. It wasn't until 1868 that the town got a new clock, a gift from Miss Brigstocke gracing the newly erected town hall clock tower. The *Observer* promptly featured a column written by the 'Town Hall Clock' itself. (*Isle of Wight Observer*, February 12th 1853 and the Historic Ryde Society)

~ February 10th ~

1890: Following the sinking of the ship *Irex* and the death of crewman Richard Sterne, an appeal was issued for donations towards a headstone. In response, Queen Victoria sent a 'gracious message stating that it is her wish and intention to erect such a memorial and to commemorate thereon the names of the other sufferers. The inscription is to be: 'Erected by QUEEN VICTORIA in memory of RICHARD STERNE who died at the Needles' Fort, on the 10th of February 1890, aged 37 years.' Poor Sterne had suffered several broken limbs and been dashed about in the storm before being rescued. The rest of the memorial was to read as follows: 'And in remembrance of CAPTAIN HUTTON, JAMES H IRVINE, ERNEST HANSEN, HARRY GRAYSON, WILLIAM OGILVIE, HATCHETT who were lost in the wreck of the *Irex* January 25 1890.' Carrying the story, *Freshwater Parish Magazine* added that engravings of the wreck 'may still be obtained on application to the Rev A H Lamb. There are also a few copies remaining of the March number of the Magazine, containing the account of the wreck.' (*Freshwater Parish Magazine*, March 1890)

~ February 11th ~

1878: Across the country, newspapers carried the report that at 8 a.m. this morning, James Caffyn, a labourer from Elmfield at Ryde, had been executed for the murder of Maria Barber. Maria had lived with the prisoner and when she threatened to leave him, he struck her on the head with an axe, killing her. He had escaped to Portsmouth but on being arrested, he made a full confession. At the petty sessions at Newport, before being sent for trial, he said that he had been determined that his victim should not deceive any more men and he had deliberately struck her with the axe. He did the deed with good heart and was ready to die for it. Caffyn maintained the same reserved, self-possessed demeanour he had exhibited at the trial. He received Holy Communion and expressed penitence for the crime. He ate a good breakfast, submitted quietly to the process of pinioning, after which he walked with a great firmness to the scaffold. Chillingly it concluded: 'The fatal scene lasted for three minutes but life was not extinct for a considerable time after the fall.' (*Somerset County Gazette*, February 16th 1878)

~ February 12th ~

1787: Under the heading 'Fair Complexions' today's *Hampshire Chronicle* was pleased to report that Hall and Co. of London had succeeded in developing 'something that will make the skin fair without injuring the complexion'. The company was so well convinced of the beautifying effects that if the customer was not satisfied, they would take back and return the full value paid for it. A description of the product was given: 'in any kind of perfumes … If in so short a space of time as that of a week, the lady does not find her face, neck and arms delicately white, fair and beautiful, and to remove any apprehensions that might be entertained as to the innocence of its nature, an affidavit has been made proving that it contains no kind of paint whatever in its composition. By candlelight in particular it gives a fair delicacy to the complexion … removes pimples, freckles or worms from the face … and if used at an early time of life, the effects will be seen for several years after.' This amazing product could be purchased in London only at their house at the Strand under the name of Turkish Wash. Certain agents were permitted to supply it in various parts of the country however, and locally Mr Nutt of Newport Isle of Wight would be pleased to oblige. (*Hampshire Chronicle*, February 12th 1787)

~ FEBRUARY 13TH ~

1889: Miss Maud Berkeley spent her young adult life under the crotchety eye of her elderly parents. Each summer was passed at their house Fernleigh at Sandown where, along with a number of visiting gentlefolk and locals, they found ways of amusing themselves. Maud kept a record of the passing days and an outing to Shanklin today was worthy of her comment: 'Walked to Shanklin in the afternoon. Saw a very strange figure on the step of the Crab inn, a gentleman in a Norfolk jacket and knickerbockers, with bicycle propped against the wall and sketching book in hand. Lilian [her companion] and I both sneaked a look at his work and later privately agreed that we thought it hardly worth his while progressing further.' It being such a cold day they felt compelled to hitch a lift from a passing coal cart – only they couldn't decide which of them should ask. As a result the cart passed by and they lost the opportunity. As Maud concluded, it was just as well because 'the cart turned round and went off to Ventnor'. (Flora Fraser (ed.) *The Diaries of Maud Berkeley*)

— FEBRUARY 14TH —

1891: Today Tom McCarthy, accredited agent of the Dock, Wharf, Riverside and General Labourers' Union paid a second visit to Newport and addressed a crowd in front of the Guildhall. He said there were grave matters under consideration, for one of the biggest strikes ever known in this country was being threatened. He addressed himself to the agricultural labourers where in Hampshire and Wiltshire he had found men working from 10½–11½ hours a day for 9s or 10s a week. He went on to denounce the 'cursed system of capitalism and landlordism' which ground down English labourers. There were strong-limbed, able-bodied labourers in the Isle of Wight – honest, respectable men, not rogues and thieves – who were anxious and ready by means of their labour, to earn sufficient to keep for themselves, their wives and children, but with the present system they could not. He said that there was a cry for 'The land for the people who work it, and not those who live on its fruits and do nothing.' He condemned the big gentlemen, swelling with wine after dinner, talking about the privilege of belonging to the great and glorious empire, but to the half-starved labourer with no present comfort and no hope for his old age the sentiment was a mockery. He concluded by saying that their first intention was to start branches of the union in all the purely agricultural villages of the Island. (*Portsmouth Evening News*, February 16th 1891)

~ February 15th ~

1900: The sailing brig *Auguste*, travelling from Freemantle to London, became the subject of one of the most dramatic rescues around the Isle of Wight. At 4.30 p.m. in heavy seas amid violent squalls, she was blown inshore by a force-nine gale and grounded stern-first on the rocks. The crew immediately took to the rigging. The lifeboat *Catherine Swift* was launched from the shore, but the sea was so rough that water filled the craft, threatening to sink her, and she had to retire. As the crew watched, the *Auguste* started to break up. The Bembridge lifeboat *Joe Jarman* then attempted a rescue, but ran aground on a sandbank. Several rockets were fired to the ship but failed to reach their target. It was not until 2.30 a.m. the next day that the *Catherine Swift* again set out and managed to save all eighteen crew. When the gale finally dropped, many of the rescued men returned to save their belongings and part of the cargo. The *Auguste* slowly disintegrated over the winter. (*Shipwreck Index of the British Isles*, Lloyds Register)

~ February 16th ~

1867: From his home at Farringford, Lord Tennyson wrote in his less-than-perfect French to the illustrator of his epic work *Idylls of the King*. Tennyson started work on the *Idylls* in 1856, at which time he had been Poet Laureate for nearly six years. It took him the best part of thirty years to complete, and the massive work was dedicated to Prince Albert. The poem retold the story of King Arthur, his rise to power, his attempts to create a perfect kingdom and the betrayals that saw him fail. For many it was viewed as a commentary on the fallen ideals of Victorian life. The man illustrating the work was Gustav Dore, a gifted and prolific engraver. Dore's drawings featured unfamiliar landscapes fraught with dangers and heroic characters risking all in the pursuit of their goals. Tennyson wrote to his illustrator that 'a l'instant combien je me sentais hereux d'avoir trouve un tel interprete mais je craignais vous importuner de mon mechant Francais' – how happy he was to have found such a telling interpretation but that he was afraid to bother him with such 'wicked' French. Dore, who was contracted to spend three months in England every year, no doubt forgave him. (*The Letters of Alfred Lord Tennyson*, 1871–70)

— February 17th —

1851: 'A fire broke out on Monday at Binstead, Isle of Wight, the seat of Sir Ulysses Baganal Burgh, Major-General Lord Downs which was totally consumed. Binstead is one mile from Ryde whence the fire engine was despatched, but it was of little service in consequence of the combustible nature of the building – part being very old, and covered in thatch. Very little of the furniture was saved. It is stated that Lady Downes has lost £30,000 of jewellery.' The couple made regular visits to Binstead and were on their way to the Island when they saw the conflagration from the steamer. They were the founders of Binstead Lodge School. Lord Downes served in Robert Peel's ministry and his last recorded votes were against the emancipation of Jews and to keep the death penalty for forgery. (*Sussex Advertiser*, February 25th 1851)

~ February 18th ~

1839: Today's *Hampshire Telegraph* printed the following notice, searching for anyone living in the Isle of Wight who might have had their child stolen: 'A poor woman with a near naked child knocked at a door at a house in Eltham in Kent, asking for alms. The owner of the house was a respectable chimney sweep who was looking for a climbing boy and the sweep's wife declared that the only way she could help would be by taking the boy in. The child's mother parted with him and he came to live with the family. Being too young to legally climb chimneys, he was fed and clothed but also a financial burden on the family. One day at dinner when a dish of potatoes was served, he suddenly remarked that the dish always used to be served with a fowl. Other memories he expressed led the couple to suspect that he did not belong to the woman who passed him on. He remembered a house with green railings and a green gate and a great dog chained up and that he had been taken in a boat.' The *Telegraph* therefore wished to know if there was a family on the Isle of Wight who had, during the last two or three years, had a child stolen away. (*Hampshire Telegraph*, February 18th 1839)

─ February 19th ─

1848: Today at the petty sessions in Newport, the following case was brought against George Lock, corn merchant of Sea Street. He was accused of stealing a bundle of his employer's straw, valued at 9*d*. It appeared that having been sent by his master with a waggon and horses to Ford Farm to collect a load of straw, he tied up a bundle of it for himself which he disposed of for the trifling sum of 4*d*. The prisoner pleaded guilty, and there being a former charge against him for stealing barley 'and his antecedents in other matters not being very complimentary to his honesty', the court ordered him to be committed to hard labour for six months. (*Hampshire Telegraph*, February 20th 1848)

‒ February 20th ‒

1753: A letter dated today came into the hands of the *Caledonian Mercury* who saw fit to publish the following extract:

Six Vessels have been wrecked this Month on the South Shores of this Island and last week a Vessel from Liverpool or Chester with 130 Ton of Cheese on board suffered the same Fate when she struck in the Night, nine of the Crew went off in the Boat, it being calm, but as they have not been heard of since, they must all have perished. The Master of this Ship, his Nephew and one Man were left on board; in the morning the two last came on Shore as on the ebbing of the Tide the Ship was left almost dry; several People came from the Countrie and went on board and told the Master that before it was Half Flood next Tide his Vessel would be beat to pieces, and persuaded Him to come on shore with them; he told them the ship was his own; and Part of the Cargo; that it was his All; and he would perish with her; These Reasons they thought so cogent that they very humanely suffered him to pursue his own Inclinations and left him singing Psalms in his Cabbin [*sic*] and in about Half an Hour, after they saw the Vessel beat to pieces, with the Sea beating against her, his Body was thrown on Shore, a silver watch &etc. and ten Guineas found in his Pocket which was given to his Nephew. The Country in great numbers gathered along the shore to catch the Cheeses.

It concluded with a postscript: 'PS I forgot to inform you that five Men of this Island were drowned in this Cheese-catching Exercise.' (*Caledonian Mercury*, March 6th 1753)

⁓ February 21st ⁓

1917: One of the worst tragedies at sea off the Island coast occurred on February 21st in thick fog. On board the troopship *Mendi* were about 800 men, mostly African, recruited to fight in France. The ship *Darro* was travelling full speed ahead as darkness fell when out of the fog the green lights of a ship were seen. Seconds later there was a violent jolt and the captain of the *Darro* thought they had been hit by a torpedo ship. Thinking that they would sink he sent an SOS but, discovering that his ship was only holed above the water line, he declined assistance when his alarm was answered. The *Mendi*, meanwhile, had suffered catastrophic damage and was virtually cut in two. Many men were injured and lifeboats destroyed. Flung into the freezing water, upward of 600 African troops either drowned or froze to death. The captain of the *Mendi*, Captain Yardley, was the last man to leave his ship and plunged into the sea. He was later rescued. At a Board of Trade enquiry, Captain Henry Stump of the *Darro* stated that the first he knew of the *Mendi*'s predicament was at breakfast when a lifeboat was picked up. In the fog nothing of the sinking or the cries of the drowning had been witnessed. The enquiry was finally completed on August 1st and Captain Stump had his license suspended for twelve months. (*Hull Daily Mail*, August 19th 1917)

~ FEBRUARY 22ND ~

1892: On this day John Robinson, a 38-year-old servant of the queen, committed suicide by swallowing a large quantity of spirits of ammonia at Osborne House. Robinson, whose wife and three children were living at Windsor, was employed in the kitchen and this was his second visit to Osborne. A witness, Mrs Hannah Houndsell, said that she saw Robinson in the silver pantry and spoke to him but he did not answer. He had a bottle in his hand that he raised to his lips and drank. She asked him, 'John, what are you doing?' and he again raised the bottle and emptied the contents. It contained 16–18oz of ammonia, occasionally used for cleaning plate; a dose of 2oz was sufficient to kill an adult. According to Houndsell, Robinson staggered against a wall and groaned very much. He was normally very cheerful but lately he had been quiet and said something about detectives being after him. This was pooh-poohed. On the previous Friday night he had said, 'That pin will be found at Windsor on Wednesday.' On her last visit to Osborne, the Princess of Wales had lost a pin but it was deemed impossible that Robinson could have stolen it as he did not have access to that part of the house. The doctor confirmed that he had not been drinking alcohol and the verdict was given that he had committed suicide while temporarily insane. He was interred at Whippinham the following Tuesday afternoon. (*County Press*, February 27th 1892)

⊸ FEBRUARY 23RD ⊸

1942: William Basterfield, a fire-watcher employed at Cowes and living at Barton Road, Newport, was in custody for a week on Saturday for demanding £150 with menaces from Lady Baring, of Nubia House, Cowes. Lady Baring was the wife of Sir Godfrey Baring, chairman of the Island County Council, county magistrate and former MP for the Isle of Wight and North-West Devon. At the previous hearing, Inspector G. Dobson of Cowes stated that Lady Baring had been recently receiving anonymous letters, and in one of them £150 was demanded under threats of personal violence. In a letter received on February 6th, Lady Baring was instructed where the money should be placed. A decoy parcel was put in the place suggested in the street at Cowes, and Basterfield was arrested when he took the parcel. At the assizes on Monday, March 9th, he was sentenced to twelve months in gaol. (*Western Morning News*, February 23rd 1942)

~ February 24th ~

1883: Today's *Isle of Wight Observer* announced the death of Farmer Watson. A well-known Isle of Wight man, he died at Shanklin at the age of 53 after an attack of bronchitis. The *Observer* did not know his exact weight but it was estimated to be 20 stone. Thirty years ago, his father, a highly respectable farmer near Ryde, was equally stout although it was not as obvious as he had a more massive frame. He had two sons and one daughter, all stout and, in the days before political correctness, they attracted the attention of nearly everyone they met in the streets. The father was a genial and friendly man with an almost-constant good-humoured smile. He was a regular for shaves in Hopgood's barber's shop in Cross-Street, Ryde and about the year 1850 he was asked: 'Varmer, what makes ye so fat?' to which he replied, 'Well, I don't mind telling thee, if it will do thee any good – I lets the world slide.' His son had recently died and, although the lad was at times afflicted with lunacy, he was always quiet and harmless. To see him leading his cow by a rope invariably created a smile from those he met. (*Isle of Wight Observer*, February 24th 1883)

— February 25th —

1892: Francis Gray Bacon, a 12-year-old boy staying on the Island, was out riding with his father along the undercliff while his mother followed in a carriage. Whilst going at a walking pace, Frank's pony stumbled, unseating the lad who landed on his head, suffering fatal injuries. After consultation with two local doctors, a third was summoned from London and in an attempt to save his life they resorted to trepanning (boring a hole in the skull), but it was to no avail. Frank never regained consciousness and died two days later. His father Hackley Bacon, a wealthy businessman from New York, arranged for his son's burial in Ventnor Cemetery, with a memorial bearing: 'Shall We Not Meet Them on the Golden Shore?' In tribute, Frank's tutor recalled, 'I have never met any boy who brought such intellect to bear on his work.' He was an only child and the spot where the accident occurred is marked with a large Portland stone block, protected by iron railings and with the inscription now eroded. (*Isle of Wight Observer*, March 5th 1892)

— FEBRUARY 26TH —

1949: The *Western Morning News* today announced the arrival of the Cabinet at Shanklin Manor to formulate their next election plans. After travelling from Waterloo by train, they crossed the Solent in the British Railways vessel *Brading*. Dr Edith Summerskill was greeted with cries of 'snoek', 'give us more fat' and 'what about the coal?' The Press Association correspondent said that the visit had shattered the winter quietude of the Island and everybody was talking about politics – often indeed Opposition politics, the Island being a Conservative stronghold. A late supper of meat and fish awaited the party with special vegetarian fare for Sir Stafford Cripps. After breakfast the next morning (February 26th), discussion began on the draft general election programme. The rumours that the meeting was a reaction to a split in the government was denied as the venue had been booked months before. (*Western Morning News*, February 26th 1949)

~ February 27th ~

1903: Today's *Western Times* reported that, after taking part in a dramatic performance on the evening of February 10th at Shanklin, Miss Marjorie Lumsden had mysteriously disappeared. That evening, Coastguardsman Manger had seen a figure in white at about 11 p.m. on Shanklin pier and about 10 minutes later he went and searched about the shelter to satisfy his own curiosity, but found no trace of anyone. He did not raise an alarm thinking that she must have gone out for a walk after supper. A £50 reward for information was offered, which Mrs Silas Kemp earned by following the indication of a dream. She told the jury she was led to a spot, and seeing a bundle she approached it until she saw rings on the fingers, and then called her husband. The body was identified by Mr Innes Smith and Dr Cowper, both of whom saw Miss Lumsden in the play that evening. Her father, Colonel Lumsden, was present at the inquest. The jury returned a verdict of 'found drowned'. (*Western Times*, February 27th 1903)

— FEBRUARY 28TH —

1889: The *Aldershot Military Gazette* today carried the following report from their correspondent:

> I hear from the Isle of Wight that there are again rumours abroad to the effect that it is the intention of the Government to erect large buildings in connection with Parkhurst Barracks. If so, the additional accommodation will come none too soon, for with the exception of the married men's quarters, the rooms are in a sad condition, and in some cases even worse than the oldest wooden huts in Aldershot. Not only are the buildings bad, but accommodation is insufficient for two regiments. The 1st battalion 14th Regiment seems to be gaining the admiration of the Islanders. It had a march out this week, accompanied by the spotted deer, brought from India, and I am informed that although weak in numbers, the battalion looked remarkably smart in appearance as it passed through Newport. The 42nd Highlanders (Black Watch) which is also stationed at Parkhurst, has secured a good share of favourable opinions. It has been suggested that the regiment should be brought over to Portsmouth on Easter Monday, to take part in a grand field day on the Common. This will be a capital idea, but one I fear which has little chance of being carried out. The first instance at Parkhurst of a recruit claiming his discharge on payment of £10 under the New Army Discipline Act occurred the other day, when a private of the 42nd Highlanders took advantage of the privilege.

(*Aldershot Military Gazette*, February 28th 1889)

~ February 29th ~

1876: Mr Henry William Nunn, formerly of Broadlands House, Newport, who had moved to the Island in order to start a lace factory, died this day at the age of 70. He left a personal fortune of nearly £400,000 and his chief beneficiary was his daughter Mary Nunn Harvey, to whom he left furniture, plate, pictures, horses, carriages, and the manor and lordship of Briddlesford. His company's lace was golden, made with silk and graced the wardrobe of many members of the royal court, including Queen Victoria. The factory was run on benevolent lines and at its height employed up to 200 workers, including winding boys and girls. As an example of his generosity, in February 1858 Mr Nunn donated upwards of 800 loaves of best Wight bread to the people of Cross Lanes, Barton village, where they were 'thankfully received'. The factory closed on his death, its demise being a blow to the local population. His heiress, Mary, devoted much of her life to good causes, amongst which was the foundation of the Girls' Friendly Society. She donated Winchester House at Shanklin to the society to provide accommodation and a holiday retreat for poor working girls. Among its patrons were Queen Victoria and later Queen Mary. (Wootton Bridge Historical Society; *A History of the Girls' Friendly Society* by Agnes L. Money, 1911)

1862: On this evening, William Wadden, a 'miserable old man' who lived at Winford and worked at Wacklands, murdered 29-year-old James White. On Monday, March 3rd an inquest was held at the Stag inn at Lake in a room that could barely hold the jury and witnesses, and the deceased's body was stored in an outhouse. The murder was spurred by a quarrel about Jane Smith, 'a good looking girl' and single woman who lived with her mother and 5-year-old son at Apse Heath. Jane and William had been childhood friends and, for the past thirteen months, lovers. They planned to marry. While White was visiting Jane, Wadden, who was a widower, called and tried to persuade Jane to let her son visit his house where he had some eggs and cakes. At this point in the cross examination, Jane fainted and had to be revived. She had tried to prevent White from going outside, but he went to face Wadden. The two men hurled abuse at each other and when Jane ventured out they were both on the ground, with White on top and neither of them moving. A passer-by dragged White from Wadden but the younger man could not stand so was rested against a bank. He died after about 15 minutes; he had been stabbed in the chest. Wadden ran away. The *London Daily News* reporter who covered the case observed that Jane's cottage was 'a wretched hovel and a disgrace to the Isle of Wight'. Jane had done some occasional domestic work for Wadden who always had something offensive to say about White, including that he would put the length of his knife into him. The knife in question had a 10½ inch blade and was believed to be the murder weapon. Wadden was found guilty of wilful murder (*London Standard*, March 5th 1862)

~ MARCH 2ND ~

1905: At 3 a.m. on the 2nd, following an operation for appendicitis, William Gilbert Grace, eldest son of the famous cricketer, died at East Cowes. He was 30 years old and had been an assistant master at the Royal Naval College at Osborne for the last two years. Like his father, brothers, uncles and grandfather, he was an enthusiastic and successful cricketer, playing first-class matches for Cambridge University, Gloucester and London County. His career lasted from 1893–1903 and he also played rugby. Like his father, William had studied medicine. William Gilbert Grace Senior suffered several tragedies during his life. Apart from William's early death, his daughter Bessie died at the age of 20 and his nephew Gerald, working as a doctor in South Africa, was shot by the police when he broke through a cordon in his haste to perform an emergency operation. William Junior was interred at Elmers End Road Cemetery on March 6th. (*Gloucester Citizen*, March 3rd 1905)

— MARCH 3RD —

1886: Today's *Hampshire Advertiser* reported on a rather rare Island event at the divorce court. An actor named Mr James was suing his estranged wife and a co-respondent named Makin for divorce on the grounds of adultery. The couple had married at Carisbrooke church in 1881, the groom being under the impression that the bride was a widow, which proved to be untrue. Within a week of the ceremony he discovered that she was addicted to intemperance and quarrels ensued. In 1882, while he was touring in the provinces, they stayed at a hotel where the wife became drunk and violent, hitting him with a poker. They continued living together but he later found her under suspicious circumstances and she was accused of committing adultery with Makin. She had been leading a loose life since they had separated and the judge therefore granted the petitioner a *decree nisi* with costs. Until 1857, a divorce could only be granted by Act of Parliament. (*Hampshire Advertiser*, March 3rd 1886)

～ March 4th ～

1917: On this day, Mary Gartside-Tipping (*née* Flynn) was shot by a deranged French soldier while on active service in France. Mary was the daughter of a captain in the Royal Artillery and in 1890, had married Henry Gartside-Tipping, serving in the Royal Navy. The pair moved to Binstead where Henry's uncle had left him a house called Quarr Wood, and had a son and two daughters. In the First World War, the pair were the only married couple to die in separate incidents while on active service. Henry, then a retired lieutenant commander, joined the Mercantile Marine Reserve, serving aboard the yacht *Sanda*. On September 15th 1915 she was fired on by shore batteries off Zeebrugge and was lost at sea. For Mary, after war work in the canteen of a munitions factory in January 1917, the 47-year-old joined the Women's Emergency Corps, a group described as an unlikely mixture of well-to-do women and radical feminists. She appears to have applied for a more active role and was posted to France where she was shot. In France, the military honour the Croix de Guerre had been withheld from women combatants, but was reinstated following the circumstances of Mary's death. Mary was buried at Vauxbuin National French Cemetery and Henry's name appears on the Nieuport War Memorial in Belgium. Both are inscribed on the Binstead War Memorial and the Island's memorial in St Nicholas Chapel Carisbrooke. (Jan Toms, *Pushing Up the Daisies*, Isle of Wight: Coach House Publications)

~ March 5th ~

The *Isle of Wight Observer* published:

Royal Isle of Wight Infirmary – Report for the week ending March 5. Patients admitted 7; Discharged 4; Died 1; Remaining in the Infirmary 40; Waiting for admission 2. Outpatients on the books 130, of whom 40 were visited in their own homes.

Fever Wards (separate from the main building), for male and female cases.

Charges for the use of Disinfecting Apparatus – from 2s 6d to 5s.

Medical Officer for the week – F. Greening Esq. Visitor – Captain Boger R.N.

[Signed] B.C. Oldham, House Surgeon.

Convalescent Home – Admitted 1; Discharged 1; Remaining 6. Reduced Charges: All Patients, 7s per week. No increase after three weeks.

The Committee gratefully acknowledges the following: Illustrated papers from Mrs Pyemont, Miss Gillson and Mr Jacobs; two dozen eggs from Miss Carter; magazines [from] Miss Whitcomb.

(Isle of Wight Observer, March 8th 1890)

⇥ MARCH 6TH ⇤

1798: It took some time for the news to travel, but the *Aberdeen Courier* of March 6th was able to report that on February 21st the Island had been thrown into confusion by a report that the French fleet was on the coast. General Wise therefore gave notice that all troops should hold themselves ready to march at the shortest notice. The Island's voluntary force turned out and the news was that scarcely a single man was absent from the ranks. In a short time the whole military force on the Island – of which there was no small number – were ready to repel the enemy should they dare to attempt a landing. In the words of the journalist: 'After continuing under arms for several hours, it was discovered that there was not any likelihood of being called into immediate active service, as the fleet on the coast was found to be Friends, and not Enemies. The mistake arose either from them not seeing or not attending to the signals made from the signal-house on the Start Point, from whence it was concluded that they must be enemy ships. It is now said that the fleet coming up the Channel, which neglected to answer the signals, was the Oporto and Lisbon convoy.' (*Aberdeen Courier*, March 6th 1798)

~ MARCH 7TH ~

1837: Today's *Brighton Patriot* reported on the burial of Robert Wallbridge on Sunday, 26th of February at Newport in the Isle of Wight, the eldest and final surviving brother of Elizabeth Wallbridge, the much esteemed 'Dairyman's Daughter'. The *Patriot* reported that:

> He was brought to the knowledge of the truth [of religion] under the preaching of the Rev John Wesley, during his visit to the Isle of Wight in 1790. And for upwards of 30 years was a useful and acceptable local preacher. He was interred at Arreton churchyard on Friday last, where also rest the remains of his exemplary sister, who was convinced of the necessity of personal salvation under the Ministry of the Rev Y Crabb of Southampton, then a Home Missionary in the Wesleyan connexion [*sic*] and shortly afterwards joined the Society, of which her deep and unaffected piety evidenced that she was a bright ornament.

Elizabeth found posthumous fame as one of the deserving poor featured in the Revd Legh Richmond's book *Annals of the Poor*, published in 1814. (*Brighton Patriot*, March 7th 1837)

⟝ MARCH 8TH ⟞

1845: Today the *Chartist Intelligence* reported from Newport that, at the usual weekly meeting held on Tuesday evening at the King's Head, the following resolution was unanimously adopted: 'After considering the recent accusations against Mr O'Connell's conduct, we beg to express our unshaken confidence in him and to assure him that so long as he continues in the straightforward course he has hitherto pursued, he will merit and receive the best thanks and confidence of the working classes.' Daniel O'Connell, who had been elected to Parliament, had been unable to take his seat due to his being a Catholic and campaigned for a change in the law. After this was achieved, he fought for the repeal of the Act of Union that united both the Irish and English Parliaments. Chartism had begun as a working-class campaign to achieve certain fundamental rights for the majority, including: votes for all men over 21 years, secret ballots, no property qualifications, pay for MPs so that poorer men could enter Parliament and reform of the parliamentary constituencies to make them of equal size. In the first Chartist petition of 1839, 547 Islanders added their signatures. (*Chartist Intelligence*, March 8th 1845)

~ March 9th ~

1839: Today the *Salisbury and Winchester Journal* reported on the trial of Mary Mew, a laundress employed at Swainston Manor. She was accused of the murder of her baby, discovered in the privy at Swainston with what was probably the string of an apron tied about its neck. Mary was initially charged with concealing the birth but, while she was in the bridewell at Newport, the charge was changed to murder and she was taken to Winchester to stand trial. Elizabeth Witthingham, who shared a room with Mary, gave evidence. She said that for a few days Mary had been ill but she had not taken too much notice, as Mary was always 'in delicate health'. On the morning of July 21st last, Mary had not gone to church and the following night the witness saw her descend the stairs with the slop pail. She remained in her bed and when challenged she confessed that she had miscarried. The doctor was called and then the police. In court, Sir Richard Simeon, her employer, gave evidence as to her unblemished character, stating that Lady Simeon and the upper servants had entreated him to do so. Mr Cockburn for the defence said that she was a poor, motherless girl of extreme youth and begged the jury to show mercy. Many of them were in tears while Mary sobbed throughout the trial. It took the jury an hour to return a verdict of not guilty to the murder charge, but guilty of concealing the birth. She was sentenced to eighteen months in prison at Winchester. (*Salisbury and Winchester Journal*, March 9th 1839)

~ March 10th ~

1881: Today at the police court at Newport, Mr Edward Heathcote, a retired solicitor, was charged with assaulting Eliza Ann Denyer, the wife of a wine and spirit merchant, by striking her with a whip. Heathcote was well known as an eccentric man; he had held a commission in an American army during the civil war and was known locally as the 'captain'. The complainant stated that on Saturday afternoon she was walking along the footpath at the top of Newport High Street when she saw the defendant outside a public house. He followed her for some distance, making remarks, and after a few yards she felt a blow on her back and saw the thong of a long whip wrap round her dress. The defendant was very close to her and she was very frightened, although not hurt. John Parkes, rate-collector, witnessed the assault and corroborated her account. Mr Hooper, for the defence, said that Heathcote had flourished his whip in order to bring his dogs together and accidentally touched Mrs Denyer. The magistrates considered the case and announced that they found the defendant guilty. Heathcote had appeared before the bench on several occasions and was regarded as a public nuisance, and if his friends could not keep him out of mischief it was duty of the magistrates to punish him. He was therefore sentenced to a fortnight's imprisonment with hard labour and was removed by the constables to the adjoining cells. (*Isle of Wight Observer*, March 12th 1881)

~ March 11th ~

1797: At the Lent Assizes the names of sixty-two prisoners were listed, many of whom for capital offences. Among them were Gaspard Koop (a German) and Nicholas Wagner, accused of assaulting and ravishing Elizabeth Lock on Carisbrooke Common. Today's *Hampshire Chronicle* stated that:

> The evidence of the prosecutrix was so clear and satisfactory as not to admit of the smallest doubt of their guilt. They attacked the poor woman as she was going across the common in the daytime, and, throwing her to the ground, the one held her down and prevented her cries while the other completed his wicked purpose. Not content with each having abused the defenceless object of their brutality, Wagner would have repeated it but for fear of detection. Wagner offered no defence. Koop, through an interpreter, pleaded his innocence, alleging that through a severe wound in his breast he was rendered incapable of committing the act. The jury without hesitation found them both guilty and Judge Buller pronounced sentence of Death.

The report ended with the news that Elizabeth Lock was two or three months pregnant. It also observed that, although illness had suspended the business of the court, this was not true of the town's inns and public houses and a sum of £250 was reckoned to have been expended – 'so piously was fasting observed'. (*Hampshire Chronicle*, March 11th 1797)

~ March 12th ~

1870: On his retirement, after twenty years as vicar of Shalfleet, the much-loved Revd Thomas Cottle was presented with a massive gold pen and pencil case and a richly chased silver inkstand, paid for by a collection throughout the parish. An elegant silver card case was also purchased for Mrs Cottle for her services to the village. The gifts were accompanied by a parchment containing the names of the main contributors. During Cottle's time as minister, the *Hampshire Advertiser* recorded the improvements that had taken place in the parish. On his arrival he was faced with:

> … a church suffering from the neglect of years and blocked up with those monstrous square pews and unsightly galleries, which happily are now becoming extinct, no parochial schools in existence nor any other agencies which exercise so beneficial an influence. All this has now changed. The spacious and ancient church has now been restored and beautified. Excellent school buildings affording ample accommodation have been erected and many other means for the relief and assistance of the deserving have been successfully inaugurated. Special mention may be made of the provision for the welfare of the distant hamlet, afforded in the shape of a school chapel.

The Revd Cottle's name was further remembered in the parish in the erection of almshouses in Warlands Lane and the provision of a Rest Home for Horses that closed in the 1970s. (*Hampshire Advertiser*, March 12th 1870)

~ MARCH 13TH ~

1858: Today's *Hampshire Telegraph* carried a round-up of proceedings at the Island's Petty Sessions and Borough Court. At Ryde on Monday, James Simmonds, a groom in the employment of Mr Wilkins the surgeon, was charged with taking away a gig harness and two stable jackets that he then either pledged or sold in order to procure liquor, having 'a strong propensity for imbibing intoxicating liquids'. Simmonds pleaded guilty but, following a request for a lenient sentence from his employer, the Bench contented themselves with afflicting a one month's term of imprisonment, even though previous convictions had been brought against him. The *Telegraph* observed that 'A few weeks previous, the County Magistrates sent an offender to gaol for six months who was far less guilty than this drunken vagabond.' (*Hampshire Telegraph*, Saturday March 13th 1858)

~ MARCH 14TH ~

1817: Starting this day in the spring of 1817, John Keats made his first visit to the Isle of Wight. He stayed in Carisbrooke with a view of the castle that gave his poetic instincts full rein. He wrote immediately to his friend John Hamilton Reynolds, saying 'I have not seen many specimens of Ruins – I don't think however I shall see one to surpass Carisbrooke Castle'. He was also taken by the colony of jackdaws, thinking how their ancestors may have looked down on King Charles during his unfortunate stay. Keats also visited Shanklin where he was particularly inspired by the sight of the Chine. Writing again to Reynolds he could not hide his excitement at the sight of 'the sea, Jack – the little waterfall – then the white cliffs – then St Catherine's Hill'. Overwhelmed by the 'shadowy sound' of the tides he was moved to write his sonnet 'On the Sea', whose 'Mighty swell gluts twice ten thousand caverns.' It was while he was staying at Carisbrooke that he took a walk along the Bowcombe Valley that inspired him to start writing perhaps his most famous work, *Endymion*. The opening line 'A thing of beauty is a joy forever,' has become indelibly associated with Shanklin, where Keats Green was later named in his honour. Keats left the Island on April 24th/25th, but returned four years later. By this time three life changing events had occurred: Keats's brother Tom had died of tuberculosis, he had fallen madly in love and he was showing the first signs of the illness that would kill him at the age of 25. (Jan Toms, 'A Poet's View of the Isle of Wight', *Island Life Magazine*, Feb/March 2010)

— MARCH 15TH —

1897: Today two ships were in trouble off the Island coast. In a south-westerly gale at about 2 p.m., the Deal lugger *Walmer Castle* was seen to pass Ventnor Pier but was struck by a wave and capsized shortly afterwards. Two of her crew of four were spotted clinging to the rigging, but shortly afterwards all four men disappeared. Wreckage was later washed up just to the west of Ventnor Pier but there was no sign of the crewmembers. The Walmer Castle was only a ¼ mile from the shore and had she managed to round Dunnose Point then she may well have avoided her tragic end. At the other end of the Island, the *Totland* lifeboat answered a distress call that evening but was unable to render assistance to the *Brigantine Gudrun* from Fowey, washed ashore on the shingle. The crew, believed to be ten people, were all drowned. Four bodies in cork lifejackets were picked up and taken to Yarmouth for an inquest. With a slightly more positive outcome, a Norwegian brig sailing that day from Cowes ran into trouble off Seaford and eight crewmembers were rescued. Unhappily it later transpired that two others had died. (*Manchester Evening News*, March 16th 1897)

— MARCH 16TH —

1754: The gathering of news across the country relied on sources that were frequently found to be misleading. Today's *Ipswich Journal* reported that: 'There is Advice from Cowes, that the Sloop from Barbadoes [*sic*], riding Quarantain [*sic*] on the Motherbank, between Portsmouth and the Isle of Wight, is ordered out to Sea, and to be sunk in deep water: and that his Majesty's Ship the *Arundel*, of 20 Guns, is to attend to the Execution of these Orders.' In the same edition, it added a further bulletin from the *Evening Advertiser* that all but three of the men belonging to the vessel ordered to be sunk off the Isle of Wight were dead. A further snippet in the same edition of the *Ipswich Journal* reported that: '13000 is ordered to be paid to the Owners of the Vessel lately sunk off the Isle of Wight; and that the surviving persons are closely confined on a small Vessel, provisions being conveyed to them with the utmost caution.' What finally became of them is not known. Such extreme measures were taken due to the fear that the plague may be spread. (*Ipswich Journal*, March 16th 1754)

~ March 17th ~

1848: The *Hampshire Telegraph* today carried a short report that Carisbrooke Water was now laid down in most of the streets of Newport, and the supply and excellent quality gave general satisfaction. This was the latest in a long and generally unsuccessful attempt to provide the capital with a water supply. Although the area is liberally fed with springs, the supply could run dry as the occupants of Carisbrooke Castle discovered to their cost in 1136 (in this case ending a siege). In 1618, one Philip Fleming planned to lay tree trunks through which to transport water around the area. He obtained a 300-year lease provided that he completed the project within three years. Clearly he failed, for by 1623 another licence had been granted to Mr Andrew Jackson. His plan was to have a central storage cistern and stand various collecting receptacles at strategic points. This too came to nothing. In 1709, William Arnold took out a lease to sink a cistern on the corner of St James's Square and the high street and to pipe the river water to local roads. The proximity of water in case of fire was clearly appealing, but again the system failed. (*Hampshire Telegraph*, March 17th 1848)

— March 18th —

1873: From the *Sheffield Daily Telegraph* of March 19th came the exciting news of a kidnapping:

> Mr Rhodes, a solicitor from the Isle of Wight went to London a short time ago. He stayed at the Inns of Court Hotel and on the second evening, went to the Queen's Theatre but did not return to his hotel. The following morning the manager of the hotel received a letter from the gentleman saying that he had been kidnapped as he left the hotel and was being held in a loathsome place near to the river. Similar letters were received by his friends. The police searched without success and a reward of £20 was offered for his safe return.

The reward, plus other money, was given to the captors before they would set him at liberty, and when they did so he was minus most of his clothes and anything of value he had with him. Information was sent to the Island that he was to be expected at Southampton this day and Mr Black, his clerk, was despatched to meet him with a suit of clothes. On arrival he quickly changed and was driven to his home in a closed carriage. (*Sheffield Daily Telegraph*, March 18th 1873)

~ MARCH 19TH ~

1871: Today at 1 p.m. as two cows were being driven to the market, one of them rushed at a regimental sergeant in Lower St James's Street and thrust him against the windows of Mr Milligan's shop. Although one horn went through the window, the sergeant was fortunately not injured as the horns overlapped his body. With great presence of mind he dropped flat on the pavement and remained motionless until the animal was driven off. The enraged bull then went into the high street where it attacked the wife and child of Mr J.R. Blake, of Blackwater, Arreton. It lifted the child on its horns and dashed it against its mother, causing them both to fall on the pavement. Neither Mrs Blake nor the child were very injured. After it was driven off it ran from street to street and when going up West Street it met an elderly woman carrying a box. She had the presence of mind to hold it in front of her; when the infuriated beast attacked her it struck the box with its horns, the force of the blow knocking the woman down. The animal next made an attack upon a lad who, in his endeavour to get out of the animal's way, fell and broke a kneecap. There was great excitement when the attack was made upon the sergeant and Mrs Blake, as it was in full view of the market. (*Hampshire Telegraph*, March 22nd 1871)

~ March 20th ~

1835: According to the *Brighton Patriot* of Tuesday, March 24th:

… some very satisfactory experiments were made on Friday last, on Bowcomb Down, with Dennett's rockets for saving lives from shipwreck, in the presence of numerous respectable inhabitants of this town and neighbourhood, who were much gratified by the admirable precision with which they were directed, not one having apparently deviated in the smallest degree from the intended line of fire. One rocket took out upwards of 1050 feet of very stout line, others of smaller size weighing less than six pounds each took out 750 feet with surprising velocity … The magnificent steamships of the Leith and London Shipping Company have been equipped with this additional security to the lives of their numerous passengers; and it is to be hoped that this valuable information will now be generally adopted on board ship, as well as along various dangerous parts of the coast. Several noblemen's yachts are also about to be furnished with these rockets as a means of defence, in which their effective powers will greatly exceed those of guns, particularly against piratical marauders (now almost the only enemy to be found at sea) … Mr H Clarke, gun founder &c has been appointed the agent for these rockets for Portsmouth and the neighbourhood.

Mr Dennett is buried in St Mary's Carisbrooke churchyard. (*Brighton Patriot*, March 24th 1835)

~ MARCH 21ST ~

1211: When the body of Simon of Atherfield was discovered, his death was at first attributed to an attack by French raiders. On the 21st March, however, his wife, Amicia was accused of murdering him. Amicia was the daughter of Hugh de Norays about which little is recorded, although in 1294 there are references to Richard and Robert de Norays of the Isle of Wight. The repercussions following Simon's death could not have been foreseen. Shortly afterwards, reports of miracles began to circulate and before long local people were leaving tributes at his tomb. Over the following months, pilgrims left donations of £7. This was not just a local phenomenon and late in the year his martyrdom was inscribed in the records of Gonville and Caius College Cambridge and he became St Simon. For whatever reason, this cult of St Simon was clearly not to the liking of the church and steps were taken to suppress it, so the site of his grave is unknown. As for poor Amicia, she was tried for petty treason, found guilty and sentenced to the agonising death of being burned at the stake. 'Saint' Simon is recorded as having been a 'martyr to his wife', although some might question which of them was the martyr.
(S.F. Hockey, *Insula Vecta*, Phillimore, 1982)

— MARCH 22ND —

1899: The first IWFA Challenge Cup Final was to go down in footballing history. The match at Church Litten was played this day between Ryde and Sandown before a crowd of 1,500 people. With minutes to go, Ryde striker William Jones scored the winning goal. Unfortunately, in the process he collided with Sandown keeper Robert Read who accidentally struck him in the chest. Jones collapsed and was pronounced to have two broken ribs and 'concussion of the heart'. He was taken to Ryde hospital where it was discovered that he had a ruptured intestine and he died two days later. The President of the Association, Dr Thompson felt bound to postpone the winning ceremony and hold an enquiry. The inquest was held the following Wednesday and only those officials from the clubs concerned were permitted to attend. Witnesses were detained outside the courtroom until they were called to give evidence. Those who witnessed the match were in agreement that they had seen no evidence of foul play and that in their opinion the collision was an accident. Reed had suffered an injury to his knee and also broke a little finger. With Jones's death, the Ryde team declared that they preferred that Sandown should be awarded the game. In turn Sandown declared that they had no wish to have either the cup or medals in these circumstances. Jones was buried at St John's church, his funeral cortege passing through the town. The coffin was placed on an open hearse and carried by eight members of the Ryde club to Ryde Cemetery, with at least fifty wreaths covering the coffin. Read was present and booed by the crowd. (Mick Bull, 'Keep it on the Island', marking the centenary of the Isle of Wight Football Association)

~ MARCH 23RD ~

1866: The *Tale Boure*, under sail and carrying oranges, figs and salt, today came to grief near Sandown Bay. A south-easterly gale was blowing and seeing the danger, the coastguards fired warning rockets which she appeared to ignore, being driven towards the shore where she became 'embayed'. Her crew cut both the fore and main masts but to no effect. Twice the coastguards tried to reach the crew but the sea was too rough and they returned ashore empty-handed. By 1.30 a.m. the vessel was going to pieces and the coastguard again set out. This time they managed to rescue one man and at a fourth attempt picked up six more. Meanwhile, a small fishing craft set out to help and managed to rescue the rest of the crew who were taken to the Sandown Hotel for dry clothes, where they received the stark message that their ship was now matchwood. Subsequently one of the rescue boatmen, Walter Main, was charged with stealing a piece of rope from the stricken ship. He was later discharged with a warning. (Richard and Bridget Larn, *Shipwreck Index of the British Isles*, Lloyds Register, Vol. 3, 1995)

⟶ MARCH 24TH ⟵

1878: It was a beautiful Sunday afternoon and the public at Ventnor were enjoying the sunshine. The sight of a ship in full sail caused many to watch and regret the arrival of the age of steam. A few sailors remarked that they should reduce sail in the freshening wind as she was clearly racing to make port before dark. Then, with freak suddenness, a storm blew up causing the sightseers to flee for cover. When they emerged it was as if the ship *Eurydice* had never been.

It was a training ship, keeping alive those skills needed when relying on canvas rather than steam. Aboard were 270 men, 26 marines, 16 officers and 7 passengers, returning from the Caribbean. The *Eurydice* sank with terrifying speed and when the schooner *Emma* reached her, only the topmost mask was visible. Nearly all of the crew had been below deck and they drowned. At the inquest at Ventnor, one of the only two survivors, Able Seaman Benjamin Cuddiford gave evidence. He had tried to save others without success and there were questions about the ship's stability and the ballast she carried. Were the gun ports open? Who was to blame? There were no obvious answers. Bizarrely Cuddiford and his follow survivor, a young lad named Sidney Fletcher, were charged with losing their ship. The captain of the *Emma* was also criticised because, being a temperance ship, she had no brandy aboard to revive any rescued men. Some bodies later washed ashore were buried at Shanklin and at Christchurch, Sandown. (Ken Phillips, *Shipwrecks of the Isle of Wight*)

~ March 25th ~

1663: Today was Lady Day and the newly instituted Hearth Tax was due for collection. Its purpose was to raise funds to support the cash-strapped royal household, whose expenses were increased by the pursuit of a war against the Dutch. In an initial attempt at 'fairness' the charge of 2s a year was payable for every hearth/chimney in a dwelling, to be collected in two halves, at Michaelmas and Lady Day. The tax was further disliked when it emerged that the distinction was not made between the owners of the property and the tenants, the latter as occupiers being deemed liable for the payment. At the end of the first period, the actual amount collected was about 35 per cent of that anticipated. Thereafter various modifications were introduced, but people resented their houses being inspected and a general reluctance or inability to find the money saw the tax withdrawn in 1689. However, the records do give an insight into the sizes of towns and villages at the time. In 1664, Newtown was liable for 12 hearths, Shalfleet for 50, Swaynton [sic] 127, Yarmouth 130, St Helens 136, Brading 56, Sandham [Sandown] 59 and Knighton 72. (Hearth Tax Returns for the Isle of Wight)

~ MARCH 26TH ~

1789: The *Hampshire Chronicle* today published the following account from the Borough of Newport:

> At a general meeting of the Corporation of this Borough, held at the Guildhall, for the purpose of Addressing His Majesty on his late establishment of Health, the following was unanimously assented to … To the KING's most excellent MAJESTY, the humble ADDRESS of the Mayor, Aldermen and Chief Burgesses of the Borough of Newport. Most Gracious Sovereign, WE … beg leave (among the just and universal acclamations of joy expressed by all Your Majesty's faithful subjects), to present our sincere and heartfelt congratulations on your late, happy recovery. Dutifully and inviolably attached to Your Majesty's Sacred Person, and the Illustrious House of Brunswick, we earnestly pray that the same Divine Providence, may grant the ardent prayers of all Your Majesty's loyal subjects, may grant the continuance of every felicity to Your Majesty and that Your Majesty may long reign over a loyal and affectionate people …

Having completed the address to their satisfaction, the *Chronicle* reported that the mayor, aldermen and burgesses then 'retired to the Green Dragon Inn where an elegant entertainment was presented by Mr Buffett, our present worthy Mayor, when many loyal and constitutional toasts were drunk, and the day concluded with every mark of joy'. The king in question was George III. (*Hampshire Chronicle*, March 26th 1789)

~ March 27th ~

1742: Today's *London Evening Post* carried a report announcing this intriguing news:

> Some small time since, a Discovery was made by a Custom-house Officer, on board an outward bound British ship at Cowes of £35,000 in British coin, which was artfully concealed with a Design to be carried abroad contrary to Act of Parliament in that Case provided; on which account the Vessel's Voyage was for some time retarded; but it was not known in the Isle of Wight to whom the money belonged.

Doubtless the hapless owner faced the dilemma of either losing a fortune or coming forward and facing a prison sentence. (*London Evening Post*, March 27th 1741)

— MARCH 28TH —

1889: Today's *Freshwater Advertiser* described how one of Freshwater's oldest cottages had been consumed by fire in an unfortunate and ironic accident. The cottage stood on the corner of The Causeway and had formerly been a mill. Its owner, Mr G. Fletcher-Jones, had the site earmarked for a gatekeeper's lodge to service the new railway passing from Yarmouth to Freshwater. At the time the cottage was occupied by Mr J.B. Tucker and he in turn, allowed a poor widow with no means of support to live in it rent-free. After visiting, Mr Fletcher Jones decided that he was unwilling both to pull down the historic cottage and also to evict the woman, so he decided to erect a new lodge on the opposite side of the road. The railway line had opened for goods traffic on September 9th the previous year and on the day that Mr Fletcher-Jones visited, a strong wind was blowing. After he left, a spark from one of the goods engines must have caught the thatch alight and the old cottage was burned to the ground. A gatekeeper's lodge therefore was erected in its place. The Newport–Freshwater Railway was formally opened to passengers in 1889. (*Freshwater Advertiser*, March 28th 1889)

— MARCH 29TH —

1873: The *Hampshire Advertiser* reported today on the latest attempts to mine coal from the cliffs at Whitecliff: 'We hear that two shafts have been sunk in the slope of the cliff at this place – under the direction of Government officials we presume – for the purpose of ascertaining the facts in reference to the existence of coal in the locality. One of the shafts has been abandoned through the slippage of the cliff, and also in consequence of being overflooded [*sic*]. The other shaft has been sunk to a depth of about 25 feet, and we are told that a large quantity of coal has been extracted therefrom.' The fuel was in fact lignite or brown coal, a softer fossil somewhere between coal and peat. It was found not to burn very well and any large-scale extraction was therefore abandoned. (*Hampshire Advertiser*, March 29th 1873)

~ MARCH 30TH ~

1869: Today's *New York Citizen* published extracts from a letter by a man calling himself a wandering Yankee who had dined with Lord Tennyson at Farringford: 'We dined at six in a quaint room … and then went into the drawing room for dessert. Tennyson and I retired to his study at the top of the house, lit pipes and talked of poetry … The first thing he did was to produce a magnum of wonderful sherry, thirty years old which had been sent him by a poetic wine-dealer. Such wine I never tasted. "It was meant to be drunk by Cleopatra or Catherine of Russia," said Tennyson … After this Tennyson and I did a bottle of the poet's "Waterloo 1815" the author of Guinivere saying "We will make a night of it!"' The *New York Citizen* continued that after drinks all round, Tennyson treated his guest to the *Idylls of the King*. Finally, at the point where Arthur forgives the queen, Tennyson's voice finally broke. The visitor reported, 'I found tears on my cheeks and Mrs Tennyson was crying …' Tennyson, however, made an effort and carried on to the end, closing "grandly.' After this, Tennyson and I, of course, had more drink, then went up to the garret to smoke and talk.' The *Citizen* concluded that Mr Tennyson, having read his own poems to his guest for the best part of the night, wound up with Andrew Marvel's 'Coy Mistress', and the Yankee and the poet separated at two o'clock. (*New York Citizen*, March 30th 1869)

~ MARCH 31ST ~

1942: Leonard Raven-Hill, the celebrated cartoonist of *Punch* magazine died today at his home in Queens Road, Ryde, Isle of Wight. He was 75 years old and came to live on the Island at the time of his retirement. Mr Raven-Hill began work with *Punch* in 1896 and remained there for forty years. His cartoons were particularly associated with farming and the sea; during his life he worked as a farmer and was also an enthusiastic yachtsman. Described as the last of the great Victorian artists, he spent his childhood in Bath and later went to France to study art. He was also an accomplished water colourist. (*Hull Daily Mail*, March 31st 1942)

~ APRIL 1st ~

1845: After a day strolling along Compton Beach towards Brook, Gideon Mantell, surgeon and geologist, recorded his impressions in his journal '... we walked along the shore, close under the Cliffs, and examined the Wealden Strata, to Brook Point ... an homeward bound Indiaman [the *Siam*], laden with silks, camphor etc., had been wrecked off Compton Chine a few days previously, and the shore was still strewn with its contents, and scores of men, women and children from the neighbouring villages, were spread over the sands collecting spoils of the wreck.' Mantell, whose medical career suffered from his passion for fossil collecting, soon became an avid prospector along the Island's southern coast from which the locals were quick to profit. On this day, having called at some cottages at Brixton, he procured several bones of Cetiosaurus, then at the customs house at Atherfield he purchased a few fossils – clearly the fisherfolk sold more than fish. Mantell later sold his collection to the British Museum for £4,000. Days before this visit, the Yarmouth coastguard cutter had rescued six of the crew from the *Siam* while the rest had made their own way ashore. Lieutenant Gould of the Coastguard Service was awarded a silver medal for bravery for his part in the rescue. (E. Cecil Curwen (ed.), *The Journal of Gideon Mantell 1818–1852*)

~ April 2nd ~

1793: After nearly seven weeks anchored off the coast, ships carrying hundreds of soldiers from the German territory of Hesse were finally allowed to come ashore. In the struggle against the French, the Duke of York had recruited troops from his German cousins but the number turned out to be far in excess of those required. In early January they arrived at Spithead. A shock awaited them for, although they were British allies, being foreigners they were not permitted to land. Apart from soldiers, the ships were packed with horses and within the next two weeks many of them died. Reluctantly the rest of the animals were unloaded, along with grooms, who had to supply their own food and accommodation, but the troops remained on board. An infectious illness broke out so as a concession the soldiers were allowed to come ashore for 2 hours. By February 21st, 641 men were sick but it was another week before they were found accommodation ashore in unheated, draughty, makeshift storerooms. Those who survived finally departed on April 2nd to continue the fight against the French, leaving eighty-two men and two women behind, buried in Whippingham churchyard, their resting places unmarked. In 1906, their sacrifice was finally acknowledged when a plaque was erected inside St Mildred's church. (Visitors' Centre St Mildred's church, Whippingham (summer only))

~ April 3rd ~

1858: Excitement at finding skeletons at Ryde on this day was soon quashed by the reporter of *Isle of Wight Observer* stating:

> It is a well-known fact to the old inhabitants of Ryde that the 'Dover' now called the Strand, was the burial place of hundreds of the men who perished by the capsizing of the 'Royal George' at Spithead in 1782, and also of an immense number of Lascars who perished by disease on board an East Indiaman near Spithead near to the same period. In putting in the new sewer in the locality during the past week it is not at all surprising therefore, to find that numerous human remains were discovered, but we should not at all have expected to find them in such a state of excellent preservation. They were re-buried with proper decorum by the contractor.

The sinking of the *Royal George* was a ghastly accident. As she was about to sail, hasty, last-minute repairs were carried out and the ship was heeled over to allow part of the hull to be above the water line. Unfortunately she tipped too far. Water rushed into some open gun ports and with terrifying speed she sank. Apart from the crew and workmen, about 200–300 friends and relatives were reckoned to be on board, saying farewell. The total number was about 1,500 people. In 2009 a memorial was unveiled at Ashley Gardens on Ryde Esplanade. (*Isle of Wight Observer* April 3rd 1858, Royal Museum Greenwich: An Account of the Sinking of the *Royal George*)

~ April 4th ~

1864: 'Cowes claims the honour of being the first spot in the Isle of Wight trod by the greatest man who ever set foot on our soil.' So wrote the reporter for the *Isle of Wight Observer* on the visit of Giuseppi Garibaldi as a guest of Charles Seely at Brooke House. Some 2,000 people greeted him with cheers and banners and marched with him the 15 miles to Brooke House; Cowes shipbuilder J. Samuel White gave his workers a day off to take part. During his visit, Garibaldi visited Lord Tennyson at Farringford where a crowd waited at the gates. Like Seely, Tennyson was a supporter of Italian unification and Garibaldi was its hero. Tennyson reportedly advised his guest against talking politics in England so they recited poetry to each other, each in their own language, where Tennyson was at a disadvantage in not understanding Italian. Whilst on the Island, Garibaldi planted two trees, an oak dubbed The Liberty Tree at Brooke House and a Wellingtonia at Farringford, both now sadly deceased. Perhaps the Italian's greatest impression was on Mary Seely who cut off a lock of his hair as a keepsake and wrote after his departure: 'When alas! you had left me yesterday and my heart was heavy with grief, I went to your little bed full of emotion and sorrow that your dear and revered head would not rest there again.' This does not seem to have worried Charles Seely who confirmed that 'my wife and I long to have you back again, all to ourselves'. Following his departure, Garibaldi was granted the freedom of London. (*Isle of Wight Observer*, April 4th 1864)

~ APRIL 5TH ~

1879: The *Aldershot Military Gazette* reported that Richard King, the former manager of the Capital and Counties Bank at Ventnor who had absconded the previous November, had today been apprehended. King had served for several years as a bank manager and at the time of his disappearance it was thought he had gone to the mainland to visit his family. After some days it dawned on the staff that something was wrong and, on investigating the Bank's accounts, several thousand pounds were found to be missing. At the time, the *Isle of Wight Observer* recorded that Mr Daniel Attrill, one of the bank's customers and an associate of King's, had been apprehended and in the ensuing struggle Attrill struck a policeman and had to be restrained. Attrill was described as a farmer and butcher and was found guilty of fraud, the judge exclaiming that he was being as lenient as possible, in sentencing him to twelve months' hard labour. King's fate was considerably worse. Having fled to Buenos Aires he was imprisoned as being insane and there suffered severe beatings and cruelty. (*Aldershot Military Gazette*, April 15th 1879)

～ April 6th ～

1853: In a letter dated today, a local man signing himself HUMANITAS, felt obliged to write to the *Isle of Wight Observer* warning the public of the potential danger in the steamers and other boats travelling to and from Southampton. The correspondent had checked out the life-saving equipment aboard the steamers, concluding that: 'The boats carried by all the companies are absolutely useless. They are common punts, not lifeboats, about 10' to 12' long and consequently scarcely able to carry the crew safely, to say nothing of the passengers. One Company carries its boats to the stern and it is doubtful whether, in a sudden requirement, they could be lowered properly. Another company carries theirs on the deck of the steamers without any equipment whatever for lowering!!! … Supposing that all should go right, how could such numbers be accommodated? Swamping would inevitably result.' He concluded by reminding the companies that 'Prevention is better than Cure'. (*Isle of Wight Observer*, April 9th 1853)

⟶ April 7th ⟵

1865: A reporter for the *Isle of Wight Observer* was shown a petrified bird's nest dug from the chalk at the Wroxall end of the railway tunnel currently being excavated to Ventnor. He described that it had been found last February and that the nest, in a perfect state of preservation, contained five eggs, four of them whole. The moss and twigs, and even the colour of the moss was perfectly discernible. It was identified as being a bullfinch's nest and would be on display in the window of Mr Dennis's shop in Ventnor. (*Isle of Wight Observer*, April 7th 1865)

~ APRIL 8TH ~

1630: Today four ships sailed from Yarmouth carrying Puritan emigrants under the auspices of wealthy lawyer Henry Winthrop. Known as the Great Migration, the *Isabella*, the *Talbot*, the *Ambrose* and the *Jewell* safely reached Salem. The colonists then moved on to form the Massachusetts Bay Company and to settle in what became the city of Boston. Earlier, on February 11th of that year, the church register for Newport recorded the following five marriages: Henry Bushell to Alice Crocker, Christopher Cradock to Alice Cook, Edmund Marshall to Marye Mitchell, Walter Beare to Anne Green and Robert Gullafer to Joan Pie. The entries carried the following footnote: 'Last fyve cupples were for Virginia.' After the marriage ceremony it seems likely that they sailed on the ship *Abigail* that was then calling at the Island en route for the colonies. In 1633, ships left the Island to form the colony of Maryland and the Isle of Wight County, Virginia was founded in 1634. (James Eldridge, *Newport Isle of Wght in Bygone Days*, Newport, 1952)

~ April 9th ~

1877: On this day at Winchester Court, Ann Stallard gave evidence at the trial of her daughter Frances who was accused of killing her 2-year-old daughter, Agnes. Agnes had been born in the workhouse and, when her mother found work with Emily Meager at Ventnor, Agnes was farmed out to a Mrs Simmons of Newbridge. News reached Frances that her daughter was unwell and with her mother she went to fetch Agnes home. The toddler was in a dreadful state and could neither sit nor use her arms and legs so Frances said that she was taking the child to the relatives of her father in Lymington. In evidence Ann stated that Agnes became very distressed during the journey so Frances 'placed a cloth over her face', after which she stopped breathing. Frances concealed her in a culvert and told her mother and employer that Agnes had been safely delivered. When the body was discovered, Frances was put on trial and although the jury recommended mercy the judge sentenced her to death. At the last moment the sentence was commuted to life in prison. Frances became a cause celebre, featuring in the book *Only a Woman's Life* by Mrs Houston. After fourteen years of campaigning she was released from gaol and returned to the Island. (*Hants Advertiser*, May 25th 1899)

~ April 10th ~

1901: The fourth annual Point to Point races took place today at Afton, Freshwater. The *Freshwater Advertiser* edition of April 13th described the event: 'Heavy rain fell in the morning but the sun broke through by midday. Afton Road was wet and muddy as hundreds of people made their way from Freshwater Railway station to the course. The Downs gave a grandstand view of the four-mile course and below one could see the fashionable turnouts as they arrived, bookmakers calling the odds ... and a good view across the Solent. The first race started at 2.00pm with the Isle of Wight Heavyweight Race, horses to carry 13 stone 7lbs or over. 1st: Mr Mearman riding Countess; 2nd Mr F Philip on Vixen; 3rd Mr W Shorthose riding Tyke.' (*Freshwater Advertiser*, April 10th 1901)

~ April 11th ~

1833: Jeremiah Sailow, a hawker, was found guilty of gaming on the Steeplechase racecourse at Ashey today. He was discovered behind the coffee tent surrounded by about forty people who he was encouraging to take their chance by laying out money. He had a board containing lots of coloured pegs and a turret through which balls were dropped and only occasionally did he pay any money out. On being discovered he ran away, but was caught and when searched, he had the sum of £1 19s 10½d in small change. After hearing his case, the magistrate decided that as he had been in custody for four days he would only fine him 2s 6d. His board and turret were confiscated. (*Isle of Wight Observer*, April 14th 1833)

April 12th

1912: Mr Alfred Ernest Nicholson of Shanklin was the only Island resident and passenger to drown in the *Titanic* disaster. Nicholson, a tea merchant who lived in Prospect Road, was on his way to visit his sister Mrs Ripley in New York. Leaving his wife behind, he treated himself to a first-class ticket costing £26. Following the accident, his body was picked up by the steamer *Mackay Bennet*. He was identified by a pearl scarf pin with the letter N, his gold watch and chain, a diamond horseshoe pin, gold cufflinks, three gold studs and £9 in gold in his pocket book. Mrs Nicholson did not arrange for the return of Alfred's body and it was forwarded instead to his sister, who buried him in New York. Also aboard the *Titanic*, serving as a steward, was Henry Charles Fairall of Ryde. As a young man he worked as a messenger for the post office, living in Surrey Street, but in 1911 he married and, with three daughters, began a new career by moving to Portsmouth and working for the Ocean Star Navigation Company. At some point before April 1912 he signed up as a steward first class in Belfast and was part of the fated maiden voyage of the *Titanic*. His body was never identified. (Information supplied by Shanklin History Society and Ryde Social Heritage Group)

~ April 13th ~

1949: In February the Labour Party Executive chose to hold their annual conference for the first and only time on the Isle of Wight. The venue was Shanklin Manor, a house owned by the Workers Travellers' Association. Sixty members were present including Prime Minister Clement Attlee, Sir Stafford Cripps, Dr Edith Summerskill, Ernest Bevin, Aneurin Bevan and a youthful Harold Wilson. Locally, curiosity and indifference turned to outrage when it was discovered that the delegates had consumed more than their permitted bacon ration. The managers of Cowes and Shanklin Co-ops, the manager of Shanklin Manor and the executive of the WTA were all accused of flouting the Food Rationing Order. Counsel for the hotel and the WTA explained that the offence had been a purely technical one and that nobody had being buying bacon under the counter; the belief that delegates were gorging themselves on bacon while it was unavailable to the local population was untrue. The Minister of Food himself had been present, as was the Chancellor of the Exchequer who was vegetarian, and in addition he had declined to accept an extra portion of cheese to which he was entitled. The *Western Morning News* of April 13th reported that a fine of £2 with £10 costs was today imposed for each summons. (*Western Morning News*, April 13th 1949)

~ April 14th ~

1877: Today's *Hampshire Advertiser* reported that on the previous Wednesday (April 11th) a meeting was held at the Fountain Hotel, Cowes to collect donations from the town's tradespeople towards the presentation of the annual town cup. The cup would be presented to the Royal Yacht Squadron at the time of the regatta in August but an early selection of the design was essential to ensure that it was ready in good time. The selection of a suitable cup was already underway and at the meeting, Mr James Dimmick, who would supply the cup this year, showed members the proposed design. He also had three cups on approval, and one of these of an entirely novel design was chosen. The *Advertiser* was confident that the RYS would admire the chosen cup as much for its intrinsic value, as for its beauty. (*Hampshire Advertiser*, April 14th 1887)

⸺ April 15th ⸺

1947: The *Worcester Journal* today reported on the success of an experiment recently carried out by Mr Nott with his electric telegraph. A single wire was sunk across the river Medina from East to West Cowes and the telegraphs were set up on each side, in the Medina Hotel and the Fountain Hotel. Enthusiastically the journalist explained that:

> The signal bells were then rung simultaneously, and the telegraphs commenced working and communicating questions and answers with the greatest precision and certainty with a galvanic battery of a low power showing that a single isolated wire immersed in the water could carry the electric current a distance of half a mile. The water brought back the current to its source without the slightest perceptible dispersion or loss of the dynamic power. This experiment demonstrates the perfect practicability of submarine communication, and the question as to its application may be said to be satisfactorily solved. The consequences can scarcely be as yet appreciated, though they are wonderful to contemplate. Instantaneous communication may be established between places divided by estuaries and channels, and islands and continents brought into immediate proximity of correspondence.

(*Worcester Journal*, April 15th 1947)

~ April 16th ~

1866: Tuesday 16th saw the second and final day of the Isle of Wight Steeplechases at Gatcombe. The *Isle of Wight Observer* of April 21st reported on the event. 'A motley and weather-beaten crowd of pedestrians attended plus the biggest number of carriages yet. The grandstand too was crowded although all around it was a complete mass of mud.' The *Observer* elaborated how: 'On the ground were the usual beer drinking booths, broken down acrobats … thimble-riggers, brass bands and their attendant paraphernalia: and amongst the company there were high and low, gentle and simple; costly dress and jewelled fingers side by side with rags and dirt, all alike in search of enjoyment.' There was a full programme of races and although the weather improved on the second day, there were a few mishaps. 'A valuable horse belonging to Mr Snowdon Henry was staked, and although every assistance was rendered, it was found necessary to kill it. The same gentleman also had to shoot a very valuable horse that broke its leg in the first race.' (*Isle of Wight Observer*, April 21st 1866)

~ APRIL 17TH ~

1880: Today the election results for the Isle of Wight so incensed Conservative supporter and chemist Francis Cory that he assaulted George Johnson, a hawker. Soon after the result was announced, the defeated Conservative candidate was being escorted along the High Street when Johnson was tripped up and as he attempted to rise he was hit on the back of the head with a thick walking stick. He was rendered insensible, his head was cut open and he suffered a great loss of blood. His face was also cut in the fall. Two witnesses positively identified Cory as the man who had struck the blow. A police sergeant and a constable who were escorting the candidate, however, said that they saw the complainant stumble but did not see anyone strike him. The bench considered that there was insufficient evidence to confirm the assault and therefore dismissed the case. Nationally it took between March 31st to April 27th for all the constituency results to be gathered in. On the Island, the successful candidate was the Hon. Evelyn Ashley for the Liberals. (*Aldershot Military Gazette*, April 17th 1880)

~ April 18th ~

1864: Today the last of a series of lectures was given to the Philosophical and Scientific Society at Melville Street in Ryde. The lecturer was the Revd W.M. Frost MA on the subject of The Telescope. The *Hampshire Telegraph* reported that his talk was a graphic and comprehensive account of the development of the telescope until it reached its present perfect state. He brought with him both examples and illustrations. The talk was deemed to be 'of a strictly scientific nature which was absolutely called for from the nature of the society'. The downside however was that 'The attendance had been very meagre, for in Ryde, as in all other towns, the masses both high and low, are not by any means scientific.' The journalist concluded that the Directors had provided an excellent bill of fare but that: 'if large audiences are desired, then popular subjects must be selected.' (*Hampshire Telegraph*, April 23rd 1864)

– April 19th –

1917: On this day, the sons of several notable families on the Island were killed in the second Battle of Gaza when the British Expeditionary Force fought against Turkey in an effort to gain control of the Mediterranean. The first two battles ended in defeat. Charles Seymour Pittis MC of the Hampshire Regiment was the eldest son of Seymour and Kate Pittis, owners of Hale Manor. Aged only 21, he was a partner in the family firm of Roach, Pittis and had been awarded the military cross for his part in the Gallipolli campaign. His memorial plaque in St George's church, Arreton was designed by Island architect Percy Stone. Captain Stephen Gilbert Ratsey, son of the sail-making family at Cowes, shared the unhappy fate of being lost at Gaza with his brothers Donald and Thomas; their memorial is displayed at St Mary's church, Cowes. In St Olave's church at Gatcombe, a memorial tomb acknowledges the death on the same day of Charles Grant Seely who 'fell gloriously, thrice wounded'. His family, who grew wealthy from coal mining, acquired land at Brook, Brighstone, Mottistone and Gatcombe. Involved locally in politics, they were also associated with the lifeboat at Brighstone and donated the Seely Library to Newport. (Isle of Wight Monuments and Memorials online records)

~ April 20th ~

1313: As a storm raged along the Island's south coast, the ship *Marie de Bayonne* ran aground near St Catherine's Point. The crew managed to get ashore safely but the locals were more concerned with retrieving the cargo – 174 barrels of white wine. They successfully rescued 150 barrels which the local lord of the manor, Walter de Goditon, promptly confiscated from the now-drunk Islanders. Unsurprisingly, the owners of the ship registered a complaint and de Goditon and three others were arrested although they swore that they had been elsewhere on the day in question. Eventually their story was worn down; the other three admitted to having accepted an odd barrel and De Goditon claimed to have bought fifty-three casks from the crew. The goods were seized and he was prepared to accept a fine as an occupational hazard. He did not know that the wine in question was en route to the Monastery of Livers in Picardy and was communion wine, blessed by the Pope. Threatened with excommunication, de Goditon prepared to save his soul by building a lighthouse and an adjoining chapel above the bay and employing a priest to pray for the souls of those in peril from the sea. The effectiveness of the light was very limited. Known locally as the Pepper Pot, its ruins remain on St Catherine's Down. (S.F. Hockey, *Insula Vecta*, Phillimore, 1982)

~ April 21st ~

1890: Wealthy yachtsman Frank James, the eldest son of 'a gentleman of American extraction', celebrated his thirty-ninth birthday by taking part in an elephant hunt in West Africa. When he twice shot at a bull elephant it, along with the herd, turned and charged, goring James in the chest. He died from his wounds. In his memory his brothers elected to build a hospital at East Cowes for the accommodation of elderly seamen. Known as the Frank James Memorial Hospital, the beautiful, single-storey, brick-built home was opened by Princess Beatrice on June 25th 1903. The running costs were covered by generous endowments and legacies from wealthy supporters. In 1948 it became part of the NHS and continued to offer both long-term and respite care. Having been bequeathed to the people of East Cowes, the building was nevertheless sold and allowed to deteriorate. There are strenuous efforts to safeguard its future. (Courtesy East Cowes Heritage Centre)

— April 22nd —

1645: The Earl of Pembroke, as Island Governor, received instructions to detain and discreetly search the ship and person of the Duchesse de Chevreuse, intercepted at sea as she made for the port of Dartmouth. The lady, known to be a friend of King Charles's wife Queen Henrietta Maria, was suspected of bringing large sums of money from France intended for the Royalist cause. She was taken to Newport to await her fate. The duchesse was in fact on a more personal mission, fleeing France having been banned from court and facing gaol. Her plan was to get to England and then take a ship to Flanders where she hoped to clear her name. She had not allowed for the inconvenience of a civil war and the presence of Parliamentarian soldiers. On discovering that Lord Pembroke was the Island's governor, whom she had met on a previous and happier visit, she wrote immediately to him stating that she 'greatly rejoiced, being assured that, in your virtue and courtesy …' He would help – how could he resist? It was decided to return her to Dunkirk but there being no ships, she had to remain on the Island for two months before the Spanish ambassador was prevailed upon to secure her release. The duchesse was embroiled in political turmoil for much of her life, featuring in Alexandre Dumas's *Three Musketeers* adventures. She died in a French convent in 1679. (Louis Batiffol, *The Duchesse de Chevreuse, a Life of Intrigue and Adventure*, Library of Congress)

~ April 23rd ~

1898: Following a report from the Women's Horticultural College Swanley, feelings ran so high among the committee of the East Cowes Horticultural Improvement Association that they felt compelled to write to the *County Press*. In the Association's view there were already many thoroughly experienced, capable, able-bodied male gardeners – many of whom had wives and families to support and who were compelled to be ratepayers. They therefore wrote, 'it is astonishing to find that this question of women gardeners is allowed to proceed with, to our mind, its damaging effects' and even questioned the validity of the report as it seems 'so near to absurdity'. They felt that any woman who laboured digging, trenching and performing numerous other important items (and so was thus qualified to judge the work of experienced men) 'could not be a true representative of her sex'. Coping with changes of temperature from the hot house to outside departments requires 'a constitution of iron to go with it. Are we to understand that the universally acknowledged weaker vessel of creation can endure such without serious and lasting injury resulting from it?' It would seem in their view – clearly not! (*Isle of Wight County Press*, April 23rd 1898)

~ APRIL 24TH ~

1753: A man-of-war, the *Assurance*, sent to Jamaica to bring back Governor Sir William Trelawny and his retinue, carried his goods including a fortune in silver coin. On this day, as it approached the western end of the Solent, the ship's master David Patterson took over the navigation from Captain Scrope and declared the ship would be 'so close [to the outer Needles Rock] that the flag of the ensign will touch the rock.' Misjudging the danger, the *Assurance* sailed too close and struck the Goose Rock. The ship was lost although the crew was rescued. At the court martial, Mr Patterson blamed himself saying he had been so confident that he had refused the services of a pilot. In giving evidence, three pilots declared that they did not know the rock on which the *Assurance* foundered was there. After 2 hours' deliberation, the jury sentenced Mr Patterson to three months in the Marshalsea Prison. In 1970, the site of the shipwreck was discovered and later fully surveyed. Various artefacts were recovered, including Spanish reale cob coins and, surprisingly, Roman coins that presumably came from another wreck. The finds are in the Royal Naval Museum in Portsmouth. Governor Trelawny returned to Jamaica where he died of a fever in Spanish Town in 1772. (*Oxford Journal*, May 19th 1753)

~ April 25th ~

1780: Today's *Hampshire Chronicle* carried an advertisement for the following event: 'Cocking Isle of Wight. A main of cocks will be fought at the house of Mr John Gregory at the Green Dragon Inn, Newport between the gentlemen of Somerset and the gentlemen of the island. To show 45 cocks all main, for 5 guineas a battle, and a hundred the odd. The fight on the 25th inst April and the 2 following days. A Good Ordinary Each Day.' The term 'ordinary' applied to a meal served to the public at a fixed price – a 'dish of the day'. Cock fighting continued legally in Britain until it was finally outlawed in 1835. (*Hampshire Chronicle*, April 25th 1780)

~ APRIL 26TH ~

1898: The *County Press* carried a blow-by-blow account of the final of the Portsmouth Senior Cup held today. The match was doubly interesting in that it was the first time the two finalists had entered the competition and they were both from the Isle of Wight. The general opinion was that there was only a hair's breadth of difference between the two teams, Sandown Bay and the 32nd Co. Royal Artillery (the RA). In the past the RA had beaten Sandown Bay three times while Sandown was successful once. Special excursions were laid on to watch the match at Southampton and both teams had many supporters. The RA was reported as full strength but Sandown was missing two key players, one through illness and the second because he had formerly played for the RA. Sandown, playing in green shirts, won the toss and there followed 90 minutes of exciting football. The only goal was scored by the RA, but was disallowed as being offside. After a further 30 minutes extra time, the game remained a draw. It had to wait until the next meeting when Sandown finally carried the day. (*Isle of Wight County Press*, April 30th 1898)

~ April 27th ~

1944: During the hostilities with Germany, news reports from that country were often reported in the press. Reuters' relayed the following information: 'A German News Agency reported today that German speedboats last night attacked destroyers and a British convoy off the Isle of Wight.' The agency described the scene of the clash as: 'off the south coast of Britain just west of the Isle of Wight' and added that 'in spite of extremely strong enemy defence the Germans sank three ships totalling 9,100 tons and torpedoed another of 200 tons, the loss of which may be presumed. In hard defensive clashes, one enemy destroyer was so heavily hit by torpedoes that its loss can be assumed but it could not be observed owing to the powerful defensive activity of the enemy and the consequent rapid displacement of the scene of the conflict. The German speedboats returned to their basis intact without loss or casualties.' (*Hull Daily Mail*, April 28th 1944)

~ April 28th ~

1894: According to today's *Isle of Wight Observer*, this year the build-up to the Ashey Races attracted a greater number than usual of rough elements. 'A large number of turfites [*sic*] came into town on Tuesday. On the evening of that day a number of them were in the billiard room of the Esplanade Hotel, when a quarrel ensued, and one man present (who is said to have been accused of welshing) was knocked down, kicked under the billiard table, and beat about in such a manner that it was necessary to send for the police, who removed the fellow bleeding and unconscious. What subsequently became of him we have not heard, but he probably deserved all he got … "Spider", also got into an altercation with one of the same fraternity in a local bar. Wordy arguments were followed by blows. Glasses were thrown, cheeks cut open, and again the police had to interfere. "Spider", was severely knocked about and could not go on the course next day.' The grandstand at Ashey burned down in 1929 and was not replaced. Amateur races still take place annually at West Ashey Farm. (*Isle of Wight Observer*, April 28th 1894)

~ APRIL 29TH ~

1876: Today's *Hampshire Advertiser* announced the winners of a Singing Bee held last Tuesday at the Forester's Hall at Cowes – the first of its kind. The event was very well attended. Twenty-two contestants performed and the event was judged by Mr R. Sharpe of Southampton. The *Advertiser* reported that 'each presentation was listened to intently with some requests for encores but of course, as is customary, they were not allowed.' The choice of both songs and prizes reflects on the tastes of the times. The results were: Sopranos – 1st: pair of gold earrings to Mrs Flux for 'Thou art so near'; 2nd: smelling bottle to Miss Williams for 'The Blind Girl to her Harp'. Tenors – 1st: pair of vases to Mr Lee for 'Sweethearts'; 2nd: meerschaum pipe to Mr Roach for 'The Death of Nelson'. Basses and baritones – 1st: a dressing case (fitted) to Mr Sibley for 'The Stirrup Cup'; 2nd: cigar case to Mr Coleman for 'Man the Lifeboat'; 3rd: copy of 'The Messiah' to Mr Humah for 'The Pilot'. Comic Song – a photograph album to Mr Cusack for 'Happy Jim'. (*Hampshire Advertiser*, April 29th 1876)

～ April 30th ～

1853: William Yelf, an actuary was today in court accused of stealing money from Newport Savings Bank. The *Western Times* suggested that his misdemeanours had been going on since 1839. More than £8,276 was at present unaccounted for and he was suspected of appropriating £1,000 a year from the working classes. The *Glasgow Herald* reported that at this time he was also a 'religious preacher'. At the hearing 53-year-old Yelf wished to make a full confession and to render every assistance to the investigators and appeared deeply affected by his situation at his trial in July. According to the *Taunton Courier*, the learned judge 'viewed the conduct of the prisoner as most unpardonable … The sentence he was about to pronounce was one he should not be performing his duty to the public if he failed to apply, and that sentence was that the prisoner should be transported beyond the seas for the term of his natural life.' (*Western Times*, May 7th 1853; *Taunton Courier*, July 20th 1853)

∼ May 1st ∼

1934: Tuesday saw the inauguration of the London to Isle of Wight Air Service which made London within half an hour's reach of the Island. A year earlier another service had been launched between the Isle of Wight, Portsmouth and London (Heston) by Spartan Airlines, their machines made by Spartan Aircraft Ltd. at East Cowes and including Shanklin, Ryde and Portsmouth. The company was next operated by Portsmouth, Southsea and I.W. Aviation Ltd. The new service flies between Croydon Airport, Bembridge, Ryde and Somerton (Cowes) this being the Island depot and is organised by Southern Railway in co-operation with Spartan Airlines, operated entirely by the latter. It will in future be known as Southern Air Services. Four daily trips in each direction were advertised. On the first day, fog in London delayed the flight from Croydon but the service proved so popular that the flights had to be duplicated. It took under 40 minutes to travel from Croydon to Cowes, calling at Bembridge and Ryde en route. Nowadays the weather should not cause a problem as the three-engined Spartan airliners, with a cruising speed of 118 per hour, are fitted with special wireless apparatus for direction finding. (*Isle of Wight County Press*, May 5th 1934)

~ MAY 2ND ~

1850: In its weekly roundup of events on the Island, today's *Hampshire Telegraph* reported that:

> ... at a public meeting of inhabitants held in Newport Town Hall it was announced that instructions had been received from the churchwardens at Carisbrooke to arrange the sale of the town gun. The gun was stored in St Mary's church and instructions were that, as it had remained useless for the last 300 years, it should be sold by auction. Being a piece of antiquity it was hoped to realise a good sum. It was described as of very superior workmanship, made of brass, and measuring 7' 3' with a 2¾' caliber [*sic*]. The inscription states: 'ROBERT AND JOHN OWINE, BRETHEREN, MADE THIS FALCONE, ANO 1594, CARASEBROWE'.

Happily for Island history, somebody must have stepped in for the cannon is now on display at the entrance to Carisbrooke Castle Museum. (*Hampshire Telegraph*, May 2nd 1850)

— MAY 3RD —

1845: From Cowes, today's *Hampshire Telegraph* informed their readers that Prince Albert had purchased the Woodhouse Estate. The property, belonging to the Hon. W.H.A. à Court-Homes, the Island's MP, consisted of 1,400 acres and included the whole of the land from Osborne and Barton to King's Quay Creek. Also included was the Isle of Wight Racecourse. The *Telegraph* stated that 'it cannot be too generally known that this gentleman has for some time discharged his gamekeepers, and declared the game on his extensive estates to be the property of the tenants on whose crops they feed'. The queen and Prince Albert were expected on the Island on about May 8th; unlike Windsor Castle and Buckingham Palace, Osborne House and its growing estate was the private property of Queen Victoria, largely purchased from the money she received for the sale of Brighton Pavilion, inherited through her uncle King George IV. The original Osborne estate was bought from Lady Isabella Fitzroy, widow of Robert Pope Blachford, she being a descendent of King Charles II and it consisted of 342 acres. By the time the adjacent farms of Barton and Alverstone were added, it covered more than 2,000 acres. (*Hampshire Telegraph*, May 3rd 1845)

~ MAY 4TH ~

1926: Island members of the railway, printers and transport unions responded to the call for a general strike, beginning at a minute to midnight on May 3rd. For the past two weeks, coal miners had been locked out of the mines for demanding shorter working hours and the slogan called on support 'in defence of the miners' wages and hours'. It was branded by the *Daily Mail* as not an industrial action but a revolution. Approximately 250 railwaymen, 250 transport workers and 60 printers on the Island joined in the strike. Immediately about 500 volunteers were recruited by the Island Committee for Voluntary Services 'willing to maintain essential services'. On the first day there were no trains but, with the help of office staff from the Railway Company, on the second day one or two trains ran from Ryde and ferried children to school. Vehicles were placed at the disposal of the strike-breakers and locally as well as nationally it became clear that the strike could not be fully effective. It collapsed on May 12th. (*County Press*, May 7th 1926)

– MAY 5TH –

1739: On this day the *Newcastle Courant* was able to confirm a rumour that had been circulating about Charles Barrington, brother of Sir John Barrington of Swainston Manor. The ship *Halifax* had brought the news that Barrington, 'an English Gent in the Swedish Service, [was] marrying an Indian Princess in Madagascar'. Rather snootily, the editor opined, 'but I suppose her father to be only totti-potti-moy Prince: But Mr Barrington is not the first English Gentleman who was so fond of Dominion as to declare publickly [*sic*] to one of our Monarchs "That he would rather be King of Mole-Hill than the greatest Subject of the British Dominions."' The *Stamford Mercury* added further morsels. Mr Barrington, it seems was employed by the Swedish East-India Company travelling out in one of the company's ships. En route they were held up in Madagascar where: 'Mr Barrington was introduced to the King's Court and was so happy as to gain the Good graces of the Princess, the King's Daughter, and in a short time was married to her and since which the king died and Mr Barrington was declared King in his room, by the Unanimous Consent of the People.' (*Newcastle Courant*, May 5th 1739; *Stamford Mercury*, April 7th 1739)

~ MAY 6TH ~

1627: A note in Sir John Oglander's diary recorded that the Island governor Sir John Conway was waiting to receive 1,000 soldiers serving under Colonel Brett who were to be billeted on the Island. There was immediate concern as to how to feed and house them. They remained until June 21st after which time Sir John Oglander of Nunwell announced his satisfaction with the way it had turned out; the Islanders had been well paid and he wouldn't mind the same thing happening again. It did. In November a further 1,500 men arrived. They turned out to be a regiment of 'Scotch' soldiers, dumped indefinitely as there was no money to return them home. The men were undisciplined and the officers (in Sir John's view) were not gentlemen. Island-wide, a series of fights, robberies, rapes and murders occurred, their officers refusing to take action and according to Sir John, their presence was a great sorrow to the whole island. On August 4th Sir John was part of a group sent to petition the king to remove them. Instead, His Majesty treated the petitioners to dinner and thanked them for being so patient. The regiment remained for nearly a year and when they finally departed they left behind as many as seventy bastard infants. As they left, Sir John declared that he hoped never to meet a 'Scotchman' again. (Sir John Oglander, *A Royalist's Notebook*, transcribed and edited by Francis Bamford, Constable)

~ MAY 7TH ~

1877: At the Isle of Wight Petty Sessions held today, George Ranney, a labourer lodging at the White Lion public house in Coppins Bridge, was charged with stealing nine growing cabbages valued at 9*d*, from the garden of Thomas Cole of the Salisbury Arms. The incident took place on the night of Saturday 5th and Police Constable Rackett deposed that at about 11.30 he found the prisoner cutting young cabbages in the prosecutor's garden on Snook's Hill. He had six of the cabbages tucked under his arms. The prisoner was drunk, and at first said that he was doing nothing but afterwards said that a Mr Uram had given him leave to cut the cabbages. He was fined 2*s* 6*d*, ordered to pay 9*d*, the value of the cabbage, and 5*s* cost of the court, which he paid. (*Hampshire Advertiser*, May 9th 1877)

— MAY 8TH —

1942: A funeral of particular poignancy took place today in Ryde. The deceased were Herbert Dewey and Colin Weeks, both members of the National Fire Service. They had died three days earlier at Marvin's shipyard in Cowes, a base for the Free French navy. During a night of relentless bombing on the 4th/5th, at least seventy people were killed in two waves of enemy fire. The firefighters were taking a moment to drink tea when the yard took a direct hit and they were killed instantly. Dewey was 40 years old and Weeks was just 19, and the pair shared a mutual interest in music, together playing the organ and the violin. The two flag-draped coffins were transported to All Saints church on fire engines and then carried into the church on the shoulders of their colleagues. After the service they were buried side by side in Ryde Cemetery. Colin Weeks' parents were the Mayor and Mayoress of Ryde and, in a cruel coincidence, on the day of the bombing the town clerk also learned of the death of his son away on active service. (Courtesy of Ryde Social Heritage Group)

— MAY 9TH —

1886: On this day, 18-year-old Emma Annie Jacobs was charged with the murder of her newly born baby. After hearing the evidence the girl was remanded in custody to await further evidence. It was June 8th when the *Portsmouth Evening News* reported on the outcome at the Newport Petty Sessions. Mr Mould from the town clerk's office appeared for the Superintendent of Police and Mr Joyce for the prisoner and one new witness was called, Dr Hutton Castle who had assisted Dr Wilkins at the post-mortem. He merely confirmed the latter's evidence. The reporter was clearly not engrossed in the case for he stated that 'After a very tedious hearing of three hours and a half, the prisoner was discharged.' (*Portsmouth Evening News*, June 8th 1886)

− MAY 10TH −

1823: Reporting the Island news sent to them on May 10th, the *Hampshire Chronicle* also felt moved to extol its virtues: 'This beautiful Island which yields to no part of Great Britain for the fertility of its soil and its salubrious air, begins again to receive a number of visitors from all parts; some who are invalids who come for the purpose of recovering and establishing their health, which they often secure more rapidly here than they can in any other parts in the kingdom, in many instances by application to the chalybeate water, originally discovered and possessed by Thomas L Waterworth Esq. But most of our visiting gentry come for the purpose of beholding the highly picturesque and infinitely varying scenery …' The chalybeate spring was discovered at Blackgang by Dr Waterworth and soon became a Mecca for those seeking relief and even cures for various ailments. A grotto sprung up from which the water could be purchased and soon a hotel was built close by for the accommodation of visitors. It was called the Royal Sandrock, and was sadly destroyed by fire in 1984. (*Hampshire Chronicle*, May 12th 1823)

~ MAY 11TH ~

1861: The arrival and departure times of the Island's coaches was as important in the nineteenth century as that of the bus and rail timetables are today. The *Isle of Wight Observer* kept the public updated with any changes to the running of the *Rocket*, a four-horse coach that plied from Ryde to Ventnor Station, passing through Brading, Shanklin and Wroxall. October saw the discontinuance of some journeys to be resumed again in June. The adverts were at pains to make clear that the *Rocket* was timed to coincide with the arrival of trains from the South-West and the southern trains from London. Earlier there had been plans by a London enterprise to break the 'monopoly' of the *Rocket*'s service and to run an alternative during the summer months. Today's *Observer* quickly came to the *Rocket*'s defence. The proposed service planned to run two coaches named the *Defiance* and the *Retaliator* but, according to the *Observer*, 'as far as coaching goes there is little room for improvement … What need then, of any interference of strangers?' It called on Islanders to discountenance the invasion that would take income from the legitimate services. (*Isle of Wight Observer*, May 11th 1861)

~ MAY 12TH ~

1915: The *Newcastle Journal* today reported how on April 8th, the tug *Homer*, belonging to the Lawson Tug Steamboat Company, had been towing the French barque *General de Souis* in the Channel when she was approached by a German submarine who called on the captain H.J. Gibson to surrender. Ignoring the instruction, Captain Gibson severed the towrope of the barque and steamed straight ahead, towards the U-boat, under a shower of bullets from the submarine's machine gun. The *Homer* missed the submarine's stern by only 3ft and headed towards the *Ower* lightship with the German boat in pursuit. A torpedo just missed the tug. After half an hour, the submarine gave up and Captain Gibson was able to bring his ship safely into Bembridge. There were thirty bullet holes in the vessel. The French ship also escaped safely and in recognition of his actions Captain Gibson was presented with a gold watch by the admiralty. (*Newcastle Journal*, May 12th 1915)

~ MAY 13TH ~

1787: On May 13th, led by the flagship *Sirius*, the first consignment of convicts set sail from the Motherbank off the Island's coast, for Australia. The *Sirius* carried the new governor, Sir Arthur Philips and the Commander of the Marines, Major Robert Ross, who was responsible for guarding the prisoners. The journey took more than eight months, reaching Sydney on January 26th 1787/8. The accompanying ships were the *Alexander*, *Charlotte*, *Friendship*, *Lady Penrhyn*, *Prince of Wales* and *Scarborough*. Aboard were approximately 1,400 convicts and en route they called at the Canaries, Tenerife, Rio de Janiero, Cape Town and Van Dieman's Land (Tasmania). Inevitably there were deaths aboard and although the convicts were chained throughout the voyage, some escaped. Twenty-two babies were born en route. At Sydney the Union Jack was planted, declaring the land for Britain, and the French arrived two days later, narrowly missing the chance to claim it for France. In spite of unthinkable hardship, the European presence in Australia survived. *Sirius* left to return to South Africa for supplies, circumnavigating the world in the process. By the time she returned she was in dire need of repairs and taken to Mosman, a suburb of Sydney, before setting out for Norfolk Island. Here, she ran aground and was wrecked. The residents of Mosman commissioned three bas-reliefs to record the epic journey 200 years later. One was presented to the Borough of Medina and erected at Appley Beach, one was given to the people of Norfolk Island and the third was placed at Mosman. (Royal Australian Historical Society)

‒ MAY 14TH ‒

1889: When the young American woman Florence Maybrick was arrested in Liverpool for murdering her husband, it was of passing curiosity to Islanders. Tried, condemned and sentenced to death, she ultimately served fifteen years in prison. After the event, however, in May 1889, members of the Maybrick family took up residence in Ryde. Michael Maybrick, brother to the murdered man, was better known as Stephen Adams, the singer, songwriter and greatly admired performer. Maybrick married on March 9th 1893 when he was 52 and threw himself into the social and political life of his new neighbourhood. A committed mason, he was soon appointed a Justice of the Peace, became the chairman of the Isle of Wight Hospital at Ryde and five times served as Mayor of Ryde. In sporting circles he went yachting and played cricket. Of his many compositions, the most enduring is probably 'The Holy City', written in 1892, with lyrics by his intimate friend Fred Weatherly. Maybrick died on August 26th 1913 and the question of his involvement in his sister-in-law's conviction for murder remained a cause for speculation, Florence being condemned as much for having an affair as for mariticide. Michael was buried in Ryde Cemetery in a substantial, some might even say ostentatious, vault. (*Oxford Dictionary of National Biography*)

⁓ MAY 15TH ⁓

1905: A picture postcard showing a photograph of a rare kyang at Parkhurst barracks was today sent from Newport, to Master Alan Long of Mill Bank, Carisbrooke bearing the message: 'Kyang is the first of its kind ever brought to England.' The 'Kyang' in question was spotted by a detachment of British Mountain Artillery Battery Gunners serving in Tibet. The terrain meant sure-footed ponies and mules were essential as pack animals and on seeing the kyang the soldiers asked about them. They were told, however, that they were untameable. About the size of a zebra, they came in various shades from black to rich golden brown, sandy yellow and white. Appearing in great numbers, they sometimes galloped in an almost military formation and the army made it their purpose to capture some. The task proved difficult but they succeeded in lassoing two mares. On crossing a mountain river one of them was drowned and the survivor was shipped back to England and installed at Parkhurst Barracks. She was later sent to London Zoo and with other importees, sent to Woburn Abbey where she died while giving birth. In total eleven foals were born in England but gradually the numbers declined and now the only examples left are at the Highland Wildlife Park at Kingussie in Scotland. (Edmund Cander, *The Unveiling of Llasa*, Gutenberg)

— MAY 16TH —

1949: The *Western Morning News* reported that 'Dr Mills, the smallpox officer for the Isle of Wight said last night that all Island doctors were receiving a circular giving instructions and advising against panic vaccination after a suspected case of smallpox at Lake. The patient, a Dutch woman of 24 and her husband and parents, have been isolated in hospital in the district of Ashey, near Ryde. For a mile around the District has been proclaimed an infected area. Road blocks state "Danger. Smallpox. No entry beyond Barrier. Infected Area."' Following a twentieth-century global campaign of eradication, the last known case of naturally occurring smallpox was in 1977. (*Western Morning News*, May 16th 1949)

∼ MAY 17TH ∼

1824: Today the arrival of King Liholiho and his wife Kamamalu from the Sandwich Islands on a 'state' visit was greeted with curiosity. The couple arrived at Portsmouth and visited various parts of the country for two months, including calling in at Ryde on the 17th where Captain Fagan of the cutter *Lapwing* acquired a very strange souvenir, part of the underdress of the queen. Kamamalu was a tall, stately woman regarded as very beautiful. There was some delicacy about the status of the couple in that they were half brother and sister. Kamamalu was also the third of the king's four wives and also his favourite, which was why he brought her on the visit. The trip was to end in the worst possible way because the royal couple and many of their entourage had no immunity to western illnesses and Kamamalu was struck down with measles from which she died on July 6th. Liholiho also caught the virus and although he might have recovered, he was so devastated by the loss of his wife that he was considered to have died of grief. Captain Fagan kept his strange memento of the Hawaiian queen and a letter explaining what it was is held in the Island's Public Record Office. (Isle of Wight Public Record Office, Newport)

~ MAY 18TH ~

1860: On this day at Sandown Granite Fort, as his wife and six children were sleeping, Serving Officer Sergeant William Whitworth cut the throats of his entire family. He was charged with their murder and being found insane, was consigned to a lunatic asylum. There had been no indication as to Whitworth's state of mind. At the time he had only nine months left to serve before he received his pension, but the decision was taken to replace the existing fort and instead Whitworth faced redundancy; perhaps the prospect of an uncertain future and ensuing poverty was just too much to cope with. The new fort, the third on the site, was constructed of blocks of granite, each weighing 6 tons, which teams of horses transported from Brading Harbour. Sandown Bay was viewed as a likely invasion point and the fort was further strengthened with special iron plating around the gun sites. It was fully armed and manned by 1876, but advances in armaments meant that it was already obsolete. Used as a training ground, in 1930 it was sold for scrap but the buyers found that it was so well constructed they could not dismantle it. During the Second World War it became a pumping station to transport vital fuel under the channel to France, the operation known as PLUTO. The Sandown Council then opened it as an Island Zoo and so it continues under private ownership, specialising in the conservation of tigers. ('Report of the Inquest', *Hampshire Telegraph*, May 26th 1860)

~ May 19th ~

1952: On Sunday an outing of 124 members of the Railway Correspondence and Travel Society descended on the Island, arriving at Ryde Pier. The party travelled first to Newport, their train pulled by the engine Ryde, with a visit to the paint shop, followed by the chance to see the site of the former Yarmouth/ Freshwater and Newport Railway Terminus. They then took in Cowes, travelling at maximum speed and thence to Freshwater and back, having lunch at Newport Station. From Newport, they travelled on a 'special', pulled by the Bonchurch and rode along the Merstone to Ventnor West line passing through St Lawrence Tunnel. Back to Merstone, the whistle-stop tour then branched out for Sandown followed by a prolonged stop at Brading and then off to Bembridge. Finally, the special carried them to Ryde St John's for a tour of the railway works before continuing up the Pier for the 7.35 boat. In all, the day-trippers covered 52 miles of the Island's 58 miles of track. Being a Sunday in May the trains were busy which raised hopes that the rumours of line closures would not be true, but a month later British Rail announced the closure of the Merstone to Ventnor West Line and the last train ran on September 14th. (Isle of Wight County Press, May 23rd 1952)

~ MAY 20TH ~

1887: For a week in May 1887, the American industrialist Andrew Carnegie and his wife Louise passed their honeymoon at Bonchurch. They had married in New York on April 22nd and then crossed the Atlantic by liner. Their first outing on arriving in Bonchurch was to visit the grave of poet John Sterling. At the graveside they picked bay and myrtle leaves, and sent them home with the sentiment, 'Their branches wave over his remains and never have these hallowed the resting place of a finer soul.' Of Louise, Carnegie wrote: 'Everything charmed her. Until this time she had only read of Wandering Willie, Heartsease, Forget-me-nots, Primrose, Wild Thyme, and a whole list of homely names.' Now, she saw them. Sterling had moved to the Island when he was already dying of that nineteenth-century scourge, tuberculosis. He lived at Hillside in Ventnor and is buried in the old graveyard at Bonchurch. (*Evening Telegraph*, September 21st 1911)

~ MAY 21ST ~

1922: It seems that a combination of love and money drove 60-year-old barrister William Hartshorne Shorthose of Stickworth Hall to shoot himself on the doorstep of the object of his affection, Catherine Coombes. His body was discovered by William Poynter, a van boy who in turn called upon Mrs Haynes, a neighbour. She stated that Mr Shorthose was a frequent visitor to the house and that a letter addressed to his daughter was on the table. The inquest was held in the schoolroom at Blackwater, attended by his widow who arrived heavily veiled in her car with the blinds drawn. The letter was read out to the court. It started, 'I cannot live any more owing to the serious illness of my dearest girl, Catherine Coombs' and was signed 'Your lovingest father'. A policeman confirmed that the dead man's skull had been smashed and his gun lay to hand. He confirmed that he knew him and saw him frequently visiting Miss Coombs' cottage at Dolcroft, Rookley. Doctor Cowper of Shanklin confirmed that it was a case of suicide. He had noticed a recent weakening of the brain and Mr Shorthose had become increasingly emotional, particularly on the day before his death. His solicitor Mr Jerome confirmed that he had many financial problems and perhaps he had worried too much over them. A verdict of suicide while temporarily of unsound mind was returned. (*The Post*, May 21st 1922)

⇀ MAY 22ND ⇀

1870: On this day one of the Island's largest landowners, Sir John Simeon, Baronet, died at Fribourg in Switzerland. His body was returned to the Island and after a ceremony in the chapel at Swainston Manor, he was buried in the vault of All Saints church, Calbourne. Chief among his mourners was Alfred Lord Tennyson who was greatly affected by his friend's demise. After the ceremony Tennyson retired to the gardens at Swainston and there wrote the poem 'In the Garden at Swainston' to Sir John Simeon. In it he mourned the loss of three dead friends (his youthful friend Arthur Hallam, his son Lionel and now Simeon – 'the last of the three'). Simeon had converted to Catholicism which troubled Tennyson but gradually the poet became more accepting. Apart from the Swainston Estate that covered nearly 6,000 acres, Sir John also owned the St John's Estate at Ryde. He gave land for the erection of St John's church at Ryde and leased land for the provision of Ryde Cemetery. A monument to him stands in Newport at the junction with Castle Road and the main Carisbrooke Road. (*Oxford Dictionary of National Biography*)

– MAY 23RD –

1874: Today the *Hampshire Telegraph* reported on the monthly meeting of the Guardians of the Poor where a letter from the War Office was considered. A pension of 1*s* 6*d* a day had been awarded to two old soldiers who were inmates of the workhouse, and the War Office wrote inquiring how it should be disposed of. The men were summoned before the board and both elected to leave the house. The sum of £7 had already accumulated and the board agreed that the two soldiers should keep the entire amount. One, named Cheverton, was 82 years of age and his wife, 78 years, was also an inmate. The *Telegraph* also reported on the recent meeting of the Sanitary Board, where it was stated that Freshwater owners were improving the sanitary state of their properties but that there were: 'several properties in Shorwell in a very unsatisfactory state and that at least two of them were overcrowded and also that several nuisances existed at Yafford.' (*Hampshire Telegraph*, May 23rd 1874)

~ MAY 24TH ~

1875: The *Isle of Wight Observer* of the 29th carried a detailed report of the Industrial Exhibition that was held in Newport the week before. The number of entries was enormous and the *Observer* listed the objects with the names of those who had kindly donated them. The entire space of one wall of the building was given over to pictures being the best of the kind ever seen in Newport including works by Hogarth, Turner and Reynolds plus a selection of rare engravings. Some models were included, amongst which were a model of St Catherine's Lighthouse and the cooking apparatus of a yacht in miniature. A special prize was awarded to Alfred Prangnell, a brick-maker of Newtown, for an inlaid workbox. Mr Wood of Carisbrooke sent a fine collection of fossils, while blind Walter Willis exhibited a number of objects in wood. A bible belonging to the Dairyman's Daughter was on display and Mr W.B. Mew lent a collection of old china. There were prizes for needlework, fretwork, penmanship, paintings and drawings, model-making, lace and cabinet-work. Over 1,000 people visited the exhibition and it was hoped to be even more successful the following year. (*Isle of Wight Observer*, May 29th 1875)

~ MAY 25TH ~

1758: The country being held in the grip of the Seven Years' War, today's *Caledonian Mercury* saw fit to print the following 'letter from the Isle of Wight', originally dated May 17th: 'You would be astonished to see the prodigious Quantities of Artillery, and other warlike Implements, that are already brought hither; and the whole Island seems full of Soldiers. Nothing was ever pushed with more Vigour than the Preparations for this grand Expedition. It is allowed on all Hands, that the whole will be ready to put to Sea in the Course of the next week; and it is confidently reported here, that the Parliament will not break up till the Event of this great enterprise is known.' The primary target was the French with whom Britain was involved in a military struggle for influence over the New World. It ended with the British having gained significant colonial territories. (*Caledonian Mercury,* May 25th 1758)

~ MAY 26TH ~

1851: Before the court were twelve local men, all described as labourers, accused that 'in the parish of Newchurch, together with diverse, other evil disposed persons, unlawfully, riotously and routously [*sic*] assembled, gathered together and disturbed the pubic peace.' The disturbance took place at the polling station in the Market House and persons wishing to vote were accosted with cries of 'rat, rat', implying that they would be hunted down and dealt with like vermin. As the crowd increased and tensions grew, the police arrested two of the inciters, but this in turn roused the crowd who were intent on freeing them. Such was the threat that the police felt compelled to let them go. In the furore, one gentleman lost his life, although this was not blamed directly on the accused. Police Constable Blake suffered injury when hit by a stone that knocked out one of his teeth. Police reinforcements charged the crowd and today's *Hampshire Telegraph* reported the view that 'some injuries were the consequence but they deserved what they got'. At its height about 1,000 people were present. Summing up, the jury was advised that no individual could be charged with riotous behaviour and it took them only a few minutes to acquit the accused. The sound of cheers echoed around the court. (*Hampshire Telegraph*, May 26th 1851)

~ MAY 27TH ~

1870: Noah Williams, unaware that he was under surveillance by the coastguard from Ventnor, prepared to come ashore on the beach near Dunnose at 2.15 a.m today. The coastguard, Thomas Hoar, declared that he had watched the white boat with a black bottom sail within about 50 yards of the beach then lower his sails and begin to row ashore just west of Luccombe Chine and opposite some cottages. He could not identify the men who were landing. A shot was fired and the boat was pushed off with one of the men aboard. Two coastguard galleys gave chase for $3\frac{1}{2}$ hours before they came aside and found the defendant on board. There was a little bread and water and no fishing gear on the boat. The beach where he had landed was searched and two and a half barrels of contraband were discovered. The evidence of the coastguard was corroborated and Noah Williams was fined £100 plus £2 costs, to be imprisoned for six months in default of payment. (*Shields Daily Gazette*, May 31st 1870)

~ MAY 28TH ~

1631: Sir John Oglander, Deputy Governor of the Isle of Wight was a great one for anecdotes. On the 28th May in his copious memoirs he recorded the following incident:

> A mason, Thomas Davis, and his sonn, digginge for erth in a barne of Nicholas Gardes att Princelade in Nuchurch p'rish, found a pewter platter, and underneath a brasse pott, and in ye brass pot, an erthen pott full of Elizabeth's shillinges. He at nigyt putt it awaye but itt came at last to be known by his over hastie spending, whereupon on ye fayre woords myxt with threates, that he said Nicholas Garde and his father used, he gave them £98, but itt is thought that there was more. I hearing of itt, sent my warrant for them all, took their several examinations, returned them to my Lord Treasuror, and thye will produce who shall have itt. But I am confident that it was hidden there by one Rychard Garde, unkel to Nicholas and owner of ye sayde lande, an envious, miserable fellowe, who dyed soome 14 years before it was found.

(W.H. Long (ed.), *Oglander Memoirs*, Isle of Wight County Press, 1888)

— May 29th —

1666: On this day Sir Faithful Fortescue, living at Bowcombe Manor, died at the age of 85 and was buried at St Mary's Carisbrooke. As a young man Faithful was sent to Ireland where he joined his uncle, Sir Arthur Chichester. One of Chichester's duties was to redistribute Irish land, handing it over to the English for which, unsurprisingly, he was reviled. In 1605, Faithful became Constable of Carrickfergus Castle, adding Irish-owned lands to his estate. Having been knighted, as Civil War threatened in England he was appointed governor of Drogheda and met with a rebellion during which skirmish, two of his sons were killed and he fled to England. He was put under the command of the Earl of Essex but Essex joined the Parliamentarian forces, placing Faithful on what he considered to be the wrong side. Belying his name, in the first fighting at Edghill Faithful arranged to change sides but in the process his men forgot that they were wearing the orange Parliamentary sashes and seventeen were killed by their new allies. After the war Faithful, on the losing side, joined the future Charles II on the Continent. At the Restoration he became a Gentleman of the Bedchamber but left London for the Isle of Wight on the outbreak of plague. A plaque was later erected to his memory by his descendant Lord Clermont. (*Oxford Dictionary of National Biography*)

~ MAY 30TH ~

1838: A letter dated May 30th from the Governor of the House of Industry to the Board of Governors reads: 'I beg leave to lay before you my report of proceedings in obedience to your commands by which I was directed to clothe, supply with necessaries and embark … 51 emigrants belonging to the Isle of Wight, inmates of this house … The clothing (though somewhat expensive for people of their condition) is such I trust that by yourself … be sanctioned as necessary to the position of comparative advantage in which you desire your people should find themselves in landing in a foreign country. With such an object in view, no expense beyond the dictates of real necessity has been incurred … the people were orderly in the movement of embarkation and gave no trouble whatsoever … they were safely aboard at 8 o'clock and I left them at 10 o'clock.' The emigrants sailed aboard the ship *Hibernian*, in the Governor's view, 'one of the best ships I have seen for the accommodation of emigrants'. She was bound for Montreal, leaving Cowes Roads at about noon on Thursday 24th. In a statement of expenses, each adult cost £7 5s; children of 7–14 years £3 13s 6d and children under 7 (of which there were four), £2 8s 4d. The total cost for bedding, clothing, food and other charges came to £587 19s 11½d (Isle of Wight Public Record Office)

᠆ MAY 3IST ᠆

1856: Today's *Hampshire Telegraph* described the victory celebrations held in Newport to mark the end of war in the Crimea. On Thursday (28th), with the promise of a splendid day, the Depot Battalion at Parkhurst Barracks carried out a mock attack on Carisbrooke Castle. Scaling ladders were used and when the imaginary garrison surrendered, the banners of the victors flew from the keep. Some 2,000 troops took part and many thousands came to watch. In the afternoon upwards of 3,000 children marched towards Carisbrooke in expectation of plum cake, oranges, coffee and nuts but before they were halfway there rain fell with such ferocity that the celebration was overturned and the soaking, muddy children returned home. The mammoth bonfire prepared for the evening in the cricket ground was damp but, with the assistance of large amounts of tar, the flames rose into the sky. The day was rounded off with a picnic and ball given by the officers at Carisbrooke Castle. (*Hampshire Telegraph*, May 31st 1856)

~ June 1st ~

1862: Today the Island's first passenger railway line opened from Cowes to Newport. While the work was in progress, the *Isle of Wight Observer* tempted the future passenger with what they would see after they boarded the train at the Cowes Station in Carvel Lane and travelled under the tunnel at Mill-hill Road. They would pass 'in succession the Cowes gas-works, brickyard, through another brickyard, past the cement mills, then across a wooden viaduct, about 100 yards in length, supported on wood piles ... the most conspicuous objects in pursuing the course of the line southward are the elegant tower and spire of St Thomas's church, the keep of Carisbrooke Castle, Parkhurst barracks and prison, Poor house, the downs above Newport, and the green and shrubberied [*sic*] banks of the Medina River.' The railway continued to operate until May 14th 1966. (*Isle of Wight Observer*, June 7th 1862)

— JUNE 2ND —

1883: Today's *Hampshire Advertiser* reported that the local board had decided not to take into consideration the subject of making a road through the Thrunge, notwithstanding the great sanitary improvement that would unquestionably result. The reason given was that the resulting road would only be 18 inches wide. The *Advertiser* reminded readers that Cowes High Street was in many parts no wider than this and that 'there is a great want of communication between the High-Street and Cross-Street.' The Thrunge was a narrow passage running between Carvel Lane and Cross Street enclosed by houses and considered an insanitary and unhealthy place to live.

The dictionary definition of 'thrunge' suggests the insertion of a large object into a smaller one, implying here that the lane was not big enough for the intended purpose. The Thrunge is now known by the more mundane name of Middleton Terrace. (*Hampshire Advertiser*, June 2nd 1883)

~ JUNE 3RD ~

1931: The *Cheltenham Chronicle* of June 6th reported that a body had been discovered on the railway line near Wootton three days earlier. It was that of Major Thomas Edward Swayne of Stroud who was a patient at Osborne Convalescent Home. Major Swayne retired from the RASC about eleven months earlier and had suffered a severe nervous breakdown in the April of that year, being placed in this nursing home for officers. He had served in the South African war and in the Great War where he saw active service in France, Belgium, Greek Macedonia, Serbia, Bulgaria, European Turkey, and the islands of the Aegean Sea. He had been rewarded the 1914 Star and Clasp, the British War Medal and the Victory Medal, and on news of his death there was much sympathy for his widow and daughter. The convalescent home opened in 1904 and closed its doors in 2000. Among its many patients were Robert Graves and A.A. Milne. (*Cheltenham Chronicle*, June 6th 1931)

～ JUNE 4TH ～

1853: Today's *Isle of Wight Observer* reported how Henry Jackson, a 'Son of Africa', had been arrested for begging under false pretences. The accused came from Halifax Nova Scotia and was raising money for the Zion Methodist church there. He had letters with him 'purporting' to be from very respectable parties and he wore a medal which he 'alleged' he gained in Algiers in one of HM's ships. He had called at the door of a Mr Minter who confirmed that he had given Jackson 1*s* as he came with the recommendation of the Wesleyan minister. The defendant said that he did not know that he was doing anything wrong. He was discharged and his money returned. In response, a correspondent signing himself 'Right is Right, Black or White' accused the police of failing to investigate the circumstances of the case before taking Henry Jackson before the magistrate. The writer had investigated all the charges and found that the persons whom Jackson was accused of conning all confirmed that he was genuine. The letter ended condemning the fact that Mr Jackson's name had been sullied and suggesting that in future, the police should investigate 'real' cases instead of supposed ones. (*Isle of Wight Observer*, June 4th 1853)

— JUNE 5TH —

1937: Today the beautiful Victorian Gothic mansion of Weston Manor at Totland opened its doors to 100 refugees from the Basque region of Spain. Following the bombing and destruction of the town of Guernica, an appeal was issued to the wider world to offer sanctuary to these Basque children. In total 4,000 were packed into a boat and shipped across the Bay of Biscay, arriving in Southampton on May 25th. The young arrivals at Totland were aged between 6 and 14 and relied on the goodwill of local people to offer them a temporary home. Weston Manor, the former home of the wealthy Catholic Ward family, was built in 1869–70 and includes a beautiful High Gothic chapel designed by August Wellby Pugin. At the time the children arrived, it was occupied by a Spanish order of nuns. Later, it became a home for adult men with learning difficulties but has since been sold and turned into a hotel. (British Listed Buildings – source English Heritage)

– JUNE 6TH –

1933: Today a serious fire broke out at Ryde Town Hall while the staff were at lunch. Although firefighting apparatus was quickly used by those inside the building, the flames were high and quickly spread downwards. Brigades from all parts of the Island were summoned and councillors and visitors helped to carry out valuable documents and other items displayed inside; the borough mace and plate were moved to places of safety while a visitor rescued the mayor's chain of office. Soon the pavement outside was piled high with saved objects, including cases of fossils and Egyptian mummies. The Ryde Roll of Honour escaped loss although two paintings, one on each side, were damaged, and the organ installed as a memorial to Queen Victoria, one of the finest in the country, was also seriously harmed. One fireman had to be carried outside, overcome by the smoke. The cause of the incident was believed to be the sun shining through the fanlight in the roof of the town hall – the largest in the Isle of Wight. (*Dundee Courier*, June 7th 1933)

~ JUNE 7TH ~

1819: Today's *Hampshire Chronicle* carried a notice advertising that materials from the barracks erected at Colwell at the time of the Napoleonic Wars were to be put up for auction. Mr Francis Pittis auctioned about 500,000 bricks, a large quantity of slating, oak and fir scantling of different dimensions, roofing, flooring and boarding. There was also a number of doors, sashes and frames, paving stones, lead pumps and a quantity of lead. Other fixtures such as racks, mangers and stall boards for the horses were all fully detailed in the catalogues that were available as far afield as the Auction Mart in London; the George in Portsmouth; the Star in Southampton; the Nag's Head in Lymington and at various locations on the Isle of Wight. The barracks, accommodating a number of German soldiers, had stood on the western side of Colwell Common. The sale was due to commence on the premises at 1 p.m. (*Hampshire Chronicle*, June 7th 1819)

~ June 8th ~

1872: Today's *Hampshire Telegraph* described an inquest held into 'an extraordinary case of sudden death' held at the Gem Inn, Hill Street, Ryde. The deceased was Captain Stellard, aged 72, who had married a young woman of about 24 years old the last October. The paper explained that the marriage had caused considerable excitement, as the captain's grandchildren were themselves old enough to be grandparents. He had apparently lived happily with his wife but recently a quarrel meant they had been sleeping in separate apartments. On the night in question, Mrs Stellard gave evidence that she had visited her husband in bed at about midnight and then again at about 3 a.m., and he was perfectly well. When she called in again at 5.30 a.m. he was quite stiff and cold. A granddaughter, who had lived with the captain prior to his marriage, said that on one occasion the couple had quarrelled and Mrs Stellard had declared, 'Oh, give him a pennyworth of arsenic, I'll show you how to use it.' The captain's son demanded that there should be a post-mortem but the coroner pointed out that the girl could not have been in earnest when she referred to the arsenic. A verdict of death from apoplexy was recorded. (*Hampshire Telegraph*, June 8th 1872)

⏤ JUNE 9TH ⏤

1800: Today's *Hampshire Chronicle* reported how troops from different parts of the Island began to amass in the morning due to King George III's birthday having been on the 4th:

> The Newport Volunteers assembled in their usual place ... then proceeded with the volunteer banner of the Island to Barcombe [*sic*] Down, under orders given by the commander in chief, Lord Cavan. The right wing was composed of a squadron of volunteer cavalry with the 4th battalion of the 60th Lancashire Militia. The left was formed of the Dutch troops and Oxford militia, and the centre which extended near a mile and a half on the rise of the down consisted entirely of volunteers of the island among which were the West Cowes artillery, the Newport regiment of volunteers, the three united companies of Godsall [*sic*] Arreton and Gatcomb, with the independent companies of East and West Cowes, Wootton, Ryde, Shalfleet, Niton, the whole comprising about 10,000 men ... The day was spent in the utmost loyalty and conviviality.

(*Hampshire Chronicle*, June 9th 1800)

∽ June 10th ∽

1898: The omnipresence of the military on the Island is illustrated by two consecutive news reports in the *Isle of Wight Observer* of June 10th. Under a heading entitled 'The Hants Carabiniers at Ryde', the paper recounted how:

> … the Carabiniers march daily through the street to the Gatehouse where they are drilled … their training ground is in some fields kindly leant by Mr Lake. Brigadier General Crichton attended the parade on Tuesday and judged the saddling competition and various field manoeuvres were carried out. On the same day Sir Charles Seely Bart JP gave a garden party in honour of the Yeomany in the grounds of the Isle of Wight College, where all the officers attended and many well-known residents of the Island were present.

The Wednesday suffered from such unrelenting rain that nothing much happened, but the week-long visit ended with sports in the recreation ground. Another account relayed how crowds of people turned out on Sunday to witness the church parade of the Hants Yeomanry and the journalist commented on the 'lively and bright atmosphere given by the fairer sex in their summer costumes'. The Ryde detachment of the Isle of Wight Rifles joined the yeomanry at Ryde Town Hall, to march to All Saints church where the service took place and the mayor and members of the corporation were all present in their robes. The reporter observed how smart the yeomanry appeared in their blue-black uniforms with white facings and white plumed helmets, making the sombre green and black uniforms of the Rifles look plainer by contrast. (*Wight Observer*, June 10th 1898)

~ JUNE 11TH ~

1951: The hovercraft, designed by Sir Christopher Cockerell and built at Saunders Roe shipyard at Cowes, today made its first public appearance. The first model, designated SR N1 (Saunders Roe Nautical 1) was capable of carrying four men at a speed of 28 miles an hour. Its potential as a military vehicle being recognised, it was then sent to France for further tests, successfully crossing from Dover to Calais. Its many applications continued to be explored, and it provided access to areas where conventional boats had difficulty in negotiating the channels. A successful and ongoing passenger service from Ryde to Portsmouth started in 1965 and there followed a cross-Channel service. Before and during the war, Sir Christopher worked on important navigation, communication and homing devices for aircraft. A plaque in East Cowes marks the spot where he lived and worked on the hovercraft. He died on June 1st 1999. (*Oxford Dictionary of National Biography*)

— JUNE 12TH —

1869: Today's *Luton Times and Advertiser* reported that on June 7th, Mr George Colenutt of Shanklin, with two others as yet unknown, was accused of wholesale smuggling. The charge was 'running' a cargo of forty-two tubs of brandy and Mr Dear, the collector of customs, prosecuted. At about 6 p.m. on Sunday 7th, the prisoner was seen leaving the shore in a boat with two others by Thomas Pyle, a coastguardsman on duty at Shanklin. At 12.15 that night, Mr John Knowler, in charge of the coastguard, saw a light on the beach between Shanklin Point and the Chine and at first light he had the area searched. In total forty-two barrels of spirits were discovered, some with slings attached to them and others buried in the furze. The prisoner's boat was searched and some cut rope, similar to that used on the tubs was discovered. This was not, however, considered sufficient evidence to convict. (*Luton Times and Advertiser*, June 12th 1869)

~ JUNE 13TH ~

1857: Alfred John Dunkit, an historian and editor of the *Archaeological Mine*, was at Niton, 'strolling through the locality in search of the picturesque' when he discovered a perfect specimen of Saxon fictile ware from the early or pagan period, on a scullery window. He most forcibly expressed his concern for this urn, 'which 'erst, perchance held the ashes of some noble Saxon warrior [and] now holds the soda of a washerwoman'. Although not uncommon, the merit of this specimen lay in its near-perfect condition. Mr Dunkit confirmed it as coming from a time when cremation was exercised and consequently it was pagan. He hoped that it would not be removed from the neighbourhood in which it was found and might be given to some local institution. (*Isle of Wight Observer*, June 13th 1857)

⤙ June 14th ⤚

1851: In their Island News section, the *Hampshire Telegraph* for today included an assault by a master on his servant. Ann Prince, hired as a children's nurse, gave evidence at the petty sessions that having smacked her charge for a misdemeanour, the child's mother demanded her husband Mr John Spickernell strike Miss Prince in return, which he did twice with his fist. Another servant of the house at Carisbrooke remarked that he gave her 'two hard ones'. Overheard saying that her master 'shall not do that again', Mrs Spickenell once more called on her husband who delivered several more blows. Mr Spickernell replied that he only slapped her once with his open hand and in turn charged Ann Prince with cruelty to the child. The chairman said it was clear that an assault had taken place and that the accused should have turned Miss Prince out if she 'misconducted' herself. Spickernell was fined 12*s* 6*d* and 7*s* 6*d* costs. (*Hampshire Telegraph*, June 14th 1851)

~ JUNE 15TH ~

1893: Today's *Isle of Wight Observer* reported on the Ryde fire brigade annual outing on a bright and breezy Wednesday morning (12th). As the town could not be left unprotected, the police and fire brigade were divided into two companies, the first travelling on Wednesday to Blackgang accompanied by the mayor (Alderman Ellery) and an assortment of dignitaries:

> Sweet music was discoursed on the whistle pipe and flute by P.C.Hayes and Mr Mundell on the kettle-drum. P.C.Taylor lent a helping hand to the 'band' by accompanying on a bell, which answered the purpose of a castanet. Songs were given by P.C.s Ryall and Hayes, PS Martin, and in fact most of the party in the second coach were musically inclined. At Ventnor lunch was partaken of after which the party strolled about the town and those who were interested therein examined the fine appliances belonging to the Ventnor Fire Brigade. The hills around Ventnor being very steep, the members of the Brigade and Police thoughtfully walked when a hill had to be traversed, thus saving the horses.

At St Catherine's they were given a tour of the lighthouse and the keeper very kindly started the foghorn, which can be heard 5 miles off. At Blackgang they sat down to a substantial dinner after which toasts were drunk and the mayor declared that a little while ago he had not expected to be there, but it had pleased God to spare him. Police Superintendent Hinks in turn thanked the mayor, and Captain Langdon thanked the organisers on behalf of the brigade. Thereafter, the outing made its way home. (*Isle of Wight Observer*, June 15th 1893)

— JUNE 16TH —

1842: The *London Standard* reported today from Ryde on the visit of Queen Adelaide, the 'Queen Dowager'. At short notice, accommodation with twenty-five beds had been arranged at the Ryde Pier Hotel. A meeting was immediately convened to discuss the propriety of local inhabitants presenting the queen with an Address. The meeting was chaired by Dr Lind, but Mr Hughes, who claimed to personally know the Earl of Denbigh, one of the queen's party, felt it behoved him to personally offer his services to the royal visitors. Having done so, he received a reply stating that the queen's health would prevent her from meeting with a deputation. Undeterred, Mr Hughes, and the other committee members felt that some written evidence of warm local feeling should be prepared. It fell to the Revd W. Spencer Phillips of Newchurch to prepare the address. It contained the following sentiments: 'We the undersigned, Magistrates, Clergy and other inhabitants of the town and neighbourhood of Ryde … cannot suffer such an opportunity to pass without … testifying our sense of the many virtues that shine forth in Your Majesty.' Not wishing to resort to flattery, they concluded by wishing the queen a happy visit to this 'salubrious and highly favoured proportion of the British Dominions'. To cheers the Address was handed over for onward transmission. (*London Standard*, June 16th 1842)

~ June 17th ~

1904: Today a large crowd gathered at the Oddfellow's Hall at Sandown for the sale of goods confiscated from local passive resisters. The goods put up for sale were mostly watches and chains. The day before, a sale had taken place at the Market House Ventnor where the property on offer included that of the Revd R. Allen Davies, the congregational minister and resister, comprising a biscuit box and a loo table that sold for £2. A brass-bound writing desk with inscription, belonging to the Revd J. Howen Rodda (a Bible Christian) was bought for £1 by Mr W. Roff, while a music cabinet and silk screen, the property of Miss James, was bought by the Revd G. Standing for £1. Outside the Market House, the resisters made speeches, having been refused permission to enter the building. The passive resisters were non-violent protesters who, as a way of rebellion, refused to pay their rates. The protest was mostly by Nonconformist ministers against the introduction of the 1902 Education Act that funded only Church of England and a few Roman Catholic schools. Nationally, nearly 200 protestors found themselves in prison. (*Portsmouth Evening News*, June 18th 1904)

~ JUNE 18TH ~

1892: Today's *Hampshire Advertiser* included a report on the annual outing of Mew Langton's Royal Brewery the previous Monday, which saw the Island employees enjoying a day out in the New Forest. About 100 members of staff met at Newport Railway Station and were transported to Cowes and then to Southampton. Here, they went to the brewery stores where breakfast was laid out, followed by a tour of the docks and other places of interest. A number of well-equipped 'breaks' (brakes, a type of pony carriage) were then provided to transport them and, in spite of a few showers, they enjoyed driving out around the Forest, their entourage accompanied by a brass band. At Lyndhurst they stopped for refreshments then went on to Minstead where they were joined by the directors of the company, who had been yachting and driven up to meet them. More eating followed on tables liberally decorated with flowers and a series of speeches and toasts continued, to the queen, the royal family, and Prince Henry for his role with the Isle of Wight Volunteers. The band provided more music as the revellers sang 'Rule Britannia' and the National Anthem before returning by carriage, boat and train to Newport. The Mew Langton brewery provided beer to Osborne House and transported India Pale Ale to India. It continued trading from Newport Quay until the 1960s. (*Hampshire Advertiser*, June 18th 1892)

~ JUNE 19TH ~

1880: At the meeting of the Board of Guardians this week, concern was expressed about the 'terribly large' increase in insanity on the Island. It was so great that one of the magistrates, Mr Snowden Henry, reported that when he was last at Winchester he had been asked to explain why the increase in lunacy on the Island was so enormous. The general opinion seemed to be that it was due to the number of families intermarrying. It was pointed out that the cost of maintaining lunatics at the asylum amounted to over £3,000 yearly and Mr F. Stratton bore witness to the great increase during his twenty years connection with the union. (*Isle of Wight Observer*, June 19th 1880)

~ JUNE 20TH ~

1931: For the third year in a row, the Isle of Wight bowling team knocked Dorset out of the Middleton Cup. Playing at Newport the Islanders won by 19 shots. Bowls had long been played on the Island; in the sixteen century Sir John Oglander reminisced about a regular meeting 'with my Lord Southampton at St George's Down, at bowls, some thirty or forty knights and gentlemen where our meeting was then twice a week, Tuesday and Thursday and we had an ordinary there and card tables'. Sir John had his own green at Nunwell House while, in order to alleviate the boredom for King Charles I, his host-cum-gaoler Robert Hammond created a bowling green at Carisbrooke Castle. Being one of the wettest summers ever, it was barely used. Bowls were so popular it was once outlawed to encourage the practice of archery instead. (*Western Gazette*, June 26th 1931)

— JUNE 21ST —

1855: The *Berkshire Chronicle* today carried the news that an inspection had been carried out by government inspectors to establish whether Appuldurcombe House at Wroxall would make a suitable naval hospital. While the outcome was not known at the time, the *Chronicle* opined that: '… it is scarcely possible to imagine that any spot in England can be better situated for such a purpose.' The house was of sufficient size to offer 'every facility for accommodating our sick and wounded heroes in considerable numbers, while the healthy climate, the spacious park and the beautiful country around it leave nothing to be desired'. Following several centuries in the hands of the influential Worsley family, the house was inherited by the wife of the Earl of Yarborough and on his death it became a school for twenty to twenty-five 'little boys' and the same number of 'lads' were prepared for life in the army or the colonies. Its next incarnation was as a home for French refugee monks who later moved to Quarr Abbey. Its fate was finally sealed by a bomb in 1943. (*Berkshire Chronicle*, June 21st 1855)

— JUNE 22ND —

1838: When widow Mary Woolfrey chose a headstone for her husband, Joseph, she had no idea that her inscription would result in a cause célèbre. Following discovery that his tombstone was incised with the words, 'Pray for the Soul of Joseph Woolfrey,' the vicar of St Mary's church at Carisbooke, John Breeks, wrote to Mary insisting that it should be removed. When Mary declined, he referred the case to the Ecclesiastical Court of Arches. Mary was called to account for having, 'unduly and unlawfully erected, or caused to be erected, the said tombstone, with the said inscription thereon contrary to the articles, canons and constitution, or the doctrine and discipline of the Church of England.' The wording of the text was offensive as it was perceived as part of the Romish doctrine of purgatory that was not recognised by the Anglican Church. The case was heard in December and it did not take the commissioners long to decide that the charge was injudicious and unchristian. It was dismissed with the costs to be paid by the Carisbrooke vicar. (*Western Press*, December 8th 1838)

— June 23rd —

1883: Under the heading 'A Singular Case', William Cotton of Atherfield was charged today with selling beer without a license. Police Sergeant Foster had the task of watching the house and at about 7 p.m. on the day in question, he observed one man go into the house and a horse and trap stop at the rear where, over the hedge, Mrs Cotton handed him a pint of beer. Having talked to her for about 20 minutes, the man then drove off. Constables Sharpe and Cousins entered the pub and found a man named Frank Cotton drinking beer out of a pint cup. In the ensuing search they found an 18-gallon cask containing 5 to 6 quarts of beer, eight pint cups, a quart jug, a funnel and a brass tap, all of which was now produced. Cotton denied the charge saying that he was the captain of a gang of fisherman and had bought the beer for general consumption among them. In dismissing the case, the magistrate said that in searching the house the police had done no more than their duty. (*Isle of Wight Observer*, July 12th 1883)

~ June 24th ~

1873: The *Freeman's Journal* today reported on the review carried out at Spithead in honour of the Shah of Persia. In an impressive display of naval might, the Shah, travelling aboard the yacht *Victoria and Albert*, was able to see the iron clads spread out in two long lines, lying at anchor way over towards the Isle of Wight. The *Journal* described how, 'throughout the livelong day, bells have been ringing, flags waving and the populace filling the streets vehemently cheering'. However, is seems the Shah must have been a difficult man to please because he was reported to not be much impressed with what he had seen so far. Having cut short part of his British tour, the *Bradford Observer* described the disappointment of the waiting crowds, not least the ladies who were 'simply broken hearted, many of them not having had an opportunity of looking upon the dusky countenance of His Majesty'. During the course of the visit, six diamonds that adorned the bridle of his horse were lost, being valued at £300. From the Island, at the request of several noblemen who were present to watch the review, Mr Arthur Fowles, the eminent marine painter from Ryde, made a crayon sketch of the naval review, showing the moment when the royal salute was given on the arrival of the Shah. The finished article was later to be presented to the Shah by local man Mr Webber. (*Freeman's Journal*, June 24th 1873)

— June 25th —

1956: Poet Alfred Noyes died today aged 77 at Ryde Hospital. He was living at Lisle Combe, St Lawrence, having returned to the Island in 1949 from time away in America during the Second World War. Born in Wolverhampton, he became a student at Oxford during which time he wrote his first volume of poetry, *The Loom of the Years*, published in 1902. The Island was a natural choice of residence, satisfying his passion for both the works of Lord Tennyson and a love of the sea. Unhappily, Noyes became virtually blind following an unsuccessful operation for glaucoma. On the death of his first wife, he converted to Catholicism, and when he died he was buried in the churchyard at St Saviour's church in Totland. As a poet, his greatest success was with the work 'The Highwayman'. (*Oxford Dictionary of National Biography*)

~ June 26th ~

1754: On this day the writer Henry Fielding boarded a ship on the Thames for a voyage to Lisbon. By July 10th they had only sailed as far as the Island when a gale forced them to come ashore at Ryde. Fielding had to be manhandled ashore, recording that 'between the sea and the shore, there was, at low water, an impassable gulf, if I may so call it, of deep mud, which could neither be traversed by walking nor swimming, so that for near half of the twenty-four hours, Ryde was inaccessible by friend of foe.' Fielding was carried by chair about a ¼ mile to a lodging house. Having sent their provisions ahead, the party arrived hoping to find their dinner on the table. Instead the landlady, Mrs Francis, flustered by the arrival of such gentlefolk, spent the time washing the rooms. Faced with a wet house, the Fieldings decamped to the barn. Their meal of beans and bacon proved so inadequate that they finally persuaded her to procure some freshly caught whiting. The weather remaining bad, the Fieldings stayed overnight. The available bedroom proved to be 'an ancient temple, built with the materials of a wreck, and probably dedicated to Neptune … Certain it is that this island of Wight was not an early convert to Christianity; nay, there is some reason to doubt whether it was ever entirely converted.' It was not until Wednesday, July 22nd that the voyage was finally able to continue. As they resumed their journey, Fielding observed that, notwithstanding their 'ill treatment' by their hostess, they had stayed in the 'most pleasant spot in the Island'. The Fieldings finally made it to Lisbon but there Henry died. (Henry Fielding, *The Journal of a Voyage to Lisbon*)

– JUNE 27TH –

1937: Today's Sunday evening entertainment on Shanklin Pier ended with the manager of the Pier Casino, Mr Horace Terry Wood, being prosecuted under Section 3 of the Sunday Entertainments Act. On the evening in question, Police Constable Lewis attended the theatre with a young lady. After the performance he lodged a complaint at the police station claiming that the performance, which included singing, dancing and other material, was not suitable for a Sunday. A double act by comedians Messrs Clapham and Dwyer, who were employed by the BBC, included offensive jokes about a fancy dress ball at a nudist colony where one man had 'painted stripes around his tummy' and gone as a naval officer. Another joke claimed that a lady had so many varicose veins that she went as a road map. One sketch involved a husband coming home drunk from the pub when his wife was entertaining a lover. The lover hid in the bed and was discovered when the husband noticed four feet sticking out from under the sheets. The cast also included the comedian Tommy Trinder, who told unseemly jokes. Police Constable Lewis claimed his companion had been embarrassed by the material but, to laughter, he admitted that he had stayed for the second half as he 'thought that it might improve'. The defending council called it a storm in a teacup and some charges were dropped, but Mr Terry Wood was fined £10 for permitting entertainment not suitable for the day and also for allowing dancing. The bench was confident that he would redouble his efforts to abide by the Sunday Guidelines in the future. (*Isle of Wight County Press*, July 3rd 1937)

— JUNE 28TH —

1902: The postponed illuminations for the coronation of King Edward VII at the Guildhall, Newport were today turned on by the mayor alderman, J.T. Mew, watched by a large and enthusiastic crowd. From the balcony Mr Mew reported that the king's condition was satisfactory in all respects and that this was a very good time to sing 'God Save the King'. The mayor was praised for his part in the week's celebration, having been drawn around the town by a number of firemen and others in a waggonette. The Guildhall was illuminated in the national colours by fairy electric lamps surrounding a sign reading 'God Save the King and Queen' and 'May Peace Attend Thy Reign' in gold letters on a red background. While these celebrations were held later than expected, at Cowes there was a premature launch as the huge pile of wood and faggots amassed in Mr Caws' field overlooking the Channel, was set alight by 'someone who had no authority to do so'. The conflagration was watched by a huge crowd and all the material was consumed. The delays in starting the coronation celebrations arose because of the king's illness, he having suffered from appendicitis. (*Portsmouth Evening News*, June 30th 1902)

~ JUNE 29TH ~

1844: Under the heading 'R.Y.S. Intelligence', today's *Hampshire Advertiser* carried a weekly account of the arrivals and departures of yachts into Cowes. On this particular week, the *Kestrel*, a yawl belonging to the Earl of Yarborough, commodore of the squadron, was in the process of being fitted out. She had been newly coppered, was 'all a tanto' and ready to be launched from Hansen's Slip on Monday (July 1st). The earl was a founding member of the squadron in 1825 and had had the good fortune to inherit Appuldurcombe House, giving him an ideal base for his sailing activities. Perhaps appropriately, he died aboard the *Kestrel* at Vigo in 1846.

The *Advertiser* also included a summary of mercantile shipping and on this day it reported that the Peninsular & Oriental steamer *Braganza* would also be launched on Monday and 'the novelty of the launch of so large a steamer will no doubt attract much company'. The ship was prepared in the yard of Messrs White. (*Hampshire Advertiser*, June 29th 1844)

~ June 30th ~

1897: Following the arrival of the telephone on the Isle of Wight, a cable was laid undersea from Stone Point in Hampshire to Gurnard Bay, connecting the Island to the mainland. The idea that the Isle of Wight should have telephones had been mooted as early as 1893, when in September of that year the Mayor of Newport convened a public meeting at the Guildhall. It was February of 1896 before the first call exchanges were up and running; initially there were six of them, based in pubs and shops, and the National Telephone Company rented these at a cost of £18 a year. The first exchange to operate was at Cowes. Early subscribers were identified by the first three letters of the town in which they lived, plus a number. Anybody asking for COW 13 would have been put through to Osborne House, the Holliers Hotel at Shanklin could be reached through SHA 3 and Doctor Dabbs of Shanklin was an early subscriber, with the number SHA 4. It is doubtful, though, whether many of his patients would be able to ring him. In 1899, the telephone dial came into service which allowed subscribers to dial numbers direct and as from the New Year began in 1912, the National Telephone Company sold their assets to the General Post Office for a massive £12.4 million, which was in turn replaced by British Telecom. (Moyra Bird, *Wight Wires*, 1996)

~ JULY 1st ~

1848: Today's *Hampshire Telegraph* was pleased to report that Ryde's 'old and favourite townsman' had written two new pieces of music, entitled the 'Garrison', and the 'Osborne Polkas', 'displaying a maturity of study and thorough knowledge of the science of music'. The composer in question was Joseph Theodore Treakell, whose very musical family ran the music publishing business of Treakell & Son in Portsmouth and also supplied pianos. Joseph was very successful, having his music published in New York, and he wrote a Swedish Polka, dedicated to the singer Jenny Lind. His 'Osborne Polka' was played in Queen Victoria's presence by the Royal Marine band and after a few bars, the queen and her husband were said to have 'polkad on the green for some minutes'. Today's *Telegraph* felt compelled to 'congratulate our Piano Forte Friends on this addition to their collection of sweet sounds'. (*Hampshire Telegraph*, July 1st 1848)

~ July 2nd ~

1898: Today's *Isle of Wight Observer* carried a notice from the RSPCA 'to the effect that proceedings will be taken against anyone who ill-treats, abuses, or tortures a horse by docking it with the mistaken motive of improving its appearance. The policy of the Society will be to make it incumbent upon the owner to prove his motives for having his horse docked. It is hardly possible that any magistrate would convict for cruelty unless it can be proved that the operation has been carried out in an improper manner. Those who are qualified to speak with authority upon the subject are unanimously of the opinion that if docking is carried out carefully by a skilled hand there can be no cruelty, because very little pain is inflicted.' Horse docking, the removal of part of the tail to change the horse's appearance, was not outlawed until 1949. The RSPCA was founded in 1824 and received its royal status from Queen Victoria in 1840. (*Isle of Wight Observer*, July 2nd 1898)

~ July 3rd ~

1824: On this day:

> ... following information against Sarah Read, an old and infirm female of the Parish of Whitwell, for knowingly harbouring and concealing upon her premises a large quantity of foreign spirits, [she] came before a full bench of Magistrates, the Rev James Worsley in the chair. Mr Cossins conducted the prosecution at the instance of the Board of Excise and upon the examination of his witnesses in chief, the case apparently operated to the defendant's prejudice, but Mr Day, in the course of an ingenious cross-examination, drew from them the following facts: That the cow-house, in a small cave under which the liquors were found, was situated 500 feet from the defendant's dwelling; that the officers ... had no reason to suspect her and did not even search her dwelling, nor hold any communication with her personally till three or four days afterwards when she admitted that the cow-house and garden were her property, but denied all knowledge of the smuggling or concealment alluded to ... That many other houses stood close to the cow house, some which officers actually searched, though without any warrant to legally authorize [*sic*] them, and in short that any other person or persons might have concealed the goods where they were found, without the defendant's knowing a single particle of the transaction.

In view of the above cross-examination, the magistrates felt bound to dismiss the case. (*Hampshire Telegraph*, July 3rd 1824)

~ July 4th ~

1721: Sir Tristram Dillington MP, major in the Guards, was found drowned in the pond in the grounds of his house Knighton Gorges. He had inherited the house in 1712 and was a devoted husband and father. When, in the space of two weeks, his wife and all four infants died from a fever, it was more than he could bear and he took his life. His butler, realising that if suicide was suspected the land would be forfeited to the Crown, immediately released his master's horse with a loosened girth and on 'finding it again', he reported that Sir Tristram had died from a tragic accident. Local people were less than convinced and after his funeral, a rumour circulated that although there was an impressive tomb in Newchurch church it was in fact empty because a suicide was debarred from a Christian burial. Having no immediate family left, the house passed to a distant relative though marriage and eventually went down to George Maurice Bisset who, having led a dissolute life and having only a female heir, decided to pull it down rather than allow her to inherit it. The heir's crime was to have married a vicar. (Henry Davenport Adams, *The History, Topography and Antiquities of the Isle of Wight*, Smith, Elder and Co., 1856)

— JULY 5TH —

1890: On this Saturday morning, an old French craft, the *Happy Bordeaux* was towed past Cliff End Fort at about 12 knots. As it drew near, a torpedo was seen to take to the water, gradually sinking until only its little flag was visible. Travelling at about 20 knots it made its way towards the hulk and passing under her stern, it turned suddenly and struck on the far side. A huge hole was torn in the vessel and two columns of smoke and spray rose into the air. Within a minute the hulk was no more than a few floating timbers. This was part of a weeklong military operation on the Island. The evening before, a night attack had been launched at Freshwater Bay, with enemy forces attempting to land under cover from shots fired from their invading fleet. On shore the artillery launched volleys of fire from around the Albion Hotel. The enemy having supposedly landed, a stout defence was launched between Freshwater Bay and the Post Office, using a machine gun. The infantry, meanwhile, advanced under the cover of the hedgerows and gave the foe 'a very warm reception'. Meanwhile, the enemy fleet sailed towards the west and, on rounding the Needles, were detected by means of electric light and fired upon from the forts. (*Manchester Courier*, July 7th 1890)

⟶ July 6th ⟵

1861: The *Isle of Wight Observer* today reported that Captain Breton of Dover Street Ryde found himself before the court on a charge of using foul language and assault. The case was brought by his neighbour, Sarah Sweatman and the cause of the dispute was Miss Sweatman's noisy parrot. The captain, having been driven to distraction, knocked on his neighbour's door and, after complaining loudly, suggested that she should cut the parrot's throat. Miss Sweatman suggested that he would be better employed if he were to cut his own throat. The captain then pushed Miss Sweatman and grabbed her arm. In his defence Captain Breton said that the parrot was an abominable nuisance to the entire neighbourhood. He was fined 5*s* with 7*s* 6*d* costs. (*Isle of Wight Observer*, July 6th 1861)

— July 7th —

1878: Following a suggestion that Germany was intending to annexe the Isle of Wight, today's *Falkirk Herald* printed a spirited column examining how such an invasion would benefit the rest of the country:

> The Isle of Wight brings no advantage to England. We are forced to keep at Newport a permanent force which is withdrawn from the defence of England itself. The returns show that the taxes levied there are entirely insufficient to pay for the expenses we are obliged to incur for its defence. The inhabitants do not like us as witness the sympathy shown for Charles I ... The very prosperity caused by our rule is an evil, inasmuch as it has increased the population and so raised the prices of the necessaries of life that we hear of men and women there dying of starvation and whole families obliged to take refuge in the work-house ... it would be a blessing and not an injury to us to be quit of this miserable island. Instead of opposing the Emperor we should go hand in hand with him.

The emperor in question was Frederick, husband of Queen Victoria's eldest daughter Victoria – and father to the future Kaiser Wilhelm II. (*Falkirk Herald*, July 7th 1878)

~ July 8th ~

1936: Amid considerable emotion, and watched by a large crowd along the banks of the River Medina, today a naval cutter left the Minerva Boatyard for her final, short voyage. The royal yacht *Britannia*, so loved by the recently deceased King George V, was to be sunk at sea. Pulled by a tug named *Irishman*, the cutter moved slowly downstream. A wreath was placed across her bow by the foreman of the yard who, throughout her forty-three years' service, had been personally responsible for the hauling up and launching of the vessel. As she passed, people cheered then removed their hats and fell silent. *Britannia* had been built in 1893 for George, then the Prince of Wales. She had a magnificent 10,000 sq ft of sail made by Cowes sail-makers Ratsey and Lapthorne. The evening following her departure, at 9 p.m., two naval destroyers, *Amazon* and *Winchester*, from Portsmouth, took charge of *Britannia*, towing her to a spot off St Catherine's Point. There a timed charge holed her beneath the waterline and she quickly sank. (*Western Morning News*, July 9th 1936)

~ July 9th ~

1884: Under the heading 'Death of an Aged Convict', today's *Hampshire Advertiser* reported that John Selby-Watson, serving a life sentence for murdering his wife, had died following an accident in his cell. Watson, who was described as a clerk in holy orders and a widower, had been the headmaster of Stockwell Grammar School and wrote numerous books on religious subjects and biographies. On losing his position at the school after twenty-five years' service, he struck his wife Anne with a heavy object, wrote a confession and took prussic acid, but it failed to kill him.

He had arrived at Parkhurst from Pentonville and was employed at the prison in the patching and darning department. Some days before his death, a warder had found him with blood on his whiskers. He said that he had fallen from his hammock and asked to go to the infirmary. The doctor confirmed that he had cut his ear right through, a very serious matter for a man of his age, being then near to 80 years. On July 3rd he was reported as dangerously ill with erysipelas, and died six days later. The jury returned a verdict that took into account these circumstances. Departing from custom, he was buried in Carisbrooke Cemetery. (Jan Toms, 'Parkhurst People, the Revd John Selby Watson, Murderer', www.suite101.com)

— July 10th —

1841: The *Berkshire Chronicle* today reported in detail the determination of Island voters to accompany their proposed Parliamentary candidate to Newport for nomination:

> A large number of carriages and vehicles of all descriptions, horsemen and pedestrians with banners and favours and preceded by a band, assembled some distance outside the town and when Mr Holmes and his friends arrived, the numbers had increased to some thousands. They accordingly ... escorted the hon gentleman along the road and through the town to the court-house where the nomination had been appointed to take place that day. Mr Sewell the deputy sheriff announced from the front balcony of the court-house the purpose for which they had assembled, calling upon electors to come forward to nominate a representative for the county of the Island of Wight ... Vice-Admiral Sir Graham Hammond then came forward and proposed ... William Henry A'Court Holmes Esq ... Captain Brigstock seconded the nomination. Mr Holmes presented himself at the balcony and was received with loud cheers and the waving of handkerchiefs from the windows in the street.

There being no other candidates, Mr Holmes was adopted as the candidate for the forthcoming election. He then addressed the crowd, thanking them for the honour that they had conferred on him and that 'he would not consent to occupy it on any other grounds than the maintenance of those conservative principles which he had always professed' to cheers from the crowd. (*Berkshire Chronicle*, July 10th 1841)

~ July 11th ~

1903: Today the Southampton and Isle of Wight Steam Packet Company made its first day trip to Boulogne. A reporter for the *Portsmouth Evening News* was pleased to announce that the passengers had a perfect trip on an ideal vessel. The *Balmoral* set sail from Southampton at 6 a.m., picking up passengers at Cowes, Ryde and Southsea. The day was breezy and the *Balmoral* kept close to the shore, enabling the passengers to identify the coastal resorts as they passed them before heading out from Beachy Head towards their destination. On board, lunch was served before they arrived where they were greeted with a rendering of 'Tar-ar-a-boom-de-ay' which the reporter suggested was mistaken by the French for the British National Anthem. In spite of a bright, sunny day, many tourists visited the museum while others attempted to shop in French, and were defeated, until they discovered that the locals spoke adequate English. The day was spoiled by an unhappy accident, when a young French woman fell beneath a tram and there was great difficulty in extricating her. The party left Boulogne at 5.15 p.m. and by 11.45 p.m. the last passengers were disembarked at the Clarence Pier. A good day seems to have been had by all. (*Portsmouth Evening News*, July 13th 1903)

⁓ July 12th ⁓

1887: On this evening, the tug *Lioness* out of Cowes was proceeding to the east when she struck on Bembridge Ledge. The captain, John Bilson, gave the order to go astern but the tug began to fill and the crew of three took to the lifeboat. Shortly afterwards the boiler burst with great violence, but the crew returned safely to Cowes. All was not quite as it seemed, however, for on November 16th the three men were at Winchester Assizes, accused of scuttling the vessel deliberately. The three defendants were John Bilson (captain), John Naylor (engineer) and T. Symes (fireman). After the accident, a diver was sent to examine the wreck and pronounced that there was a hole in the vessel's bottom, probably made by an augur, and so his view was that the tug had been deliberately scuttled by the prisoners. Symes and Naylor were found not guilty but John Bilson was sentenced to seven years' penal servitude. (*Isle of Wight Observer*, July 16th 1887, *Bristol Mercury*, November 17th 1887)

~ July 13th ~

1935: The *Taunton Courier and Western Advertiser* informed their readers that, for their annual summer outing, this week the staff of Messrs Bovril Ltd had visited Ryde and watched the ships massing in formation along the Solent in preparation for the Royal Naval Review. Bovril had been the brainchild of John Lawson Johnston, a Scotsman who had first run his uncle's butcher's business in Edinburgh, then moved to Canada. The product had developed first as a personal drink, boiling off-cuts of beef until they reduced and became concentrated. Johnston discovered that this also made it keep longer. At the time of the Franco Prussian War, Napoleon III was looking for tinned beef to feed his troops and 'Johnson's Fluid Beef', supplied a convenient answer. Bovril went on to nourish the troops in the First World War as well as the civilian population, and is said to have sustained Ernest Shackleton's team when marooned on Elephant Island. The company passed to George Lawson Johnson who was granted the title Lord Luke of Pavenham, the title still existing today. (*Taunton Courier*, July 24th 1935)

~ July 14th ~

1860: Today's *Isle of Wight Observer* announced that 'Cook's circus will make an entry into the town [of Ventnor] and perform for two or three days wonders that will astonish everyone, if we may believe all that is contained in the flaming bills numerously posted all over the neighbourhood'. Among the 'wonders' was a 'real life bull and steeds innumerable'. The circus was a regular summer visitor touring the Island. In September 1857 it was reported as being in Ryde, where it was patronised very liberally, so much so that many were unable to witness 'the graceful riding of Miss Kate Cooke on her beautiful charger, the skilful equitation of Miss Emily Cooke, and the daring equestrian feats of Mr James Cooke'. At the end of the tour, the circus was to carry out a final morning performance with the proceeds going for the relief of the sufferers from the Indian Mutinies. The following March, the paper carried the unhappy news of a fire that occurred at the circus while camped at Portsmouth in which eight horses died of suffocation. Gas jets in the building were said to be turned off and the tragedy was blamed on 'an act of incendiary'. (*Isle of Wight Observer*, July 14th 1860)

⹀ July 15th ⹀

1901: The *Navy and Army Illustrated* reported today that a verdict of Accidental Death had been reached after four men died and several others were injured in an explosion at Fort Redoubt, above Freshwater Bay. The redoubt was used as the School of Gunnery's instructional unit by the garrisons based at Golden Hill Fort. On the day in question, the breech-block of a 12-pounder gun blew out, killing an officer and three gunners. Captain Arthur le Mesurier Bray, standing behind the gun and observing the proceedings, was killed, as was Gunner Charles Dornan who was loading the shells. Gunner Rickets and Bombardier MacDonald died a few hours later from their injuries. In addition, Gunner McGlocklan lost his right hand while Gunner Malone's arm was blown off. Gunner Pratt suffered chest injuries. The deceased men were laid to rest with full military honours at All Saints church, Freshwater, accompanied by 1,500 troops. The redoubt was built following an invasion scare in 1851 above Freshwater Bay, as this was the only landing place along the south-western part of the Island that would not entail climbing the cliffs to reach the inland area. The diamond-shaped fort was reached by means of a drawbridge and stood above a cave in the cliff that had to be strengthened to take the weight. Sold to private owners after the Second World War, the water tank supplying the fort was turned into a swimming pool. (*Navy and Army Illustrated*, July 15th 1901)

~ July 16th ~

1897: The American poet, Henry Wadsworth Longfellow
came to visit the Tennysons at Farringford, staying for two days
in the area. On the morning of the 16th he arrived and wrote
a detailed description of the house. It was a simple, rambling
mansion, plainly furnished but the walls covered in pictures, the
whole length of the stairway hung with photographs of people
and places hung one above the other in rows like steps. All of the
pictures were in oils except a print of the queen and Prince Albert,
of which Tennyson said: 'There's a hateful picture hanging
there, but as the Queen presented it to me I felt obliged to hang
it up.' Longfellow noted the busts of Dante and Shakespeare
and thought that Mrs Tennyson was 'lovely and attractive [but]
exceedingly delicate looking in health'. Tennyson's sister he
disregarded as 'dispeptic [*sic*], angular and not so attractive'.
The drawing room contained books, papers, writing materials,
a sofa, couches and a variety of chairs. Lord Tennyson had kind
things to say about his guest's work *Hiawatha*. They also discussed
the subject of spiritualism at length. To celebrate the visit, on the
second day Lord Alfred invited forty or fifty neighbours to tea,
all of which were anxious to meet the great man and Tennyson
picked out Mrs Fraser-Tytler, wife of the painter F.G. Watts, for
special mention. Longfellow was equally enamoured, declaring
'it was worthwhile coming to England to see such young ladies'.
Wordsworth also spent some time in Shanklin staying at the
Holliers Hotel. He was so taken with the drinking fountain
opposite, at the top of Chine Hollow, that he wrote a verse for the
occasion and declared Shanklin to be 'the quaintest little village
you ever saw'. (Anne Longfellow, *A Visit to Farringford*, Pierce)

⟶ July 17th ⟵

1880: Today's *Isle of Wight Observer* carried several paragraphs devoted to the opening of the Ryde Pier Railway, linking the town by means of tunnels at Ryde and Wroxall on to Ventnor. In the words of the reporter, 'this was the completion of a gigantic work, achieved at enormous expense and by the exercise of no little engineering skill; and also something like a revolution as far as relations existing between the old town and the pier are concerned'. In spite of this, as the first passenger set foot in the carriage at the pier head, there was no ceremony and comparatively little attention. The paper claimed 'there are not a few amongst us, throwing our memories back forty or fifty years who assure us that the Island is becoming gradually spoiled'. The writer, however, contended that this being a democratic age, it was no longer possible to 'preserve for such a charming spot, aristocratic seclusion and hauteur'. The day of the seaside holiday was fast arriving. The earlier problems had arisen when the council gave permission for the Pier Company to use some land along which to run the railway line. The company spent out a small fortune and when the assignment was nearly complete, the public awoke to its impact and a huge protest arose. As a result, the plans were changed at great cost to the company, as the only way around was by tunnelling under the Esplanade. With this history of changes, protests and huge costs, unsurprisingly the Pier Company felt little desire for a celebration. The *Observer* noted that 'The British traveller is an irritable person and prone to grumble'. (*Isle of Wight Observer*, July 17th 1880)

— JULY 18TH —

1635: On this day Robert Hooke, scientist, inventor, geologist, mineralogist and architect, was born at Freshwater where his father was curate at All Saints church. He was a sickly boy who spent a solitary childhood before being sent to Westminster School, and from there to Oxford. Later he went to Gresham College in London where he worked with the great scientists of his day, including Boyle, Newton and Christopher Wren. With no personal fortune, he worked to design various items that enabled his colleagues to carry out experiments. Among his many inventions and discoveries were the air pump, the spring, the spirit level and the pocket watch. Going against the belief of the day, he asserted that in the past various species of creature had died out, which was later proved right. He was a member of the Royal Society and a close friend of Samuel Pepys. In 1665, he published his book, *Micrographia*, illustrating the discoveries made with the microscope; his fine insect drawings were still the standard learning aid two centuries later. Following the Great Fire of London in 1666, he was appointed assistant to Christopher Wren who was Charles II's surveyor general. Many of the innovations and designs for the Wren churches in London are now known to be, at least in part, Hooke's work. It was he who suggested to Wren the curve that enabled him to construct St Paul's Dome and Hooke was responsible for the 202ft-high monument, commemorating London's great fire. Hooke died in London, unmarried, in 1705. Having lived a penurious existence, he left behind a small fortune. (Stephen Inwood, *The Man Who Knew Too Much*, Macmillan, 2003)

~ JULY 19TH ~

1881: A group of Gypsies setting up camp on St Helens Green outraged Mr Moody, who demanded to know if the Local Board had the power to evict them. The party had seven or eight vehicles with them and set up camp without getting permission from anyone to do so, and he believed that they were so pleased with their reception that they intended to come again. The chairman agreed that Gypsies and hawkers were a nuisance but as far as he knew there was no law by which they could be stopped. The only exception was if they failed to produce a licence and he believed that they were able to do so. Neither did he think they could be treated as rogues and vagabonds, as they would have to show that they had no means of subsistence. The travellers, it seemed, were making a good living from local attendance at their fair. The chairman continued that he thought that they had the right to pitch their tents on any waste ground or green. The only advice he could give to Mr Moody was to persuade the local people not to patronise the Gypsy fair. (*Isle of Wight Observer*, July 23rd 1881)

~ JULY 20TH ~

1832: On this day, local man Mr Ruddick of Brading received a letter from William Cobbett enclosing a petition that demanded the reform of the House of Commons. The letter urged Mr Ruddick to 'Get the inclosed [*sic*] as numerously signed as you can by Saturday night, and then send it by post to Daniel O'Connell Esq, MP, Parliament St. London. Do this quickly and as well as possible and it will produce prodigious effect.' In a work entitled *Retrospections* by Mr Roach Smith, he referred to an Island visit by William Cobbett and declared that his brother Richard had driven the visitor from Landguard to Newport, where he gave a lecture. Mr J. Woodrow of Brading also produced a letter in which 'The fact of Cobbett's being on the island is confirmed by the enclosed letter from him to Mr Ruddick of this place, and also that Cobbett had partaken of Mr and Mrs Ruddick's hospitality. William Cobbett (1763–1835) was a farmer, writer, MP and campaigner. He particularly opposed the Corn Laws and worked towards Catholic emancipation. He is mostly remembered for his book *Rural Rides* that commented on conditions throughout the countryside and is still in print today. According to the *County Press*, in the 1830s Brading had been one of the most radical places in England. (Charles Roach Smith, *Retrospections*, 1883)

~ July 21st ~

1894: An inquest was held today on the victims of a shocking accident. *Hampshire Advertiser* had reported that two yachts had been wrecked off Brambles, near to Freshwater, and were considered a hazard to shipping. Two days ago Trinity House had given instructions that they should be blown up and it fell to the captain and men of the *Mermaid* to carry it out, accompanied by the captain of the *Nab* lightship. They proceeded with five men and two ships to the scene of the wrecks. The men were William Cook, Henry Hutchens, Alfred Snow, William Oatley and Fred Cotter, all residents of the East Cowes area. Four of them were married. They took with them about 110lbs of cotton powder in different charges. A 20-pound charge was prepared, the fuse lit and it was placed at the site of the wrecks. The boats retreated to a safe distance but, although they waited for nearly 30 minutes, nothing happened. A second torpedo was prepared and this time, it worked. While a third charge was prepared, the faulty torpedo was recovered and an apprentice named Rennie was in the process of picking it up when there was a fearful explosion blowing the *Mermaid* to pieces. As the *Advertiser* graphically described, 'the water was strewn with small pieces of human flesh, hands, thumbs etc … and to collect these remains it would need the smallest mesh net possible to obtain.' Two of the men, Hutchens and Cook, were alive when a rescue boat arrived but died soon afterwards. The *Advertiser* further reported that East Cowes did not boast of having a mortuary, so several sheds were used instead. The inquest returned a verdict of Accidental Death. (*Hampshire Advertiser*, July 21st 1894)

~ JULY 22ND ~

1936: Whilst staying at Ventnor with friends, Charles, the 17-year-old son of actor Ronald Squire, was discovered drowned in the bath. The news reached Ronald while he was on the mainland, nursing his terminally ill brother, who died the following day (July 22nd). Mr Squire returned to the Island to attend the inquest that took place today and gave evidence that for the past six years his son had suffered from fainting fits. A verdict of accidental death was returned and the funeral took place on July 24th. Mr Squire was a familiar figure in dozens of films shot between 1916 and 1959, the most famous probably being *Round the World in Eighty Days*. He died in 1958. (*Nottingham Post*, July 23rd 1936)

– July 23rd –

1873: In an attempt to eradicate smallpox, an Act of Parliament required the Board of Governors to appoint vaccination officers for the Island. Whenever the practice lapsed, new outbreaks occurred and financial incentives were offered to medical officers to ensure that the job was done. In July 1873, Dr Hoffmeister of Cowes received a payment of £15 16s for efficient vaccination in his district. This was the sixth time he had been awarded such a gratuity, and the fifth time in succession. The uptake was still not universal and the guardians resorted to prosecution of those parents failing to have their children immunised. Failure to vaccinate continued until as late as November 1897 when Alfred Hill, Edward Savage and James H. Taylor, all of St Helens, appeared in court. It had been long since observed that, although milkmaids working with cows suffered from cowpox, they then seemed to be immune to the more deadly smallpox. As a result, a vaccine taken from an infected cow was injected into humans with good effect. The Chairman of the Board was of the opinion that all parents should make private arrangements for their children to be vaccinated and, if it were his own case, he would have it done direct from the cow. (*Hampshire Advertiser*, July 23rd 1873)

~ JULY 24TH ~

1933: The wills of the rich and famous naturally attracted interest and local celebrity, the late Mr Harmsworth of Pilot's Point at Totland was no exception. He had been crippled in a motorcycle accident in France and on his death he left an annuity of £600 to the two nurses who had cared for him. He bequeathed his body to the Royal College of Surgeons and, when they had finished with it, he left instructions for it to be cremated and his ashes cast into the English Channel. The rest of his £83,000 estate was to go to his relatives.

His predecessor at Pilot's Point, the first Lord Northcliffe, had grown rich through the formation of *Amalgamated Newspapers*. Among his many ventures, he had founded the *Evening News*, the *Edinburgh Daily Record*, the *Daily Mail* and the *Daily Mirror*. A man with a fascination for speed, he had donated the Harmsworth Trophy, the first international prize for motorboat racing. In 1920, when film stars Douglas Fairbanks and his new wife Mary Pickford were visiting London, the media interest in them was so intense that they escaped to Pilot's Point to evade the paparazzi. When Lord Northcliffe died, he left three months' salary to each of his many employees. (*Isle of Wight Gazette*, July 24th 1933)

~ July 25th ~

1885: On this day the marriage of Princess Beatrice and Prince Henry of Battenburg took place at Whippingham church. The preceding week had been a whirlwind of activities and a series of well-wishers came to deliver gifts: a Bible from a deputation of young women dubbed the 'maidens of England', a mirror from the citizens of West Cowes and an opal candelabra from the children at Whippingham School. A special train transported fourteen horse-boxes and carriages from the Royal Mews at Windsor, and the day before the wedding the queen laid out a dinner for the estate servants. A collection had been made locally to give to the poor of Cowes a special treat. Prince Henry, in his role as Colonel of the Isle of Wight Volunteers, received a silver sword while the queen presented Beatrice with a wedding gift of her own militia – the Isle of Wight Rifles. Forty members of the royal family stayed in Osborne House but other guests had to take accommodation in the neighbourhood.

Her Majesty was dressed in black satin with a sparkling array of diamonds, amongst which was the famous Koh-i-Noor and she gave the bride away. Princess Beatrice wore a white satin gown, liberally trimmed with Honiton lace and small orange flowers, part of the decoration coming from her mother's wedding outfit. Prince Henry was resplendent in a white uniform of the Prussian Cuirassiers. The couple made their vows, the queen kissed her daughter on the cheek and then, to the tune of Mendelsohn's 'Wedding March', the newly-weds walked down the aisle. At 5 p.m. the couple left Osborne to spend their honeymoon night at Quarr Abbey. (*Isle of Wight County Press*, August 1st 1885)

~ JULY 26TH ~

1910: About 2,000 people gathered at the Needles Golf Course to witness the departure of the first bi-plane ever to have landed on the Island. Six days earlier on a cold, wet, blustery afternoon at Alum Bay, a local resident had reported that, at about 3.45 p.m., the solitary plane had skirted the cliffs and made an emergency landing at the golf course. At the scene was the pilot being helped out of his cork lifejacket; his name was Robert Loraine, a well-known stage actor, flying under the name of Robert Jones. Nonchalantly lighting a cigarette, although numbed and wet, he explained to the gathering crowd that, it being Bournemouth Aviation week, he had set off from Bournemouth but a storm blew up and he had lost his bearings. Unwilling to fly below 1,500ft because of the cliffs, and in danger of running out of fuel, he chose the golf course as an air strip. His was the first heavier-than-air flying machine to land on the Island. Preparing for the return journey, the plane was turned towards the beacon to take advantage of the wind while Loraine took tea at Alum Bay House. Again the weather was bad, but he elected to leave anyway. It took a dozen local artillery men to restrain the surging aircraft, while Loraine climbed into the cockpit and gave the signal at which point they let go and, with a wave, he departed. The return journey took 25 minutes and Loraine is credited with having introduced the word 'joystick' into the language. (Major W.F. Smith, *Robert Loraine, a Pilot's War 1915–18*)

⟶ July 27th ⟶

1812: Today's *Hampshire Chronicle* reported that 'on Wednesday last a private of the 63rd regiment, of the name of Webster, in attempting to descend the short distance [down] the awful and tremendous cliffs at High Down, in the Isle of Wight, about 200 yards east of the Signal House, lost his hold, and precipitated to the bottom, a distance, it is supposed, of about 630 feet. A boat containing some gentlemen, who were making a tour of the island, and were going by water from Allum [*sic*] Bay through the Needles, to Freshwater Gate, happened to pass within a few minutes of the fall, and immediately carried the poor sufferer, in the boat, to Freshwater Gate. Surgical assistance was procured without delay, and the supposition is, that the unfortunate man may recover! Amputation of the right arm, which was most dreadfully broken, was about to be performed, when the Gentlemen left Freshwater Gate.' (*Hampshire Chronicle,* July 27th 1812)

~ July 28th ~

1788: Today a grand sailing match took place in the Solent and was enthusiastically reported in the *Salisbury and Winchester Journal* of August 4th. In the words of the reporter:

> All that tends to encourage the art and activity of our seamen, merits national reward. As a spectacle there has been nothing to equal this contest. On the Isle, all inhabitants were in motion to get on the different heights, while the opposite shores of Lymington and Christchurch were all lined with spectators. By six in the morning the vessels were all in their respective stations off Cowes Harbour, and started precisely at ten minutes after. Ten vessels sailed – two were distanced. They came in according to the following order: Dove, Master, Loving Corke, 4hrs 57 minutes; Palmer, T Wassel, 5hrs 6 mins; Fortitude, M Francis, 5 hrs 6½ minutes.

The other ships finishing were the *Three Brothers*, *Jane*, *Seven Brothers*, *Fame*, and last, *John and Sally*. The winner received fifteen guineas, the second ten guineas and the third five guineas. The manoeuvring of the *Palmer* was much spoken of. (*Winchester Journal*, 4th August 1788)

~ July 29th ~

1949: With three prisons on the Island, the authorities were always anxious to emphasise the small number of escapes and the failure of most prisoners to get further than the coast. On the 29th, however, the *Bath Chronicle* and *Weekly Gazette* reported an exception to this rule. 'Dennis E. Carter, a 17-year-old Borstal boy, who escaped from an institution in the Isle of Wight on Thursday, last week, was recaptured on Wednesday night by a Stothert and Pitt night-watchman as he was trying to enter a shed at Stother's storage dump at the Turnpike, on the main Lower Bristol Road. Mr E.F. Rudkin of 18, Norfolk Crescent, Bath, grabbed the boy and phoned for the Keynsham police, who quickly arrived and took the youth into custody. Carter escaped from the Isle of Wight by commandeering a dinghy in which he made his way to the mainland. He is one of very few prisoners who have been able to escape from the island in this way.' (*Bath Chronicle*, July 29th 1949)

~ July 30th ~

1913: As Professor John Milne lay ill at his home at Shide, his seismometer made a last recording of an earth tremor during his lifetime, taking place in Gibraltar on this day. He died the next day.

Professor Milne had returned from Japan in 1896, having experienced an earthquake first-hand which subsequently became his life's study. Setting up home at Shide House near Newport with his wife Toni, he continued to work on the global recording of earthquakes. He was frequently called upon to lecture on the subject and he wrote books on both earthquakes and seismology. In 1908, the Royal Society presented him with their Royal Medal and he was recognised as the world's leading authority on the subject. Professor Milne was buried at St Paul's church, Barton, on the outskirts of Newport, and his wife returned to Japan. The seismograph that has added so much to our knowledge of earthquakes can still be seen working in Carisbrooke Castle Museum. (Isle of Wight Society and East Cowes Heritage papers)

~ July 31st ~

1875: Admiralty Circular No.33 of July 31st had unforeseen and widespread repercussions, not least on the Island. A question arose when a British officer, Commodore Sir L. Heath, serving abroad, asked for guidelines as to the treatment of runaway slaves seeking refuge on board Her Majesty's ships in territorial waters where slavery is the law of the land. The admiralty replied that the fugitives in question should be returned to their masters. On August 13th, having received a 'numerously signed requisition', the Mayor of Newport convened a public meeting to consider what action should be taken in response to the circular. In the meantime, it caused such national furore that it was suspended. The mayor, therefore, made a few remarks and dissolved the meeting.

On August 14th the *Morning Post* congratulated the government in having done the right thing, in that fugitive slaves should be received aboard Her Majesty's ships and that 'very little, if any exception can be taken'. The *Post* declared that the settlement of the question 'is in exact accord with the feelings and desires of the people of England'. (*Hampshire Telegraph*, August 13th 1875, Admiralty Circular No.33, July 31st 1875)

~ August 1st ~

1857: Before the bench at Newport was James Garnett, a vagrant accused of feloniously stealing a snuffbox, the property of Edward Mew. Mew lodged at the Crown inn, Shorwell and, having seen him place his coat on the stairs, Garnett left the taproom and picked the pocket. Garnett was observed in the act and the police were sent for; the snuffbox was found under the seat the accused had occupied. He offered a desperate resistance, but was captured and brought before the court. He pleaded drunkenness as an excuse, having drunk 'five quarterns of rum and six quarts of sixpenny beer, plus porter' at the Crown that day. He asked for the mercy of the court on the grounds that his wife and four children would be left destitute and was sentenced to one month's hard labour. (*Hampshire Chronicle*, August 8th 1857)

~ AUGUST 2ND ~

1891: There was no shortage of entertainment on the Island during the summer months and the *Isle of Wight Observer* was pleased to give notice of the forthcoming events:

> The Georgia Minstrels have been giving very successful performances at Ryde, Sea View and other parts of the Island during the past week. They are certainly worth hearing. On Sunday evening next (August 2nd) they give a sacred concert at Sandown Town Hall. The 'Silver King' is announced for Bank Holiday and two following nights at the theatre. This successful drama should draw full houses. Mr Ellis Miller has engaged a special company who bring their own elaborate scenery. Miss Elizabeth Bessle supported by her sister Miss Mary Bessle and accompanied by a company of artists chosen from the London Theatres including amongst others Miss Theodore Wright, a lady who has recently come in for no small share of admiration for her performances at the Vaudeville Theatre … [the performances] are to be given at the Isle of Wight College … and we think that we may expect large and fashionable audiences on Thursday and Friday next.

(*Isle of Wight Observer*, July 31st 1891)

‒ August 3rd ‒

1900: Following the events of this day, a Cowes man, named H. Nobbs, lived to tell the tale of a shipwreck en route to Walfisch Bay, on the coast of Namibia. He was a crewman on the ship *Primera*, carrying a cargo of coal and on August 3rd a fire broke out and 300 bales of hay were jettisoned. Unfortunately, the coal also caught fire and a terrific explosion left no choice but to abandon ship. The fifteen people on board, twelve crew and three passengers, prepared to leave in two boats. The lifeboat accommodated ten, including Mr Nobbs plus the passengers – one of whom was taking the voyage for his health – with five in the smaller boat. Casks of water, tins of corned beef, condensed milk, jam and ship's biscuit were taken aboard. Unhappily, while launching the boats, a lurch from the stricken ship damaged the smaller boat that then had to be bailed out all the time. The castaways were stranded for days, and in hope of rescue the lifeboat attempted to sail in the direction of St Helena, but the wind dropped and they were unsuccessful. Daily they drifted, their supplies diminishing. Eventually they approached Ascension Island where the navy came to their rescue. They had been at sea for twenty-five days and were near to death, but were treated in hospital and happily recovered. The fate of the smaller boat was unknown. (*Isle of Wight Observer*, September 29th 1900)

~ AUGUST 4TH ~

1855: On this day the *Isle of Wight Observer* reported that, at the last petty session held at the Guildhall (Saturday, July 28), William Hayles, a lace maker, was summoned by the Guardians of the Poor for not maintaining or assisting to maintain his father. Mr Hayles Senior was not an inmate of the House of Industry and, after considering the defendant's circumstances, which were fully explored, the magistrate made an order for 2*s* a week to be allowed the father by the defendant. Not only were parents expected to look after their children, but the roles were reversed in old age. (*Isle of Wight Observer*, August 4th 1855)

~ AUGUST 5TH ~

1836: During Sir Robert Peel's visit to the Island, the inhabitants took the opportunity to present him with an address that went as follows:

> With the sense we entertain of the imminency [*sic*] of the present crisis to all our great public interests and institutions, and of the wisdom, dignity, firmness, moderation, and patriotism by which your public conduct has been regulated, how is it possible for us not to gather around you with the attachment which it becomes the children of the common-wealth to rally around him who has earned himself the proud distinction of being hailed as PATER PATRIAE, the Father of his Country. We are sensible that our congratulations will be but a drop to swell the tide of feeling and reverence which our grateful country is pouring at your feet.

The address continued in much the same vein, ending with the claim that 'no one has ever arisen among us with talents and temper so well fitted to conduct us safely through the present crisis, in which we are as much in danger from rashness on the one hand as from timidity on the other'. The crisis in question was financial, rising from the rapid fall in the bank's reserves, the situation in Ireland and President Jackson's monetary policy in America. (*Chelmsford Chronicle*, August 5th 1836)

‒ August 6th ‒

1897: On this, the 'natal day' of Alfred Lord Tennyson, the wooden cross erected on the High Down at Freshwater was replaced with a cross of Cornish Granite reaching 37ft into the sky. The *Hampshire Advertiser* described how the poet's admirers gathered on 'the bold land … where the Laureate loved to roam'. Present were the Archbishop of Canterbury and Mrs Temple, the Dean of Westminster (Dr Bradley), the Bishop of Minnesota, Lord and Lady Tennyson, Deputy Governor Estcourt, and 'several representatives of the principal Island families'. Punctually, at 3 p.m., the ceremony commenced with the singing of 'Oh God, Our Help in Ages Past', accompanied by a band, after which the Dean unveiled the monument. It bears the inscription: 'In memory of Alfred Lord Tennyson, this cross is raised as a beacon to sailors by the people of Freshwater and other friends in England and America.' In their 'Literary Notes' of August 12th, the *Morning Post* felt bound to comment that they knew of no other place where so many 'obelisks and pillars and beacons of various styles and periods can be seen at one time'. With regard to the new memorial they pronounced it 'a fine work of art and the most admirable of all the Island landmarks'. (*Hampshire Advertiser*, August 6th 1897; *Morning Post*, August 12th 1897)

~ AUGUST 7TH ~

1879: An Egyptian sailor from Alexandria was today in court for a 'murderous assault' on a Maltese man, Ernest Earer. Both men were crew on the steam tug *Constantine*, bound for Smyrna. The weather being bad, the captain had docked at Cowes roads waiting for it to improve. On Thursday evening a quarrel broke out between the pair, and witnesses stated that Earer struck the prisoner, George Hasey, with a wellington boot. Hasey then rushed at him and inflicted three serious wounds to the head. Earer was a stranger to the crew, working his passage to Melbourne, and on being injured he asked the captain for a boat to take him ashore, but the captain refused so he jumped overboard, aiming for a shore-boat seen nearby. Having reached the shore, he was taken to the house of Dr Hoffmeister where he was in a 'dangerous condition'. The captain was refused permission to continue their voyage until the case had been investigated. (*Illustrated Police News*, August 16th 1879)

~ AUGUST 8TH ~

1805: Sir Richard Worsley, 7th Baronet Worsley of Appuldurcombe, today died at his St Lawrence cottage aged 54. His life was dogged by the aftermath of his very public separation from his wife, Dorothy Seymour, *née* Fleming. Following her affair with Maurice Bisset, owner of Knighton Gorges, Worsley sued him for adultery, expecting £20,000 in damages. To punish Seymour, he denied her a divorce. Because of his apparent collusion in the affair, Worsley instead received a settlement of 1*s* and was the laughing stock of the aristocracy. Unable to escape his humiliation, Worsley fled to the Continent, hoping to salvage his good name as a collector of antiquities. Many of his amassed treasures were lost at sea as he made his way back to England while the French Revolution was gaining momentum. Still the object of ridicule, Worsley hid away in Sea Cottage along the Undercliff with his 'housekeeper', Sarah Smith, which is where he died. He was buried in Godshill church, having arranged the erection of a huge, classical sarcophagus in his memory. The object only caused more ridicule, being dubbed 'Worsley's Bath'. His errant wife Seymour survived him, regaining her £70,000 dowry on his death and marrying her lover, the musician Johan Hummell. (Hallie Rubenhold, *Lady Worsley's Whim*, Vintage Books, 2009)

~ August 9th ~

1940: The *Isle of Wight County Press* today reported on the dwindling stocks of cigarettes, tobacco and matches in the shops. Desperate smokers, finding that their local store had sold out, refused to believe the tobacconist and in some cases the traders had shut shop rather than face the abuse. The *County Press* reported that the problem was not so much a shortage of tobacco as the loss of staff at the factories, employees having joined the armed services. The Minister of Supply advised smokers that they should try to make ten cigarettes last as long as they would normally smoke fifteen. Blame was heaped upon the selfish and unpatriotic people who had been shop crawling and hoarding cigarettes. They also blamed the soldiers who shopped in local stores rather than getting their supplies from the army canteen. (*Isle of Wight County Press*, August 9th 1940)

~ August 10th ~

1865: Poet and diarist William Allingham, a friend of the Tennysons, made the following entry in his diary on making a visit to Ryde:

Steamer to Ryde, Spithead, ships of war, Ryde pier, rich idlers, white shoes, yachts, boats. Steep streets, photographers, libraries, fruiterers, hotels. Old town, country road, man mowing barley. Sun Inn, old fashioned, cold meat and ale. Portrait of Ellen Terry on the wall; I say to the girl who waits, (the landlady's daughter) 'I know who that is.' Says she to me 'Yes, it's Mrs Watts – she's staying here,' which much surprised me. It seems she used to put up here in old times, when playing at the Ryde Theatre, and now, being married – and separated – she goes about by herself from place to place, and has come for a while to her friendly old quarters. She gave them this likeness on some former visit. I was in hope of seeing her fair face again but she was gone to Sandown for the day.

(*William Allingham's Diaries*, August 10th 1865)

— August 11th —

1868: On a visit to Farringford, the diarist William Allingham made the acquaintance of Captain Tristram Speedy. The captain had been instructed by Queen Victoria to take charge of Prince Alamayu, the 7-year-old son of the former Emperor of Abyssinnia. Alamayu's young life had been shattered when his father, defeated in battle, committed suicide and the child was handed over to the British. Captain Speedy showed him much tenderness but such was the trauma suffered by the boy that he could not sleep other than in the captain's arms. Allingham was amused to overhear Alamayu, along with his Abyssinian attendant, aping English conversations, saying: 'How you do?' and 'How you like this country?' The reply to each question being 'ver' mush'. Unhappily, and to the queen's chagrin, in 1871 Alamayu was handed over to the headmaster of Cheltenham College who pronounced that he had no academic future and enrolled him at Sandhurst, an act the queen considered totally inappropriate for the boy. In 1879, he caught a fever and died, and was buried at Windsor. Queen Victoria regretted that 'His was no happy life'. (*William Allingham's Diaries*, August 11th 1868)

~ AUGUST 12TH ~

1950: News of the outbreak of Infantile Paralysis (polio) on the Island was followed nationally by the press. On the 12th the *Hull Daily Mail* reported that Dr John Mills, infectious diseases expert, was at Fairlee Hospital assessing the situation. The confirmed number of cases was now twenty-nine and children's cinemas and Sunday schools were being closed. The medical authorities asked that swimming pools should also be closed. Over the coming week the number of cases rose to fifty-one and Dr Warren Brown, MOH for East Wight, confirmed that cleaning was being intensified and that food, milk, water and unwashed hands all spread the virus. Mr Butler, owner of the Beaconsfield Hotel and three cafes in Shanklin, stated that many Island hoteliers were in a 'disastrous position' and would not be able to pay their rent during the winter. The disease was not limited to the Isle of Wight and the first suspected cases appeared in June but the climax, when the Island was particularly affected, was in August.

In December 1950, a woman who had cancelled her holiday because of the outbreak, was ordered to pay £11 4s compensation to the hotelier. (*Hull Daily Mail*, August 12th 1950)

— AUGUST 13TH —

1934: On this day a fascist meeting was held in the western enclosure at Ryde. It had been advertised and Blackshirts had paraded around the town handing out literature, but did not arouse any great interest. At 8 o'clock about forty to fifty people sat outside the enclosure but of the hundreds of canvas chairs inside ready for use, only four were occupied, and three by reporters. After some delay about thirty of the chairs were occupied and Prof. W. Boyce, who wore a black shirt and trousers and a large leather belt, appeared on the platform and gave an address from the side of a table covered with the Union Jack. He said that his party had nothing in common with the old political parties and they were opposed to any movement which could not combine within itself the principles of patriotism and economic reform. They were sometimes accused of being a foreign movement but, although fascism did not take its origins in Britain, they were a nationalistic movement willing to adopt foreign ideals. It was true that they admired Hitler and Mussolini who had brought discipline to their own countries, but theirs was a British fascism and their efforts were concentrated on building a new and better country and reviving their imperial glories. (*Isle of Wight County Press*, August 18th 1934)

~ August 14th ~

1826: The *London Morning Post* today revealed that a duel had taken place the previous Thursday (August 12th) between Lord William Pitt Lennox and the Earl of Glengall, on the shore in front of Cowes Castle. The cause of the dispute was a rumour that Lord Lennox had been writing for a scurrilous London weekly paper called *The Age*. As the *Post* observed, its 'constant publication of tales of scandal and scurrility, is greatly annoying to the feelings of individuals and families in the higher classes of society'. The Earl of Glengall refused to confirm that Lennox was not a contributor to the magazine and Lord Lennox took this as a slur on his honour. Again the *Post* took up the story:

> William sent his friend to demand for him the usual satisfaction of a Gentleman. A meeting was immediately appointed, and an exchange of shots took place, without doing personal injury; the seconds then declared that enough had been done by both parties, and the principals left the ground without explanation, or having any direct communication with each other in the affair.

The event was caricatured by George Cruikshank in a cartoon entitled 'Cowes and Asses or pat on the Affair of Honour' and issued as a print by his brother Isaac Robert Cruikshank. The cartoon suggested that paper bullets had been used and the 'asses' in question were the duellists. (*London Morning Post*, August 14th 1826)

— August 15th —

1885: The first Ryde Royal Dog Show opened on Wednesday morning at the Esplanade Gardens at Ryde. It was scheduled to take place over two days under the patronage of the Prince of Wales under Kennel Club rules and forty-four classes were planned. The entry fees were to be modest and the prizes would range from £3 to 10s. There were 360 entries and the judging took place in a marquee measuring 300ft long. The dogs would be benched and fed by Spratt's Patent, the Ryde Gas Company provided the lighting and the show was disinfected by Jeyes Sanitary Compound Company, who presented a cup worth 5 guineas. A special year's subscription to the *Shooting Times* was presented to the winners of the class for pointers and retrievers. There was a special silver cup presented to the winner of the dachshund class and a series of classes for Isle of Wight residents only. The Prince of Wales's alsatian wolfhound Ciaus of Seale won two prizes. Such was the success of the show that it was planned to repeat the following year with 100 additional competitors. Entrants came from as far afield as Hampshire, London and Birmingham. (*Hampshire Advertiser*, August 15th 1885)

~ AUGUST 16TH ~

1720: Two days before his death on August 16th, William Cromwell of Horringford Farm made his will, leaving his property to his beloved wife Martha for her lifetime. William, a descendant of Oliver Cromwell, seems to have settled at Horringford a few years earlier and set about remodelling the seventeenth-century house to his satisfaction. A stone dated 1718, marks this new incarnation.

William was undoubtedly very comfortably off and apart from his property of Horringford Farm, he left a sum of £10,000 to relatives, the majority to James Crew of 'Smithbanks, Isle of Wight' and Crew's children, among whom William includes his nieces Hester Crew and Jane Bull. It would appear that James Crew was his brother-in-law as a marriage of James Crew at Newchurch is recorded for September 18th 1709. In contrast, William left a measly 20s to his brother-in-law William Blow of Widcome, plus one or two other beneficiaries. There is a Widcombe Manor near Bath, although allowing for the spelling of the time it might possibly refer to an Island location such as Whitcombe. A marriage between William Cromwell and Martha Cook of Brading in 1692 seems likely to refer to this William. William is buried in a redbrick tomb near to the porch at St George's Arreton. He was 53 years old. (Isle of Wight Public Record Office, August 16th 1720)

~ August 17th ~

1899: Today's *Morning Post* reported Queen Victoria's visit to Carisbrooke Castle to attend a fundraising evening for the benefit of the Newport parish church restoration fund. Thirty-five years earlier, on August 24th, Prince Albert had laid the foundation stone for the new St Thomas's church with the words: 'We place this stone in faith and hope and to the Glory of God through Jesus Christ our Lord.' The Bishop of Winchester consecrated the completed church on December 21st 1856. The clock installed in the tower was given by John Woodward of Rookley and the bells were recast by Francis Foster of Romsey and dated 1668. Ever mindful of safety, the fire engine was stored in the northern aisle of the church. As the *Morning Post* now explained:

> … although the edifice is comparatively new, it had gone to decay and become a menace to the public safety. On several occasions pinnacles and other portions of the building have fallen to the pavement when a strong wind has shot through the valley between the Downs on either side of the town, and the architects had reported that it was absolutely necessary that the dangerous portions of the structure should be removed, and the building reconstructed as far as those portions were concerned. The break up of the structure is attributed to the presence of Caen stone in certain parts, and it is alleged that this material is not fitted to resist the effect of sea salt in the air. The cost of the necessary alterations is estimated at £3,000, to which about £1,000 has been scribed or promised.

The tower has twelve bells and in AD 2000 the church underwent another major renovation and was recategorised as a minster. (*Morning Post*, August 17th 1899)

~ August 18th ~

1917: An Isle of Wight converted seaplane from the yard of J. Samuel White at Cowes today bombed and sank a German U-Boat in the English Channel, the event going down in history as the first direct hit of a submarine by an aircraft. J. Samuel White's yard already had a long history of boat building, starting at Cowes from 1802. By 1850 the firm had several yards on both banks of the Medina, employing 500 craftsmen building boats for the navy. The expansion into aircraft lasted from 1912–1916, concentrating on flying boats. Earlier attempts had ended in failure. A maiden flight of very short duration was witnessed at Cowes on May 13th 1913 during which *Seaplane 1*, piloted by Mr Howard Wright, reached an altitude 40' before the engine stalled and it plunged into the water. The pilot escaped with bruises and back injuries. The plane was towed back to White's yard where it was virtually rebuilt and the cause of the crash was kept secret, but on July 10th *Seaplane 2* set off on its maiden flight. Howard Wright watched from the shore as another pilot named F.P. Raynham was at the controls. Failing to gain much height, the wing hit the water and the plane turned on its side. Mr Raynham jumped free and once again the damaged vehicle was hauled back to the yard. The company's long marine-building history came to an end when they ceased trading in 1981. (David Williams, *Wings over the Island, the Aviation Heritage of the Isle of Wight*, Isle of Wight; Coach House Publications, 1999)

~ AUGUST 19TH ~

1819: The *Cheltenham Chronicle* today reported that 'The Isle of Wight is in a complete bustle at the present moment, by the presence of the Prince Regent whose rendezvous is appointed in the Channel. The inhabitants are elated with joy at the event, no Monarch having ever been upon the Island since the imprisonment of the unfortunate King Charles at Carisbrooke Castle.' The Prince Regent visited the Island on several occasions, having developed a passion for sailing. He sometimes stayed with his friend John Nash at East Cowes Castle and when he succeeded to the throne in 1820, his room at the castle became known as the King's Room. The castle was demolished in 1960.

The *Chronicle* is misinformed in that after the departure of King Charles I, his son Charles II made at least two visits to the Island and stayed with his friend Sir Robert Holmes at what is now the George Hotel at Yarmouth. (*Cheltenham Chronicle*, August 19th 1819)

~ August 20th ~

1890: The Annual Freshwater and Yarmouth Horticultural Society held their event as usual in the grounds of Farringford today. There were numerous classes divided into sections, the first being for professional gardeners who worked within the grounds of the big houses. In each case, the prizewinner was identified both by his own name and that of his employer, some kudos going to the person who paid his wages. The section for amateurs attracted local men who grew fruit and vegetables in their gardens. As ever, there were certain competitors who regularly swept the board. The young exhibitors in the section for children inevitably bore the same surnames as those adult enthusiasts in the amateur section – keen fathers instilling their youngsters with their expertise. Perhaps the most curious class was the special section for 'Window Boxes for Soldiers at the Western Forts'. The winners turned out to be 1st Captain Coomber, 2nd Corporal Miller, 3rd the Royal Artillery Band-room, all serving at Golden Hill Fort. One wonders whether there were entries from the other local forts and how their fellow soldiers viewed their flower-growing compatriots. (*Freshwater Parish Magazine*, September 1890)

~ August 21st ~

1860: The *Isle of Wight Observer* was pleased to announce that Mr Rarey, the famed horse tamer, would be appearing at Ventnor on August 21st as part of his Island tour. Travelling with Messrs Howes and Cushing's circus and employed at huge expense, he would give a series of lectures in the afternoons and evenings in addition to the circus performances. Such was his reputation that he had appeared before all the crowned heads and courts of Europe and his system of horse training had met with the approval of the nobility, the clergy, the gentry, the newspaper press and the general public.

Whilst at the Alhambra Palace in London, Rarey had procured and tamed many vicious and unmanageable horses including the notorious stallion Idle Boy. Coming from York, the horse was so savage that no one dared approach him and he was kept in a box lined with iron because wood could not survive his vicious kicks. The horse had been led into the arena muzzled, kicking and biting furiously. In less than half an hour Rarey had entirely subdued him and led him around the arena with a straw. Desiring to face the most severe of tests, Rarey asked any gentlemen in the neighbourhood who had ugly and dangerous horses to bring them to the circus for him to operate on. (*Isle of Wight Observer*, August 18th 1860)

~ August 22nd ~

1873: In a letter signed Vectis, an Island resident wrote to the *Isle of Wight Observer* expressing his thoughts on the implementation of the new Licensing Act and how the magistrates in the adjoining boroughs of Ryde and Newport might respond. The problem arose because, while the two boroughs recognised 'closing time' as 11 p.m., in the rest of the Island the time was midnight. The result was an unseemly rush at 11 p.m. from one place to the other.

Mr 'Vectis' feared that the magistrates were 'leading Liberal artisans, creatures of the Gladstone government' and that 'there is a numerical section of Liberals, comprised of Permissivites and Puritans who sympathise with them in the movement to restrict the individual freedom of the many with the view to restraining the vicious to some trifling extent'. He believed that the Liberals in both boroughs were holding a rod over the magistrates who felt compelled to administer the new act with severity. Happily however, the county magistrates were not constrained by the same political ties and could therefore deal with each case on its merits. 'Some outcry has been raised by the Puritans that, in the interest of morality, the county inns ought to close at the same time as the borough inns and they point to some trouble that has been experienced by the county police on the borders of the early closing boroughs ... The county police have had to deal with some disorder at inns near Coppins Bridge and at Oakfield adjacent to Ryde consequent on guests at the borough inns turning out at 11 o'clock and passing over the boundary line to finish up.' This, concludes 'Vectis', is reflected in the increased number of convictions for drunkenness in the county and the corresponding decrease in numbers in the boroughs of Ryde and Newport. (*Isle of Wight Observer*, August 22nd 1873)

~ August 23rd ~

1870: Today a public meeting took place at Ryde Town Hall where a painting of the ironclad ship *Monarch* was presented to the people of the town. The picture showed the *Monarch* leaving Spithead for America, carrying the body of the philanthropist George Peabody. Vivian Webber, a member of the Royal Yacht Squadron, had commissioned the work from local artist Mr A. Fowles and it was the second work of art that he had presented to the town. In a speech Webber expressed his admiration for the skills of Fowles who had succeeded in capturing the solemnity of the occasion, with flags at half mast, and showing Portsmouth, Haslar Hospital and Southsea Castle in the distance. On the other side, Osborne House and 'the Garden Isle' completed the view. Mr Webber also praised the craft of frame maker Mr Joyce of Ryde, saying that the frame was a work of art in itself. He expressed comfort in the fact that the *Monarch*, a ship of war, was on a peaceful mission and that George Peabody himself had dedicated his life to peace and helping people. The mayor replied that he hoped the town would value this second gift and assured Webber that it would be taken great care of and held in high esteem for all time to come.

Unfortunately, it seems that both paintings were later destroyed in a fire at Ryde Town Hall. (*Hampshire Telegraph*, August 27th 1870)

— August 24th —

1872: 'The members and officers of the First Battalion of the Isle of Wight Volunteers today go under canvas in the beautiful park of Appuldurcombe as they are determined not to be deprived of their autumn exercise of out door service' today's *Hampshire Telegraph* reported. 'About £200 has been required to defray the expense of this encampment, and in answer to an appeal made by Quartermaster D. Garnett of Ryde, the gentry have responded nobly, nearly the whole of that sum having already been subscribed. Appuldurcombe will be the great centre of attraction this week, for irrespective of this unusual event, the whole neighbourhood is full of charming scenery. The Isle of Wight Railway Company too, are offering easy facilities for the public to attend to witness the manoeuvres of our gallant defenders and we expect a large company of visitors.' (*Hampshire Telegraph*, August 24th 1872)

~ August 25th ~

1867: On this day, Michael Faraday died at his home in London. Faraday had important connections with the Island and during his life he had made numerous visits. It was partly thanks to him that the problems arising from the recently installed lamp at St Catherine's Lighthouse were resolved. Until 1841 the lighthouse had been beset by difficulties, firstly being too high so that the light was obscured by fog then, when the height was reduced, the sediment from the lamp oil coated the glass reducing its visibility. Following his visit, Faraday worked on a siphon lamp that resolved the problem.

In 1824, he visited the Island enjoying what appeared to be a family holiday, but during that time he compiled a document 'Geological Notes on the Isle of Wight'. His reputation as a chemist was increasing and he was much in demand. This work, however, was later overtaken by his experiments with electricity.

In 1834, he was again planning to visit Ryde, although he did not expect to stay for longer than a week, and took regular winter breaks, sometimes to Brighton and to the Island, throughout his life. In 1854, he was again staying on the Island. At this time he had been suffering from depression while his wife Sarah, although nine years his junior, suffered increasingly with difficulty in walking and deafness. When he died, among his effects was a scrapbook containing a print of Niton church. (Michael Faraday, 'Geological Notes on the Isle of Wight')

⸺ August 26th ⸺

1852: Keeping the troops entertained at Parkhurst proved something of a challenge but the Parkhurst Barracks Amateur Theatre rose to the occasion by performing a dramatic romance entitled *The Castle Spectre* followed by a popular farce *P.S. Come to Dinner*. The reporter of the *Isle of Wight Observer* rather tantalisingly records that 'From some slight misunderstanding, the entertainment did not pass off quite so well as is usual.' There was, however, a second performance the following evening (27th) 'it being the custom to perform each play three times as this allowed all the soldiers in the garrison the opportunity of witnessing it, there not being sufficient room to admit more than a third at a time'. The paper was also pleased to report that 'since the commencement of this amusement in the garrison, less drunkenness and crime of every sort has been committed than is usually the case'. Meanwhile, the band of the 88th Regiment was out and about entertaining the public although their first performance, attended by a very numerous and fashionable company, had only time to enjoy the first March 'Prince Albert' and part of the Overture 'Horia du Namur' before the heavens opened. They would return to Carisbrooke Castle the following Saturday to complete the programme. (*Isle of Wight Observer*, August 28th 1852)

⚊ August 27th ⚊

1842: Today's *Hampshire Telegraph* announced:

> We are happy to state that one hundred shares are now taken in the
> new Cemetery for the Isle of Wight (to be open to all for interment),
> and that at the meeting of shareholders on Wednesday evening,
> it was moved and carried unanimously, that the chairman do write
> immediately to Mr Thomas Cooke and Mr J Cooke, to say the
> shareholders had decided that they would purchase the land offered
> them by those gentlemen. A public meeting of the shareholders and
> others favourable to the Cemetery will shortly be called, when a
> statement of the constitution of the company, a table of fees, prices
> for vaults, brick graves &c, will be submitted for their approval. There
> is every prospect of its being cordially and extensively supported; and
> the entrances will be made, walks laid out and the land prepared for
> the purpose of interment.

There had long been a lack of burial places, many churchyards
being full. In the same paper in October a letter complained
that at the funeral of the infant son of John Weeks of Barton
Villa near Newport, the grieving father walked 4 miles to find
that the vicar was not there. He and his wife had gone for a walk
and the mourners waited for more than 2 hours for his return.
On another occasion, the corpse had to be left in the church
overnight. New public cemeteries at Fairlee and Mountjoy
opened in 1858. (*Hampshire Telegraph*, August 27th 1842)

— AUGUST 28TH —

1861: For three years, Alfred de Vidil, a graduate from Cambridge, had been held as a lunatic on the Isle of Wight allegedly unable to take care of himself. At a trial at the Old Bailey, however, a family relative gave evidence that although he was peculiar in demeanour, he was perfectly sane and capable of looking after himself. In court today was Alfred's father, the Baron de Vidil accused of attempted murder. On June 28th, Alfred and his father had gone riding near Twickenham and at some point during the ride Alfred was badly injured about the head, having received a blow both to the side and the front. A witness who had been out walking came upon the baron and on being approached the baron leapt a fence and ran away. Two riderless horses were found shortly afterwards and Alfred arrived feeling very unwell, his face covered in blood. When questioned he said that he had fallen off and had hit his head on a wall but this did not explain the two separate injuries. A motive arose because the baron was heir to his son's considerable fortune left by his mother and the circumstances of the 'accident' gave rise to suspicion that Vidil had attacked his son with intent to murder. Although called upon to give evidence, Alfred refused to do so for which he was sentenced to one month in prison for contempt of court. Having heard the evidence, the jury found his father guilty of unlawfully wounding and he was sentenced to twelve months' imprisonment with hard labour. (*North London News*, August 31st 1861)

— AUGUST 29TH —

1894: Labourers and bricklayers employed in building the new asylum at Whitecroft went on strike yesterday, the bricklayers demanding 8*d* per hour wages and the labourers 5*d*. This was virtually a penny increase all round. The contractors, Messrs Garlick and Norton said they had already done all that they could in paying the skilled men 7*d* and 4¼*d* which was higher than any other wage in the Island before. The workmen refused to back down and having been paid off, marched to Newport with their tools shouldered, whistling and singing en route. This was a double blow to the contractors, the County Council Committee having already complained at the slow progress of the work.

In Newport the strikers were joined by about a dozen bricklayers working on the new barracks at Parkhurst who had a similar complaint. The Whitecroft men had been expecting a larger turnout but it emerged that at the last minute, the labouring workforce of nearly fifty had had second thoughts. The strike lasted for two days after which the men returned to work without their demands being met. The asylum opened in 1896 and closed in 1992. (*Portsmouth Evening News*, August 29th 1894)

~ AUGUST 30TH ~

1835: On this day, Ann Longden aged 32, a single woman with five children, died at Ryde and was buried at St Edmunds' church at Wootton. Her unmarried status belied her true situation for Ann was the beloved partner of MP Benjamin Leigh Smith, a wealthy social reformer. Benjamin's father, also a strong believer in social reform, was nevertheless anxious to secure his children's financial future and had successfully arranged two marriages for his daughters into the Bonham Carter and Nightingale families. Benjamin had other ideas and on meeting Ann Longden, working as a milliner's apprentice, he fell in love. The difference in their social status meant nothing to him but he refused to marry on principal, as both Ann and her belongings would then become his property. The couple visited America and by the time they returned they had five children and were generally accepted as man and wife. The only person to utterly shun them was Benjamin's cousin, Florence Nightingale.

When Ann fell sick, Benjamin employed nurses to help with the children and took her to Hastings to benefit from the sea air. When that failed he sent her to his relatives the Smiths at Ryde where she sadly died. Her epitaph states 'Ann, the wife of Benjamin Smith'. Among their five children, their son Ben became an Arctic explorer and their daughter Barbara Boudichon a renowned painter. A friend of John Stuart Mill and George Eliot, having been refused entry into university Barbara was a founder member of Girton College Cambridge. When Benjamin died, he was buried at St Edmund's in Wooton with Ann. (*Oxford Dictionary of National Biography*)

~ August 31st ~

1939: On this day, the Admiralty issued orders that the ferries running excursions from Southsea to Sandown, Shanklin and Ventnor were to cease operations. Four days later, war was declared against Germany. There were ten ferries belonging to Southern Railway that ran scheduled services to the Island and some excursions further afield. With the outbreak of war, the services were cut to a minimum as the steamers were called into action for war work. The *Sandown*, the *Ryde* and the *Southsea* were requisitioned and converted to minesweepers and in 1940 the plight of the British Expeditionary Force stranded on the beaches at Dunkirk saw every available ship made ready for action. The Southern Railway vessel *Whippingham*, along with the *Portsdown* and the two car-ferries *Wootton* and *Fishbourne* all answered the call. The *Whippingham* and *Portsdown* alone rescued more than 4,000 troops. In the meantime, access to and from the Island was strictly limited and the three oldest paddle steamers *Shanklin*, *Merstone* and *Portsdown* maintained the service from Portsmouth to Ryde. Only the *Portsdown* was lost, sinking as she made a night-time crossing near Sandbank Fort following an explosion on board in which many of the crew and the passengers perished. (From history.inportsmouth.co.uk, Cynthia Sherwood)

~ September 1st ~

1898: Today's *Isle of Wight County Press* reported that Silvester Lee, a Gypsy of Brading, was charged with doing wilful damage to a hedge belonging to John Henry Brown of New Farm, Brading. Farmer Brown had noticed that a lot of hazel and withy had been cut from it and reported this to PC Bungay. In evidence a quantity of sticks, peeled and cut of equal lengths were produced. They were intended for making clothes pegs and the prosecutor identified them as his property. He estimated the damage done to be about 5s. On asking the defendant where he had got them he had replied, 'I bought it off Mr Webb, wood dealer'. This was found to be untrue and PC Bungay showed that the stumps taken from the plaintiff's hedge corresponded exactly. Lee did not appear and, there being eight previous convictions against him, he was fined 10s, damages of 5s and costs 11s, in default, fourteen days' hard labour.

On October 8th this same year Lee again appeared, with Francis Hughes, summoned for obstructing the footway at Bear Lane Niton. At the hearing, PC Holding for the prosecution stated that the Gypsies had two carts drawn up right across the footway and declined to move until the following morning. Hughes stated that they had camped for the past thirty years to which the chairman replied, 'Then you have broken the law for the last thirty years.' Hughes was fined 5s with 4s cost. Silvester, who had been sleeping in his tent, was fined 2s 6d with 4s costs. Sylvester was a regular attendee at the petty sessions, his death was reported in the *County Press* (September 11th 1926) and he was estimated to be about 90 years old. He was the brother of Sussex Gypsy Lily Lee and lived in a shack in Woodvale Copse. As he got ill he was helped by local people, moving into a cottage at Cross St Cowes, but he found it difficult to live inside. (*Isle of Wight County Press*, September 1st 1898)

— SEPTEMBER 2ND —

1854: A meeting of the Philosophical and Scientific Society took place at the Bugle Inn in Newport, where a paper was read by Mr George Hillier on the recent excavations on the tumuli on 'Buccombe [*sic*] Down'. A large number of members and friends attended and the talk contained a clear and concise account of this mode of cremation. The talk included an account of the contents of the tumuli, some of which the speaker exhibited. There had been fourteen or fifteen sites in total, all of which showed some sign of cremation. In the first was found a skeleton, less the head, a fibula of rare character, the metal top of the sheath of a dagger, a horse's tooth between the legs and portions of a buckle near the pelvis. In the second a skeleton, as in the former case without a head, and some broken pottery, in the third an urn, buried in brick earth and flints containing bones, in the fourth evidence of cremation with a coin and iron dagger. In the fifth, a cyst was composed of five stones but no remains, with a heap of sand brought most probably from Shide for making urns. The sixth and seventh contained an urn of a different shape, the eighth contained pottery and bones while the ninth contained a large urn unfortunately broken. The race settled here at this time were Anglo-Saxons and a more detailed account of these finds would be given at a later occasion. (*Isle of Wight Observer*, September 3rd 1854)

~ September 3rd ~

1926: Today's *Nottingham Evening Post* reported that St Helens village, nationally feted as a paradise, was about to see a new housing development proposed by the urban council. Eighteen cottages were planned at a cost of £10,000, to be let for between 8*s* 2*d* and 8*s* 6*d* to working class people only. Earlier in the year a correspondent calling himself Claude reported that the St Helens police station had been closed as being redundant as 'a policeman from Seaview always cycles over once a day purely as a matter of form. Nothing is ever stolen in St Helens; people do not trouble to lock their doors; and mothers leave their purses wide open in baby's lap while they go into a shop to order goods.'

He concluded that while it must be gratifying to live in such a law-abiding community, it must have its disadvantages too: 'I mean to say, the strain of living up to such a standard as that must be very great. Imagine the agony of mind which a native of St Helens would suffer should he be fined by a Magistrate's Court for having a smoky chimney or for riding a bicycle on a footpath! … He would feel that nothing he could do would ever wipe out the stain; he would be a pariah and an outcast to the end of his days!' Claude therefore concluded that he preferred to stay where the standard of conduct was not so painfully high. (*Nottingham Evening Post*, July 18th and September 3rd 1926)

— September 4th —

1893: Cecil Hambrough, son and heir of Major Dudley Hambrough of Steephill Castle and an heir to the Hambrough banking business, was on holiday in Scotland when, taking an early morning walk across the Ardlamont estate, he was fatally wounded by a gunshot. Victim of a tragic accident, Cecil's body was accompanied to the island by his sorrowing tutor Alfred Monson and interred at St Catherine's, Ventnor. At the time of his death, Cecil was a week short of his twenty-first birthday, when he would have come into his inheritance. A few weeks later it emerged that a week prior to Cecil's death, Monson had taken out a life insurance on his pupil and in the event of his demise the sum of £20,000 would be paid to Monson's wife. Suspicions now aroused, it was ordered to disinter Cecil and today his grieving father stood at the graveside while the body was exhumed. On examination it was revealed that the shot had been fired from Monson's gun and that the perpetrator had been standing at least 9ft away from Cecil, so it could not have been an accident. Monson went on trial on December 2nd in Edinburgh and evidence showed that in spite of his lavish lifestyle he was heavily in debt. Only days before the accident, Cecil had nearly drowned when a boat they had shared on a lake capsized. Cecil could not swim but kept himself afloat by clinging to a rock. In spite of some damning evidence, Monson received the uniquely Scottish verdict of Not Proven. The story was widely covered nationally over a period of weeks. (*Isle of Wight Observer*, December 30th 1893)

— September 5th —

1855: Today's *Isle of Wight Observer* reported on a celebration held at the home of Dr Leeson, Pulpit Rock, Bonchurch, which was followed by a parade, to mark the fall of Sebastopol and the anniversary of the Battle of the Alma. The *Observer* recorded that: 'On entering the grounds through Ethelwolf's garden (so called from a cave being situated in them in which some coins of Ethelwolf were found) one stopped to admire the view. Gaily dressed people paraded, including the children of the National School. It was difficult to dissuade them from ripping apart a bear made of straw with a turkey on its back representing the "great northern Despot".' The only disappointment was that the band arrived late, but the flag staff was "dressed" with the standard of the Allies, under which was placed the Russian ensign inverted. There followed a procession along the cliffs of men with burning tar barrels on their heads. A royal salute was followed by the firing of rockets, shells and fixed pieces. The bonfire of tar barrels and furze on the Down was burning from Tuesday until Thursday, the day on which the report was written. (*Isle of Wight Observer*, September 5th 1855)

— September 6th —

1882: Wednesday the 6th and Thursday 7th September 1882 saw the first Isle of Wight Agricultural show, held in the fields leading to Carisbrooke Castle. The event received a boost when Queen Victoria herself entered livestock in five of the classes and the organisers promptly added the word 'Royal' to their event. Admission to the show was not cheap, costing half a crown per day while afternoons cost 1s and after 5 p.m. just 6d. Entrance fees amounted to £70 14s 6d.

There were plenty of classes to choose from; horses, cattle, sheep, pigs, poultry, pigeons and rabbits all attracted a lot of interest while exhibitions of skill by farriers and plough teams added to the fun. The judges may have faced some difficulty in judging those classes where the queen had entries and in the event they seem to have made their decision according to merit. In the class for a mare with foal at side, Her Majesty's 'Smart' was 'commended'. For cows in milk, the queen entered Gypsy aged 8, and Rose aged 7; Rose came second. In the class for heifers under 3 years, the queen's unnamed entry aged 18 months was also 'commended' while perhaps fortuitously, Her Majesty was the only entrant in a class for ten chid lambs, therefore coming first. The Society did well from advertisements in their catalogue and received generous donations, so that at the end of the show they had a profit of £249 13s. (Entry books, Isle of Wight Public Record Office)

⸺ SEPTEMBER 7TH ⸺

1807: Henry Sewell, New Zealand's first prime minister was this day born at Newport. Qualifying as a solicitor, he joined the family firm and married Lucinda Needham, daughter of a general. They had six children before Lucinda died aged 31 in 1844 and was buried at Carisbrooke. The family was faced with crippling debt when Henry's father died and rather than face bankruptcy, the children agreed to pay off the liability. While Henry shouldered some of that responsibility, a greater part fell on the shoulders of his sister Elizabeth, who also took Henry's motherless children and supported them all by writing moralistic stories for young ladies. Henry moved to London representing the interests of the Canterbury Association, intent on the colonisation of New Zealand. This brought him to the country where he served in various roles until in May of 1856 he was appointed the first premier. His administration was, however short-lived. Described as too reserved and elitist for the cut and thrust of colonial politics, he was distressed when the Land Confiscation Policy introduced a bill to claim Maori lands. He resigned in protest from the government and returned to England in 1873. Henry remarried and settled in Cambridge and it was there that he died on May 14th 1879. (*Oxford Dictionary of National Biography*)

— September 8th —

1770: The *Kentish Gazette* was not averse to a bit of scandal and today gleefully recounted the following incident on the Island:

> A great personage whose amour with a particular Lady has for long (indeed too long) been the subject of public conversation, went lately with a party of ladies (Mrs B, Miss S and two others), from Southampton to the Isle of Wight. The inn they put up at was the sign of the Sun; but it not being able to furnish lodging for the whole party, and there being no other public house that could, one of the great Person's train waited on a gentleman of fortune who has a seat there, to beg that he would accommodate for a single night, H.R.H and his suite – 'Sir (said the gentleman) if there is not room for you all at the Sun; pray go and find a lodging at the Moon; for the reputation of my wife and daughter is too dear to me to admit of my having the honour of entertaining the great Person in my house when they are in it.'

(*Kentish Gazette*, September 8th 1770)

– September 9th –

1830: A rare feeling of Anglo-French accord was celebrated at a dinner at Brading today. The *Hampshire Chronicle* reported how the inhabitants of Brading, supported by a number of respectable friends from other parts of the Island, celebrated the momentous achievement in France by a public dinner with Henry Day Esq. in the chair. The health of William IV was first proposed, followed by that of Queen Adelaide, both preceded by ardent and sincere expressions, and received by every demonstration and attachment. Philip I, King of the French, was next toasted, 'The chairman, after adverting to, and plainly pointing the general object of the meeting, dilated with emphatic force and eloquence upon the unparalleled triumph of personal patriotism, private valour, and public virtue, which the heroic population of Paris had recently displayed, in subduing the machinations and violence of bigotry and unrelenting despotism.' The toast was received with cheers and acclamations, which lasted for several minutes. Silence having been obtained, appropriate sentiments were opportunely offered by Messrs Wilkins, Sandys, Reddick, Thomas Harvey, and many other gentlemen. Many excellent songs were interspersed, and one in particular, having been composed expressly for the occasion, was rapturously encored. The dinner, wines and dessert did infinite credit to the liberality and taste of the worthy landlord of the Wheat Sheaf Hotel. The meeting separated about midnight, in perfect harmony and peace. Tri-coloured flags waved from the windows of the tavern, and everyone present ornamented himself with a cockade. (*Hampshire Chronicle*, September 9th 1830)

― September 10th ―

1881: On this day the first shareholders' meeting of the Newtown and Beaulieu Oyster Fishery Company took place at Busigny House in Cowes. The main players were two significant landowners: Sir John, Barrington Simeon of Swainston Manor who owned much of Newtown Creek; and Lord Henry, John Douglas Scott of Beaulieu who owned the land along the Beaulieu River. Oysters, once the food of the poor and wretched, had been decimated by disease, turning them into a rich man's delicacy. The pair then saw a chance to launch a profitable venture and 540 shares valued at £10 each were offered to the public. At the inaugural meeting those present were encouraged to persuade their friends to invest in 'an undertaking which has begun with so fair a promise of success'. Unhappily for the shareholders, that promise failed to materialise. In spite of various optimistic forecasts, at the fifth meeting the shareholders were advised that 'it was expedient that the company should be wound up in August next and … the necessary meetings for that purpose should be called.' Thus ended another good idea. (Simeon Papers, Isle of Wight Public Record Office)

~ September 11th ~

1866: Yesterday's opening of the Ryde to Ventnor railway line was 'under very favourable auspices' at a cost of upwards of £300,000. This was achieved by the completion of Ventnor Railway Tunnel, 1,312 yards long. The previous October a correspondent for the *Isle of Wight Observer* visited the site and recorded his impressions. He found 'a number of men engaged in blowing and cutting away the rock on the side of the hill where the station is intended to be … We were struck with the dangerous nature of the work, the men being on the side of the cutting which is nearly perpendicular and 60 to 70 feet deep, drilling holes for blasts of gunpowder.' A little further on, having narrowly missed being blasted by debris from an explosion into the chalk, he described the tunnel in progress. An employee being 'civil enough to hand us a tin with some candle we entered the tunnel but it was some time before we could distinguish any object. The first thing was a number of candles appearing like stars on a dark night, and on coming closer we could observe the tunnel for some length bricked to full size, and at the end of the brickwork was a lot of bricklayers … working in a style never before witnessed – all as busy as bees.' It took two years to complete the tunnel and at the halfway point, the navvies broke through and celebrated with a fight. Having been in operation for nearly 100 years, the line closed on 17th April 1966. (*Morning Post*, September 11th 1866)

─ SEPTEMBER 12TH ─

1874: Today's *Sheffield Independent* reported:

> … there is movement on foot among the sporting gentlemen of the
> Isle of Wight to get up some special steeplechases for the Empress
> of Austria, who is staying at Steephill Castle, Ventnor. Her Majesty
> has promised to give a cup to be run for. Her Majesty is in the habit
> of taking daily exercise on horseback, and this week has followed
> the Isle of Wight Hounds, almost invariably leading the whole field
> and clearing the hedges and ditches in a thoroughly equestrian style.
> Judging from her frequent remarks to those near here, her Majesty
> admires the beauty of the scenery through which she has ridden in the
> Island and enjoys the sport of the district.

The empress, along with her daughter and a large entourage, had
arrived on September 1st and amongst her engagements was her
presence at the Grand Fancy Bazaar and Promenade Concert
at the Royal National Hospital for Consumption to raise funds
for a new meeting room at the hospital. While there, the empress
planted a tree. On her departure from the Island, Steephill Castle
welcomed the Empress of Russia. (*Sheffield Independent*, September
12th 1874)

⁓ September 13th ⁓

1899: Under the heading 'Slice of the Isle of Wight Wanted' the *Hampshire Advertiser* today reported the following news:

> A telegram from Washington says that a Baltimore family of the name of Clavell will lay a claim to 8,000,000 dollars worth of property in the Isle of Wight. This great slice of Island real estate, Mrs Caroline Clavell of Baltimore, believes, belongs rightly to her children. Lawyers, after a careful examination of the papers, think she has a right to the property, a portion of which comprises a large section of Cowes.

The Clavells had indeed been resident in the Cowes area and as early as 1841, John Clavell of East Cowes had made an unsuccessful claim to an area of land called the Ropewalk adjoining the sea. In the 1850s, Clavells were landlords of both the White Hart and Bell Inn and on February 8th 1851, John Clavell was appointed Harbour Master at East Cowes. What became of their claim is unclear. (*Hampshire Advertiser*, September 13th 1899)

~ September 14th ~

1866: Mr Hudson of Ventnor was so moved by the local discovery of a message in a bottle that he passed on the news to the *Louth and North Lincoln Advertiser*. The letter was picked up on September 14th by William H. Whitewood, a lad living in Ventnor, who discovered a bottle floating in the sea and waded in to retrieve it. The cap and neck were thick with grease and inside was the following message:

> Her First Voyage to England. June 17 1866. The Spanish Queen bound for Bristol with timber from Quebec, having left on 5th March and owing to the rough weather lasting nine days, the old ship leaks like a sive [*sic*] and we are settling down fast. All hands are worn out at the pump. The captain is ill upon deck but is writing a note to put it in a flask. It is my last wish, if this bottle is picked up, that it may be published in some papers, as I have a Dear mother and father and I should like them to know I died happy. There is no hope for us. I shall not throw this over till the last. I remain yours, George J. Mills.

(*Louth and North Lincoln Advertiser*, September 22nd 1866)

— September 15th —

1923: Today's *County Press* reported that a body had been found at Amos Hill in Totland. It was thought it might be that of a woman camp follower who had been in the area when the Black Brunswicker soldiers were camped in fields around Windmill Farm at the time of the Napoleonic Wars. Back then a murder was said to have been committed but no body had been found. The Brunswickers, named for their black uniforms and sporting a death's head and crossed bones on their hats, had been fighting with Austria against the French before they were forced to the coast where they were evacuated to England, arriving in August 1809. After some months they were reformed and sent to serve with Britain troops in the Peninsular Wars, but not before creating mayhem on the Island. (*County Press*, September 15th 1923)

— SEPTEMBER 16TH —

1845: The resignation of the Governor of the Poor House resulted today in a heated debate at the meeting of the Guardians of the Poor at Newport's Guildhall. The disagreement was over what to pay the next appointee. The previous salary had risen from £60 to £75 and the sum of £100 was mooted for the next governor. A debate immediately followed about the provision or not, of perquisites – the 'perks' that went with the job. The chairman said the governor, like his predecessor, had been allowed to keep poultry and a dog and it was assumed that they both were supplied with barley and meat from the poorhouse. One member moved that the new salary should be set at £60 with the produce from the garden known as the Governor's Garden, plus board and lodging for himself, his wife and one child. An earlier document was produced stating that no perquisites were allowed but that £10 a year was paid in its place. Further dissent followed over the character of the governor. While the majority wished it to be on record that he was 'good', one guardian replied that he could not consent to this statement. Various combinations of pay and conditions were put forward without agreement. The Revd White felt that the salary should not be less than that previously paid and pointed out that until the last governor had been appointed there had been a series of unfortunate incidents. 'The first was guilty of peculation, the next robbed his neighbour's till and the next, who was a cheap one, was also removed for peculation.' It was then proposed that the salary should be £85 a year with board for his wife and he be allowed to have his children in the house on his paying a certain sum, say £8 each above 2 years old and £10 a year after 12 years old plus washing and instruction in the house school. The motion was carried. (*Hampshire Telegraph*, September 20th 1845)

~ September 17th ~

1879: The *Isle of Wight Observer* today reported the arrival of a messenger on horseback at Newport police station to report that a large wheat rick had been set on fire at Gatcombe. The *Observer* described how 'the fire bell was immediately rung and the fire brigade, under Mr Reynolds was instantly assembled. Messrs Urry, the occupiers of Hill and Newbarn farms, and the owners of the rick, immediately sent in two powerful horses for the fire engine which was soon on its way. Hundreds of persons flocked to the spot from Newport. On the firemen reaching the scene of the fire they found the large rick ignited in every part and although there was an abundant supply of water and every possible exertion was made to save the rick, it was by half past six completely destroyed. The rick was the produce of a large field in which it was erected. The rick belonged to Newbarn Farm, just to the north of the village of Gatcombe Mr Seeley MP being the proprietor of the farm.' (*Isle of Wight Observer*, September 17th 1879)

— September 18th —

1743: A letter from Portsmouth bearing today's date brought the following worrying news to the Island:

> Notwithstanding all the Precautions we have taken here, on Friday last the Dutch Ship *De Resolute* supposed to have the Plague on board, came to the Back of the Isle of Wight; and two Men, who were catching Crabs, one of them Brother to Boyce the famous Smuggler (now in the Fleet Prison) were so indiscrete as to go along Side of her. They told them they were homeward bound Indiamen, and wanted Provisions; on which the two Men came on Shore, and carried off a fat Sheep and some Butter, and then returned to their Houses. By this time the Country was alarmed, and arming themselves went directly to kill them, or at least make them return to their Boat; they surrendered immediately, and went where they were ordered, the Guard following at a distance. They are now at the Mother-Bank, where they are to perform Quarantine in their small open Boat. They said they saw but 8 on Deck, all seemed well in Health. The folly of these Fellows has put us all in the utmost Consternation and the chief Talk is cutting off Communication with the Island; if so, we are in a fine Condition, for Provisions will be excessive dear. God preserve us from Danger.

(*The Caledonian Mercury*, September 26th 1743)

— September 19th —

1619: On this day died one of the most flamboyant characters to live on the Island. William Keeling, a sea captain commanded an expedition to the Orient in search of spices. On April 1st 1607 he set sail aboard the *Hector* with two other ships, *Dragon* and *Consent*. Disobeying company rules, Keeling smuggled his wife aboard but she was put ashore again. Keeling was in no hurry and the other ships went ahead. By the time he arrived at the Spice Islands, the *Consent* was already back in England. His voyage was beset by 'gusts, calms, rain, sickness and other marine inconveniences' but this did not prevent him from stopping off to perform Shakespearean plays; his crew were kept busy learning their lines and making costumes. On one occasion, a crewmember had his leg bitten off by a crocodile as they washed their clothes. Keeling's presence was not welcome by the Dutch in the East Indies, especially as he negotiated for spices and nutmegs under their noses, but the local people, incensed by Dutch behaviour, came to their rescue and they returned to England with a full hold. Back in England he served as captain of Cowes Castle and Groom of the Bedchamber to James I. On his demise, his wife Anne erected a plaque at St Mary's Carisbrooke where he is buried. (*Oxford Dictionary of National Biography*)

September 20th

1911: The *Aberdeen Journal* reported that on a clear and peaceful day, in the middle of the afternoon, the Wight Star Liner *Olympic*, the 'most gigantic vessel afloat', was steaming in an eastward direction towards Spithead. At the same time the cruiser *Hawke* travelling at about 15 knots came from the west, crashing into the liner and seriously damaging both vessels. There were immediately claims and counter-claims, both sides stating that the other vessel had been the one overtaking and had not taken sufficient care to keep out of the way. At the time they had first sighted each other they were 3–4 miles apart but when the *Olympic* began making a turn to enter Spithead the two ships were only 100–150 yards apart. At the hearing it was ruled that, as the *Hawke* was the vessel to starboard, it was up to the *Olympic* to take avoiding action and so the blame lay solely with her. The *Olympic* had at that time been under compulsory pilotage and therefore the blame was laid the pilot's door. Damages apart, the other costs were to be equally shared by the two complainants. Appeals were immediately launched and it took another two years to finalise the case. Occurring a few months before the *Titanic* disaster, the *Aberdeen Journal* commented, with chilling foresight, 'The great liners may, as it has been claimed for them, be practically unsinkable, but they are far from being invulnerable.' (*Aberdeen Journal*, September 22nd 1911)

⌐ September 21st ⌐

1888: On this day a whale about 40ft long was seen at Sea View, Isle of Wight. A correspondent stated that a good deal of excitement was occasioned onboard the passenger steamer *Bembridge*, plying between Portsmouth and the Isle of Wight, owing to the departure of the steamer from the Island being blocked by the whale. Eventually the vessel got under way, followed by the whale, which kept close to the paddle box of the steamer and blew so violently as to almost deluge the deck. After a time the whale put out to sea, followed by fishermen in open boats, who succeeded in driving it onto the sandbanks where it was shot at until it was killed. (*Reynolds Newspaper*, September 23rd 1888)

~ September 22nd ~

1936: There was a persistent rumour on the Island that today a mutiny had occurred in Parkhurst Prison. The *Evening Telegraph* relayed the news that 'A reporter, who had made inquiries was informed on good authority that there had been nothing in the nature of an open disturbance. It was revealed, however, that on Tuesday a convict "ran amok" with a saucepan. Climbing to the roof of the building, which includes the governor's house, he smashed one of the faces of the clock in a turret on top of the building and hurled slates at prison officials below. A fire hose was turned on him and after delaying capture for an hour, he came down and surrendered. The prison clock is still out of action.' (*Evening Telegraph*, September 24th 1936)

⁓ September 23rd ⁓

1890: The *Isle of Wight Observer* printed a stroke by stroke account of a swimming challenge from Ryde to Portsmouth that took place today. Professor Albert, the Scandinavian swimming champion announced his intention to make the swim and before the event, he was challenged to a race by Portsmouth swimming professional S. Sargeant. The professor declined the offer but on the day, Sargeant aboard a wherry was present at the starting point. At 3.30 p.m. the professor dived off the pier and started off doing a sedate breaststroke, accompanied by two boats. Sargeant gave him 5 minutes' start and then dived off the wherry, cutting his way through the water. Within 300 yards he had caught up. Albert, who had been leisurely enjoying his swim, upbraided the challenger who took little notice and struck out for the Island shore. According to the *Observer*, Sargeant was 'splendidly steered which was more than could be said for Albert and after they had been an hour into the water the Portsmouth man was more than an hour to the good and drawing away.' Albert ran foul of the spit and although he took several doses of brandy in the water he failed to make any headway. At 5.20 p.m., having 'warmly vituperated' the men steering him, he announced his intention to give up. At 6 p.m. Sargeant came ashore at Ryde Pier, achieving what the *Observer* called 'a remarkable feat'. Professor Albert's take on the event was that 'it vos damn humbug'. (*Isle of Wight Observer*, September 27th 1890)

⭤ September 24th ⭤

1899: Today Edwin Snow of Newport died, who, until a recent illness, had tolled the curfew bell in Newport both morning and evening. This ended an unbroken tradition dating at least from Norman times. The word curfew is said to derive from the French *couve feu* meaning to cover the hearth at night and stifle the flames. Edwin had tolled the evening bell at dusk and at 7 a.m. each winter morning (6 a.m. in summer) and he was so reliable and accurate that local people depended upon him. He was a member of the Newport Company of Chimers and also the chief organ-blower in St Thomas's church. If you walk down the appropriately named Watchbell Lane in Newport the curfew bell still hangs high on the wall. After a break of several weeks the tradition of ringing the curfew in Newport was taken up again, for a while, by Mr Percy Pinhorn who died in 1923. (*Shields Daily Gazette*, October 4th 1899)

~ September 25th ~

1839: The *Hampshire Advertiser* reported today on the last meeting of the season of the Carisbrooke Archers held at the castle, when a cup given the previous year by Miss Ward was again contested for and won by Mrs Smith. Afterwards 120 members and guests sat down to a picnic dinner in the governor's apartment and dancing continued to a late hour. The first meeting had taken place on August 7th in an extremely high wind but it did not deter 'a large assemblage of the elite of the neighbourhood'. The first prize for the ladies was an elegant gold bracelet and for the gentlemen was a silver inkstand. Other prizes included an elaborately chased card case and enamelled gold shirt studs attached with gold chains. At 4 p.m. the trumpet sounded the call for dinner to which an overflowing number sat down and the evening was passed in merry dance to Mews Quadrille Band. The attention of the assembly was called to the fact that unless strenuous exertions were made at once, the whole of the beautiful lands and plantations adjoining the castle would be disposed of in small lots under the auctioneer's hammer. (*Hampshire Advertiser*, September 25th 1839)

— SEPTEMBER 26TH —

1871: Overnight, an emigrant ship, the *Underlee*, bound for Melbourne, ran aground at Dunnose Head, between Bonchurch and Luccombe Chine. On board were 150 emigrants plus the crew. The ironclad *Underlee* had left London two days earlier. The following morning two tugs were sent to her and one of them succeeded in taking off the fifteen female passengers and transporting them to Portsmouth. In the meantime, with the help of two steamers, it was hoped that at high tide it would be possible to refloat her but she was caught on the rocks and within hours began to break up. It was afterwards observed that, had the crew used the anchor instead of struggling to reduce the sail, the accident could have been avoided. All day during the 27th, crowds of people from all parts of the Island hurried to view the spectacle. By this time the shore was strewn with debris. On the 28th the rest of the passengers were rescued by tug and on the 29th the crew abandoned ship and were brought ashore by the use of rocket apparatus. The house of MP Mr Henry at Bonchurch was made available for their use. Unhappily one person, the chief steward, was washed overboard and drowned. (*Grantham Journal*, September 30th 1871)

— SEPTEMBER 27TH —

1899: On this day, Private Jennings, a Ryde man serving in South Africa found time to write a letter to his mother describing the battle against the Boers at Bergandal. Mrs Jennings of Lind Street allowed the *Isle of Wight Observer* to print it:

We have done ten days march and covered 120 miles, nothing but hills. Ashey Down is nothing to be compared to them … We are following up a commando of Boers and had a little skirmish with them but have not been able to get to them since, as they fly when they see us coming. We are driving them into three of our columns … We have had no tents for 25 days and not likely to get any. If we don't have to keep watch on the hills we just drop down where we are. My chum, Private Rider is still with me – the only other Isle of Wight man in the regiment. I have just received some cigarettes and no one knows what a gift it was. We can't get much to eat, but the smoking business is worse, the poor fellows sell their biscuits … for tobacco … We are three weeks now without a change of underclothes … I have patched my underclothing till I can't put another stich [*sic*] in them.

Having delayed the letter he then wrote: 'After playing cat and mouse with the enemy we attacked them properly. This makes the fifth hard battle that I have come through. I had two narrow escapes … but I thank God that I did not get a scratch … We move on today; it is nearly up with them now. I hear we killed about 500 of them. I was sorry to see some of the poor wounded they left to die. Those we captured were pleased to have fallen in our hands.' (*Isle of Wight Observer*, March 17th 1900)

— September 28th —

1844: Today's *Hampshire Telegraph* reported how the week's petty sessions at Newport had been kept busy with the following misdemeanours. On the previous Sunday morning, Thomas Calloway of Yarmouth had allowed his public house to be open at the time of divine service and was fined £2 with 7s 6d costs. At the same time, James Smithers, a licensed victualler who kept the Folly Inn at Whippingham, was fined 17s 6d for the same offence. A series of cases involving various assaults followed, after which Charles Linington, an apprentice to James Butcher, tailor of Cowes came before the court. He was accused of absenting himself from work and sentenced to twenty-eight days in the treadmill. The last item on the agenda concerned Martin Ferguson aged 16 and formerly residing in Parkhurst Prison, he being one of the prisoners who had died of consumption. A verdict of Natural Death was recorded. (*Hampshire Telegraph*, September 28th 1844)

~ September 29th ~

1838: The *Hampshire Telegraph* reported in detail on the two-day horseracing event that ended on September 29th. Despite unfavourable weather it was well attended. The first two races were 1-mile heats for horses bred in the Island that had never won a race other than a handicap and 'No grooms or servants allowed to ride'. A Hunter's Cup followed, again in two 1-mile heats. It was described as a very excellent race, the first heat being won by a neck. There then followed a free-for-all in 2-mile heats, the winner to be offered for sale for £30 should anyone wish to acquire it. The following day started with the Isle of Wight Cup followed by the Ladies' Cup – although the jockeys were all to be gentleman riders. A handsome whip was offered as a second prize. The final race of the day was the Hurdle Race. The *Telegraph* described how Miss Jenny Jones and the nearest rival took the first two hurdles together. At the third she was slightly behind but for the next hurdles they were again together. Unhappily, Miss Jones had suffered some injury at the first jump and was obliged to withdraw; Miss Jones was a bay mare belonging to Mr Jolliffe. The event was rounded off with a ball at the town hall and unfortunately, when returning home, Lady Holmes and her son-in-law the Hon. W. A'Court Holmes, were going in opposite directions, collided and the wheel of the Hon. gent's carriage was kicked out. (*Hampshire Telegraph*, October 1st 1838)

— SEPTEMBER 30TH —

1950: Between September 26th and October 1st, the exploits of Joseph Purton, a 28-year-old convict who escaped from Parkhurst Prison kept the press busy as he remained at large for a week. His companion, William Smith from Manchester, was recaptured at Cowes but Purton continued to avoid arrest. He narrowly evaded capture when the occupier of a house discovered him hiding in a wardrobe but Purton made his escape by stealing a bicycle. The *Hull Daily Mail* of September 30th reported the latest details. Taking shelter in a barn near Cowes, a cowman, suspecting that Purton was hiding in the hay, dug into the stack with a pitchfork causing him to leap out and head for Ruffin's wood. The man gave chase but lost him. Thirty policemen drafted in also failed to find him. The following day he was finally discovered by the military in a disued army camp at Whippingham and was described as 'unkempt and exhausted'. He offered no resistance and his face was injured with a deep gash over his right eye caused by the pitchfork. Prior to his escape he had trained like an Olympian athlete, winning a prison 2-mile race by 30 yards. Purton had twice before escaped from prison in Chelmsford. He was known as Dragon Man because of the dragon tattoo on his right forearm. (*Hull Daily Mail*, September 30th 1950)

~ October 1st ~

1810: In a report headed 'Newport October 1', the *London Morning Post* carried the following report:

I hasten to inform you of a dreadful commotion among the troops at the Depot, which took place at 8 o'clock last evening, which for some time, caused a considerable alarm, as all were panic struck within the garrison. The Brunswickers, a part of the foreign corps here, had been, during the day of Sunday, guilty of several irregularities, one of the East India recruits being wounded in affray. But the party being intoxicated, in the evening, entered the canteen, and demolished every thing that came in their way, and did the same in a second room; they then sang some national songs, rushed out in a body, went to their quarters, brought out their rifles, with four rounds of ball cartridges, and fired up and down every division at random. One report mentions 150 balls having been fired; another account makes them but 105. One man, I am sorry to say, was killed, and another was shot so badly in the arm, that it had to be amputated; another through the body, but whether dead or alive is not known. The drums at last beat to arms, and the garrison was ordered to ground arms, which was at length done, after some little hesitation on the part of the foreigners. A coach from Cowes to Newport was passing at the time, and the lives of the passengers were endangered. A woman was undressing a child in the sergeant's quarters, and a ball absolutely passed between the woman and child without injury.

(*London Morning Post*, October 4th 1810)

~ October 2nd ~

1897: Today's *Hampshire Telegraph* reported that James Duke of Leslie House, Hope Road, Shanklin, a former deputy chief constable, was accused of cutting a plane tree of about 14ft high in Hope Road, belonging to Shanklin Urban District Council. In an epidemic of tree cutting, in one night fourteen had been cut down in one road and two in another. Rewards of between £5 to £10 had been offered without success. The prosecution said that on September 12th, Police Constable Wooldridge had seen the defendant in the full light of the moon cutting a young tree outside Leslie House. The constable shouted out, 'Hullo, what is the meaning of this? I am a police constable and I charge you with cutting this tree.' The defendant replied, 'What do you mean? Me? A respectable citizen? I will make you prove it.' The Police Constable replied, 'I can do so for I saw you do it.' When summoned, the defendant said that he was glad to be arrested for when he got 'Old Lees' (the chief constable) in the witness box he would shoot him with his revolver then place it in his own mouth because 'he has been trying all his life to ruin me'. The defence asked whether the bench could be certain that the prisoner had done it and whether or not he was responsible for his actions. Some five or six years earlier he had suffered a mental aberration and had had to be watched. He was returned to the court for sentencing, the chairman of the magistrates saying that he was sorry to see someone who had held such a superior position reduced to this and he regretted having to deal harshly with him. Dukes was sentenced to six weeks' hard labour. The prisoner had to be dragged from the court and he later was despatched to Kingston Prison by train, at which time he seemed indifferent to his fate. (*Hampshire Telegraph*, October 2nd 1897)

~ OCTOBER 3RD ~

1884: As part of a lecture tour, playwright Oscar Wilde was present at Ryde Town Hall to deliver a lecture on the styles of dress of the period. Oscar had earlier declared that 'One should either be a work of art or wear a work of art' and the reporter for the *Isle of Wight Observer* surmised that the large audience had come hoping to have a laugh at this 'apostle of Aestheticism'. They were soon won round. His own dress was sober and the reporter declared that 'the rather long hair which he still affects was rather becoming than otherwise ... Mr Wilde is an enthusiast in a good cause, and like a good many enthusiasts he has had to go a long way up the hill in order to induce people to follow him ... Mr Wilde had the hearty concurrence of every sensible person present when he denounced the ugliness of the modern costumes.' *The Isle of Wight Times* also reported the lecture although with rather less enthusiasm, the journalist concluding that it was nothing but a lot of 'namby pamby notions' that would be better suited to milliners' girls. (Jan Toms, 'Dedicated Follower of Fashion', www.suite101.com, February 2010)

OCTOBER 4TH

1879: At the court of petty sessions in Newport today, before Sir Francis White Popham (chairman), Alfred Wynn of West Cowes was summoned for riding in a carriage of the Ryde Newport and Cowes Railway Company without having a ticket. Mr W.H. Woodridge prosecuted. William Strawn, stationmaster at Mill Hill, deposed that on the 20th, on the arrival of the 8.28 train from Newport, he found the defendant in a second-class carriage under the seat. He had no ticket and no money and when the witness asked him his name, the defendant struck him several times. He was fined 20s and costs. (*Isle of Wight Observer*, October 11th 1879)

~ October 5th ~

1912: Today a celebration took place in Cowes to mark the launch of an ocean-going torpedo-boat destroyer. *Tome* is the largest ship ever built in the East Cowes yard of J. Samuel White and also the second largest destroyer in the world. Six further vessels of the same design were planned for the future. Crowds of onlookers jostled along each side of the River Medina to see the event. The Chilean flag was flying and the Chilean Minister, the naval attaché and the director of J. Samuel White were all present for the ceremony, as was a representative of the Royal Naval College at Osborne. A short religious service was conducted by Father Clark RC from St David's at East Cowes, resplendent in a white and gold satin cope. Holy water was carried by his acolyte Joseph Milligan. Following tradition, a bottle of champagne was smashed against the ship by Madame Duble, wife of the captain and the occasion was marked by the presentation of a silver engraved box to Mr White. The ceremony was followed by lunch. (David Williams and Richard P. de Kerbrech, *J. Samuel White and Co. Shipbuilders*)

October 6th

1896: Today Sir James Abbott of Everslie, Ashey Road in Ryde, died at the age of 89 having retired to the Island following a lifetime of military service. As an army captain he had been tasked with limiting Russian influence in the East following British intervention in Afghanistan. To this end he was posted to Khiva, 'to a Court, of the language and manner of which I am utterly ignorant'. He failed to persuade the Khivan leader to release Russian slaves, which gave the Russians a reason to invade. Taking the initiative, Abbott offered to personally negotiate a settlement with Russia but was captured en route to St Petersburg and had several fingers severed in a skirmish. His overtures failed and he returned to England where he received a pension of £50 per annum for his troubles.

Returning to India, in 1845 he was appointed Commissioner of Hasara, securing the safety of the province and when he left the town was named Abbottabad in his honour. Sir James, who had been at school with Benjamin Disraeli, was married with a son. He was knighted in May 1894. Recently, 'his' town of Abbottabad went down in history as the place where Osama bin Laden was captured. (*Oxford Dictionary of National Biography*)

~ October 7th ~

1894: The *Portsmouth Evening News* reported today on a meeting of the Amalgamated Society of Carpenters and Joiners held at the Clarement Hall. The *News* reported that there was not a large attendance. Mr G. Fellows CC presided and said that he was sympathetic to trade unionism. In his view, unionism and education were responsible for the much-improved conditions of the working man compared to fifteen or twenty years ago. The London organising secretary of the union, Mr George Drew was in attendance and gave a lengthy talk on the benefits of membership, in particular to those who found themselves unemployed either because of illness, accident, or for those who lost their tools either by fire, water or theft. Mr D. Barret, organising secretary of the General Labourers' Amalgamated Union, also addressed the meeting. He stated that the low wages paid to labourers on the Isle of Wight was a scandal to the British Empire. Captain carpenter R.N., who was asked to speak, expressed himself in favour of working men forming themselves into these associations. (*Portsmouth Evening News*, October 7th 1894)

~ October 8th ~

1832: News of a shipwreck and rescue on this day was sufficiently exciting to be featured in newspapers as far afield as the *Westmorland Gazette*. The American ship *Bainbridge* carrying a cargo of rum came to grief at daybreak off Atherfield. For 7 hours the crew watched for signs of help from land while the men of the Preventive Service armed with Captain Manby's gun made three attempts to fire a line to the ship, but on each case it failed to reach its target. As it was about to try for a fourth time, a man by the name of Grimes discharged a rocket that carried a line directly to the stricken vessel and the crew of nineteen was saved. Grimes's rocket was the work of Newport man John Dennet and with the help of a breeches buoy it became the primary method of carrying shipwrecked sailors to the land. Captain Manby was a childhood friend of Lord Nelson. (*Westmorland Gazette*, October 20th 1832)

~ October 9th ~

1809: The *Salisbury and Winchester Journal* carried a regular list of prisoners committed to the county gaol at Winchester to await the next assizes. Among those for today was German soldier Henrick Schneider, charged with the murder of Moses Mitier of Freshwater. Unrest among the garrison of the King's German Legion (also known as the Black Brunswickers) was commonplace with numerous offences committed. At a later date, while on trial for libel, William Cobbett called on the example of the Isle of Wight when defending why he opposed permitting German soldiers to discipline their English counterparts. He thought that, 'The Isle of Wight could bear witness to their brutal outrages while in that place, from which they were obliged to be removed, being charged with two murders [in] the short time that they were there.' When the case of Schneider came to court on March 5th 1810, he was sentenced to six months in gaol and fined 1*s*. (*Morning Post*, June 16th 1810)

~ October 10th ~

1879: The *Portsmouth Evening News* today carried details of an awful accident that occurred at Parkhurst Prison. One of the guards had returned his carbine to the rack where weapons were stored but had failed to make it secure. The son of the governor, Major Noott, being in the room, took the gun down and discharged it. In so doing he shot both a warder named Dockerill in the left side and the principal warder by the name of Prendergast close to the jugular vein. At the time of the story's publication, the shot had been removed from Officer Dockerill but 'the other sufferer has not yet had similar relief and is reported to be in a serious condition'. The *News* condemned such thoughtlessness and carelessness and stated that 'It is time such negligence with loaded firearms should be punishable in some way.' They also questioned how the boy had been permitted to stay in the area. (*Portsmouth Evening News*, October 10th 1879)

— OCTOBER 11TH —

1836: Of all the local shipwrecks, the sinking of the *Clarendon* is the most remembered. The homeward-bound *Clarendon* had set off from St Kitts carrying a cargo of rum and molasses and eleven passengers. They must have had an uncomfortable time for throughout the voyage they were buffeted by strong winds. At 6 a.m. on the 11th, forced ashore by the tide, the *Clarendon* hit the beach at Blackgang and with chilling speed rolled onto her side and broke up. Local fishermen were quick to respond but the result was the tragic loss of twenty-five lives, of both crew and passengers. There was particular shock as the news reached the shore that an entire family, consisting of Lt Shore of the 14th regiment, returning from service in the West Indies, with his wife and four daughters (the youngest being just 9 months) had all perished. A few days later, news reached the island that another passenger aboard, a young woman named Miss Gourlay, had been washed up across the Solent at Southsea. Her body was found at the foot of her father's garden. Local fisherman John Wheeler was singled out for praise, having tied a rope around his waist and waded into the sea to rescue whoever he could. He managed to drag three crewmen ashore, one of whom turned out to be a former shipmate, John Thompson, who had previously served aboard Lord Yarborough's yacht *Falcon* with him. (*Isle of Wight County Press*, October 15th 1836)

~ October 12th ~

1825: An inquest was held at Yarmouth this day on the body of Ann Acres, a child who had been washed out of the vessel *Happy Return* wrecked at Totland Bay. The bodies of Mrs Arthur, Mary Oats, and Miss Colenso were taken out of the wreck, and on Sunday a coroner's inquest was held. A week later the remains of the lamented Mr Wavell and another of the passengers from the *Happy Return* were recovered. John Wavell Esq, was picked up by the cutter *Rose*, near the spot where the vessel sunk, and conveyed to Yarmouth where an inquest was taken. On Thursday a further inquest was held at the same place, into the death of the unfortunate woman to whose assistance Mr Wavell had been called, and also Miss Arthur, daughter of the above mentioned Mrs Arthur, both of whom were picked up the day before at Christchurch. The verdict in each case was 'Accidental death, a consequence of wind and storm, and the sinking of the vessel.' The victims were passengers from Penzance to London. Two other passengers were saved by clinging to the rigging, together with W. Woolcock (the master), John Davis, and Thomas Toby, the crew of the vessel. The remains of Mr Wavell were on Thursday conveyed to Newport and interred in the family vault. Mr Wavell, a local surgeon, was not a passenger but had attempted to rescue the lady in question. (*Hampshire Chronicle*, October 15th 1825)

~ October 13th ~

1921: Today's *Nottingham Post* reported the excitement on the Island following the discovery of bodies in the garden of Craigie Lodge at St Lawrence, the former home of novelist Pearl Craigie, who wrote under the pen name John Oliver Hobbs. The following day, on the 14th, the *Western Times* described how a gardener planting apple trees had unearthed the body of a child of about 6 years. She was believed to have been buried about twelve years ago and was in a crouched position. Her skull had been fractured. The story continued the next day, adding that the body of a woman had now been unearthed, buried only 12 inches under the surface. An inquest took place a few days later and according to the coroner, the bones were of 'extremely ancient origin'. An inquest was only convened because a local clairvoyant Mrs Pollack had aroused interest in the discovery. The *Exeter and Plymouth Gazette* set minds at rest, explaining that 'an octogenarian resident related the discovery of a skull in the neighbourhood fifty or so years ago. One doctor expressed the opinion that the bones had been there about thirty years, while another doctor put their age at beyond 100 years, and said the bodies were buried at a time when it was customary to place them in a crouched-up position.' (*Nottingham Post*, October 13th 1921; *Western Times*, October 14th 1921; *Exeter and Plymouth Gazette*, October 13th 1921)

~ October 14th ~

1883: This morning, as people were looking out to sea from Esplanade Gardens at Ryde, they noticed a pheasant fly out from the gardens and head out over the sea before falling into the water. As they had been watching the pheasant they also witnessed a seaman in a skiff. He was preparing to board a barge and as he did so he fell overboard. A group of young men who had witnessed both incidents from the shore immediately procured a boat and rowed out to rescue the mariner. They were just in time as he was reported to be quite exhausted. As a postscript, the *Portsmouth Evening News* added that the pheasant was also secured. (*Portsmouth Evening News*, October 15th 1883)

~ October 15th ~

1940: Following an attack on his plane by a British fighter that punctured the petrol tank, a German pilot bailed out his aircraft and was later spotted sheltering near a hedge on the Calbourne to Carisbrooke road by lorry driver Harold Blow. The pilot submitted to a search and was taken by Blow into Newport. During the journey, the driver was amazed to hear his passenger say, 'Will you pull up at the Blacksmith's Arms at the top of the hill? I could do with a drink.' On being questioned, the German said that he knew the Island well and also Southampton where, in past days, he had visited by liner. Blow took the pilot to his home where he gave him a meal as he appeared to be very hungry. Afterwards he telephoned the police to come and get him. His guest thanked him for the food and left with a police escort. Mr Blow observed that 'he did not seem worried by his fighting days being over for the present'. (*Nottingham Evening Post*, October 16th 1940)

~ October 16th ~

1826: At Yarmouth today, Henry Salter, a hay warden, 'on going his rounds, found on the Common Three Cows belonging to George Woolgar, one tied as is the custom and two loose. Salter proceeded to drive the two Cows that were loose to the pound, but on their way these were forcibly taken from his custody by George Woolgar, who at the same time threatened him with Violence.'

The hay warden was one of the officials appointed annually, along with the constables, to ensure that law and order was observed. Any infringement went before a jury to pronounce on the case. In Yarmouth, certain freeholders had the right to graze cattle on the common but it was strictly controlled. Most freeholders were permitted to graze only one cow and each animal was to be secured by a chain no longer than 12 yards in length. Animals infringing this rule were carted off to the town pound that once stood on the south side of the Yarmouth–Newport Road, roughly opposite the eastern end of the common. In this particular case, we don't know how the jury responded to Woolgar's misdemeanour. (C.W.R. Winter, *The Ancient Town of Yarmouth*, Isle of Wight County Press, 1981)

~ OCTOBER 17TH ~

1876: Today's *Edinburgh Evening News* reported on the fate of two small children rescued from Bashi-Bazouks – 'murderous marauders' attacking helpless refugees on the coast of Bulgaria. Captain Hyde Parker of the ship *Firebrand* discovered a young boy and a baby with the corpses of their parents. The boy was about 4 years old and the baby about 10 months and both were wounded. He took them aboard his ship and the boys, Yani and Georgy, were named John and George Firebrand. When Captain Hyde Parker was killed, Queen Victoria got to hear of the case and the children were brought to Osborne. She announced that 'I shall have the greatest pleasure in watching over these innocents …' She placed them in the care of Mrs Jackman, an estate worker living at Barton Cottage, who only had one child of her own. Both boys grew up and entered the navy, although with mixed fortunes. John left the navy and went to America but did not find the fame and fortune he hoped for. He married and returned to London where he died at the age of 78. George went on to become a paymaster sergeant in the army in the Rifle Brigade. He died in 1896 leaving a widow and a daughter. (*Edinburgh Evening News*, October 17th 1876; *Sofia Echo*, April 19th 2013)

~ October 18th ~

1941: Islanders had a mixed response to the call by the Minister of Munitions that, because of a shortage of materials to build tanks, iron railings should be sacrificed to the war effort. In Newport there was particular concern about the railings surrounding Church Litten burial ground as the railings were viewed to be of historic importance, each bearing the date of erection on the spearhead tops (1849). The *County Press* confirmed that they 'are so faced that they repeat the number in succession all along the line'. The only reasons that one could object to the removal of railings were on the grounds of public safety or historic value. The reporter forecast that if the railings were to be removed, it may well be the first step to moving the gravestones and placing them along the wall, then developing the open space into a pleasure garden that was 'already beautified by many fine trees'. The railings were in fact removed and the General Purposes Committee instructed the borough surveyor to erect a fence around the weeping beech, to protect it from damage by children. The mayor declared that if the children were told not to touch the tree then they could be relied upon not to do so. After the war the graveyard was indeed cleared and unhappily most gravestones were broken down for paving. The weeping beech still holds pride of place. (*Isle of Wight County Press*, October 18th 1941)

~ October 19th ~

1883: On this date, on the second day of the autumn meeting of the Royal Isle of Wight Golf Club at St Helens Dover (Duvver), a south-west gale and rain was so unrelenting that many members who attended chose not to compete. A series of valuable prizes was, however, on offer. Mrs Hambrough of Steephill Castle donated a case of silver gilt spoons and any competitor winning them twice within three years would become the outright owner. If this did not occur, the six winners would then compete for the prize at the 1886 meeting. A second and a third prize of golf clubs and golf balls were also offered. Colonel C.D. Chalmers presented two antique spoons for the best aggregate of two day's play, and a sweepstake. The *Isle of Wight Observer* reported that eight and a half couples took part. Mrs Hambrough's spoons went to Mr E.W. Hamilton; the golf clubs to the captain of the club, Captain Howard Brooke; the golf balls to Mr Alexander Crawford; while Colonel Chambers' spoons were carried off by Mr E.W. Hamilton. During the play, the ground was visited by the president of the club, HSH Prince Edward of Saxe-Weimar. In the evening a dinner was held at the Spithead Hotel where Prince Edward presented the prizes. Among the many toasts, was one to 'Golfing Societies all over the World'. (*Isle of Wight Observer*, October 27th 1883)

~ October 20th ~

1886: The hazards of sea travel were underlined in today's report in the *Hampshire Advertiser*. Under the heading 'Shipping Casualties' the difficulties suffered by the Swedish barque *Ornen* from Bergen were recounted. She had been brought into Cowes by the steam tug *Malta* three days earlier whilst en route from Mobile to Goole, carrying a cargo of resin and having suffered a most disastrous passage. Early in the voyage the crew had been struck down with an ague from which three had died. The captain was the only crewmember to remain fit and worked the vessel with the help of the cook. When they ran into gales the crew was unable to take in the sails, many of which were blown away. On reaching the Lizard Point, a pilot and an extra crewmember were taken on board to bring the ship into the nearest harbour. This they were unable to do and therefore ran for the Isle of Wight, where they were towed from Ventnor to Cowes. As they approached the harbour a further member of the crew died. Another Swedish craft, the *Kosmos* was also brought into Cowes carrying a cargo of deals (a type of pinewood). She lost half of her deck load as they crossed the Bay of Biscay. (*Hampshire Advertiser*, October 20th 1886)

~ OCTOBER 21ST ~

1830: A preventive boatman of Freshwater named Foulkes appeared to answer a charge made by some gamekeepers. They claimed that, on October 21st, he used wires to destroy game in a wood called Salter's Wood Coppice. The prisoner, through his advocate, William Griffiths Esq., made the following defence. On the day in question, Foulkes had strong reason to suspect that contraband goods were concealed in the wood, especially as a four-oared galley belonging to a notorious smuggler was moored on the verge of the wood at the time. This, combined with the orders of his superior officer, caused him to make a most minute and particular search of the area. As he did he was suddenly assailed by two men named Phillimore and Singer, who charged him with poaching and having a lure and wires in his possession. When it appeared that these two men were in the habit of conveying smuggled liquor by night round the neighbourhood, the charged was considered vindictive and fallacious and the information was dismissed. (*Hants Chronicle*, November 8th 1830)

~ October 22nd ~

1864: A visitor wandering in the graveyard of the Independent Chapel at Brading was shocked to discover the following inscription on a tombstone: 'The three bodies here interred were denied Christian burial by the clergy of their respective parishes – the two children, because they died un-baptised; the youth, because he had been baptised by a Wesleyan minister.'

The discovery resulted in the following response: 'This stone is erected as a tribute of affection for those whom Christ hath received, and as a standing testimony against clerical intolerance.'

The visitor asked whether we have a right to boast of our superior civilisation when such a record as this is found in the burial place of the dead. (*Dunfermline Saturday Press*, October 22nd 1864)

~ October 23rd ~

1582: On this day Bishop John Watson was granted a licence by Queen Elizabeth I to open a graveyard at Church Litten in Newport. A meeting was called a week later and all the inhabitants assembled on the plot of ground at Cosham to see about enclosing it against animals. This land had been first land of God's House Southampton, then Queen's College Oxford. The need for a graveyard was in response to an outbreak of plague in Newport when it had become impossible to carry the number of victims to Carisbrooke for burial. Cosham was the most deprived area of Newport on the Southern border of the town. (*Isle of Wight Curiosities*, Jack Jones, 1950)

~ October 24th ~

1793: In a news summary headed 'London, Thursday October 24', the *Hereford Journal* passed on the news that:

> A few days ago the neighbourhood of Steephill in the Isle of Wight, was alarmed by the following melancholy event. A gentleman, as he was taking his morning ride alone, alighted from his horse which he fastened to a hedge nigh a churchyard, went into the church porch and despatched himself with a pistol charged with two balls which shattered his head to-pieces: he had pinned a letter to the bosom of his shirt directed to the Clergyman of the parish, accounting for his rash act from the threats of his brother to arrest him for debt. There are several children to lament him.

(*Hereford Journal*, October 30th 1793)

~ October 25th ~

1897: More than forty years after her birth on this day in London, Pamela Arland was to turn the spotlight on the Isle of Wight as a centre for spying and treason. Originally named Dorothy O'Grady, she was the only woman to be sentenced to death for spying during the Second World War. Dorothy had moved to Sandown to run a boarding house with her newly retired husband, but as the war broke out he returned to his firefighting job in London. Dorothy, now alone, took to wandering the cliffs and beaches with her dog, being caught several times in prohibited areas. Her behaviour was bizarre (at one time she wore a paper swastika) but as her trespassing persisted and she was caught signalling out to sea, it was no longer possible to ignore it.

She was arrested and charged with spying. The case was held in camera (in private) and, with the penalty for treason being death, the judge duly doffed the black cap and announced that she should be hanged. Later Dorothy claimed to have felt excited as the sentence was handed down, but was shocked to find that she would be hanged rather than shot. Her sentence was commuted to fourteen years in prison and when she was released she returned to her Sandown home. Interviewed on many occasions, she stuck to her story that she had been suffering from some sort of 'kink' and that she had been playing a joke. Questions, however, remained and when the trial papers were released, the *Times* concluded that 'she was no innocent … but a dangerous Nazi agent.' Later examination of her early life and mental history showed a complex and damaged woman. Dorothy died in 1985, still leaving unanswered questions. (Adrian Searle, *The Spy Beside the Sea*, The History Press, 2012)

October 26th

1944: Today the death of 87-year-old Princess Beatrice occurred at the home of the Earl of Athlone. Her daughter Queen Victoria Eugenie had flown in to be with her. As the Island's governor, Beatrice had also been the country's only woman coroner but had never discharged these duties. She spent the greatest part of each year at Carisbrooke Castle and became the governor on the death of her husband Prince Henry of Battenberg, who died after the capture of the town of Kumasi during the Ashanti Wars. Of her four children: her daughter Victoria was the ex-Queen of Spain; her eldest son became the Marquis of Carisbrooke; her second son Prince Leopold died in 1922, a sufferer from haemophilia; her youngest son, Prince Maurice of Battenberg, died of wounds suffered in the First World War. She is interred with her husband in the Battenberg Chapel at St Mildred's church, Whippingham. (*Gloucester Echo*, October 26th 1944)

~ October 27th ~

1797: On this day a group of Eastbourne fishermen working at sea fell in with a cutter-rigged sailboat, which had foreigners in uniform on board, whom they took and conveyed to shore. The following day (Saturday) they were escorted thither by a file of men belonging to the Monmouth militia, and examined before H. Shelly, Esq. It appeared that they were deserters, from the Emigrant regiment of York hussars, stationed at Cowes in the Isle of Wight, from whence they had stolen the boat and embarked, with a view of getting to France or Holland. (*Ipswich Journal*, October 27th 1797)

~ OCTOBER 28TH ~

1854: The *Isle of Wight Observer* today took pleasure in reporting a 'Marriage Extraordinary' taking place in Ventnor. The groom was the recently retired curate the Revd J.C. Campbell and at eight o'clock in the morning the Ventnor Band accompanied him as he escorted his 'invalid bride to the Hymenial altar'. The bride in question was Miss Thompson whose delicate health had dictated that she spent the past thirteen years in bed. Carrying out his parish duties, the Revd Thompson had visited her and 'such an impression did he make on the sick and afflicted lady, that she was prevailed upon to be married'. The groom carried his bride to the altar where a chair was found for her. After the ceremony the new Mrs Campbell was carried to a carriage and, accompanied by the band, they drove to Shanklin. The reporter was undoubtedly a man as there is no mention of what the bride was wearing! (*Isle of Wight Observer*, October 28th 1854)

OCTOBER 29TH

1853: The *Isle of Wight Observer* reported that an inquest was held at Brixton last week on the body of an unknown man. Stephen King, a store agent at Shepherd's Chine, gave evidence that he saw the body between 100 and 200 yards from the shore. In his words:

> It had no clothes on but a flannel over the shoulders. There was a blue mark under the left arm; no wounds on the body; features gone; must have been some weeks in the water; found on the left arm the letters TS and WM and at the back part of the same arm the word HOPE in small letters; a figure of a lady and a union jack on the same arm. On the right arm is also the figure of the union jack and a man and a ship. No doubt deceased was a seafaring man. Jacob Barton has seen the body but it is neither of his sons who were drowned near Ventnor. Verdict: Found dead – cause of death unknown.

(*Isle of Wight Observer*, October 29th 1853)

~ October 30th ~

1878: Increasing resentment greeted the actions of Mr Dabell at Blackgang Chine when he placed a barrier across the path to the chine and demanded payment to use it. Dabell claimed there had never been a right of way on the path and that he had been the one to maintain the route to his bazaar that happened to straddle the footway. The issue attracted widespread interest and provoked artist and illustrator George Brannon to write and challenge the claim that this had never been a right of way. Notices were displayed telling visitors that they must either purchase something from the bazaar or pay 6*d* in order to pass through to the chine. The headline of the *Illustrated Police News* read 'Disgraceful Imposition'. The board's surveyor visited the site and reported that, although he had not been challenged over using the path, there was a barrier erected across it. Faced with this report, Dabell said that in future he would leave the gate open at all times. The commissioners declared themselves satisfied and no further action was recommended. The path to the chine was now open free of charge. (*Illustrated Police News*, November 2nd 1878)

~ OCTOBER 31ST ~

1846: Today's *Hampshire Telegraph* carried the following advert:

> East Cowes Castle For Sale. This splendid building, the masterpiece
> of the late John Nash Esq. was offered for sale by public auction on
> Wednesday last at the Medina Hotel, East Cowes and was bought in at
> £15,000. We expected there would be a good deal of competition and
> that many of our nobility would have been anxious to obtain so beautiful
> a place in such a desirable situation, but alas! Not one purchaser could
> be found; even curiosity had drawn but few persons together.

Nash had died at his home on April 12th 1835 'at a very
advanced age'. His finances being in a precarious state, his coffin
was transported at night to St James's church, East Cowes lest
it should be taken until his debts were paid. (*Hampshire Telegraph*,
October 31st 1846)

– November 1st –

1861: Mr Woodyear of Cowes, aged 74 and recently unwell, did not think twice before leaping into the sea in the vicinity of the Solent Baths when he heard a young woman crying for help. The girl in question had been swimming, got out of her depth and was being carried away by the tide. Woodyear reached her and she clung to his arm while he began to swim towards the shore. As he drew near he became exhausted and sank beneath the waves, still holding his charge. With great effort he managed to struggle to shallow water and saved both their lives. Although he refused any reward from the girl's father, on November 1st he received a letter of thanks accompanied by a very elegant silver bowl by way of appreciation. Woodyear had now passed his seventy-fifth birthday and declared that the adventure had done him no harm. (*Hampshire Advertiser*, November 7th 1861)

~ NOVEMBER 2ND ~

1804: On this day Harris Bigg-Wither of Manydown Park in Hampshire married Jane Howe Frith of Carisbrooke. Jane's father, Beddington Bramley Howe was a lieutenant colonel in the North Hampshire militia, posted to the Island to help counteract the prevalence of smuggling. Jane was his only daughter and the heiress to Brooke House. The bridegroom has a long-lasting claim to fame because, for nearly 24 hours, he had been engaged to Jane Austen. Harris had been 8 years old when he met the future novelist who was then 14. A lasting friendship developed and thirteen years later, Harris proposed. Although he was variously described as plain and somewhat uncouth, it would be an advantageous match very much in the Austen tradition. Overnight, however, Jane changed her mind after a night of considerable emotion. Two years later, Harris recovered sufficiently to propose to Jane Howe Frith and embarked on a happy marriage that produced ten children. (Claire Tomalin, *Jane Austen: A Life*, 2012)

~ November 3rd ~

1914: On this date Joan Kennard, the married daughter of John Oglander of Nunwell House, wrote '… they asked me on Sunday morning to go down to see Prince Leopold. He is stricken so with grief at losing Maurice. It went to my heart to see him lying there in bed, ill himself. He seems turned to stone over it. I think he feels it so hard to understand that he could not have died instead – of course he can never marry and Prince Maurice was everything, almost to him.' Prince Maurice was serving in the Royal Rifle Corps and killed in the first battle of Ypres. He was the younger son of Queen Victoria's youngest daughter, Princess Beatrice, and is buried in the War Graves Commission Cemetery at Ypres. When Beatrice unveiled the war memorial at Whippingham, the first name on the list was that of her son. Joan wrote from France where she was nursing casualties of the war. Prince Leopold suffered from haemophilia and died in March 1922 following a hip operation. He is buried at Frogmore at Windsor. (Oglander Correspondence held in Isle of Wight Public Record office)

~ November 4th ~

1848: Following the discovery of a girl's body at Gurnard Bay, a jury of local Cowes people were today summoned to an inquest. The girl was identified by a boatman as being named Young and had dined with his family the previous evening. During a heavy snowstorm they proceeded to her home to convey the bad news of her drowning only to find that the information was false. The body was picked up in Gurnard Bay and placed temporarily under a hedge. Among many sightseers, Captain James Wilkinson who lived nearby went to view it and recognised it as that of Miss Trickett, his niece, the 18-year-old daughter of 'an opulent farmer of Thorness'. At the inquest, so many witnesses were called that the jury were 'mixed up with spectators and witnesses … divided from each other.' It seemed that Miss Trickett had been greatly distressed by the fact that her mother had fainted and, following a quarrel with her sister, had been forced to leave home. She did so only partially dressed, with no shawl and her hair in papers. The conclusion was that she was returning to her uncle's house but because of her appearance felt unable to go in and had wandered to the beach where she succumbed to the mud and drowned. Deciding that there was no evidence that she had taken her own life, her body was returned home prior to burial. (*Hampshire Advertiser*, November 11th 1848)

— NOVEMBER 5TH —

1807: Under the heading 'A Public Declaration of Guilt' the following notice was issued by Josiah Hart:

> Whereas I, Josiah Hart, formerly of Yarmouth in the Isle of Wight, and now of Portsmouth, Mariner, have traduced the Character of Miss Sarah Lumley, of the Parish of Freshwater, in the Isle of Wight, in the county of Southampton, in the most shameful and scandalous manner; and in consequence of such, she has most lastly threatened me with a prosecution for same; I do hereby make this public declaration, that the same is false and unfounded, and most humbly ask her pardon; and do agree with thankfulness to pay the expence [*sic*] of acknowledging my error in this public manner, for the great lenity she has shewn [*sic*] in dropping a prosecution against me. As witness my hand, the 5th day of November 1807. JOSIAH HART. Witness, Wim Treadgold, jun.

(*Salisbury and Winchester Journal*, November 5th 1807)

– November 6th –

1875: Today's *Hampshire Telegraph* passed on the news that following the activities of Doctor Monck of Ryde, a 'fake medium', certain local gentlemen who had attended a private seance were dissatisfied with the supposed 'manifestations' and so made a second visit. The good doctor requested that if any of the previous manifestations were raised, then they would drop any complaints against him. They replied that nothing would persuade them to change their minds about the 'clumsy trickery' but agreed to witness a second seance. In a darkened room, two of the gentlemen held Dr Monck tightly by each arm and although he writhed and groaned, saying that spirits were taking possession of him, nothing happened until his chair was propelled violently against the wall behind him. Those present were confident that he had done this by pushing it with his foot. When the gentlemen threatened to put on a light, Dr Monck begged them not to, saying it would kill him. They did so and with a scream he hurled himself across the room, dragging the men with him. In the scramble he grabbed a piece of string from the corner and then secreted some matches in his pocket. The report closed with the words 'utterly disgusted, the séance was terminated and, Dr Monck having been roundly abused and threatened, they parted – possibly to meet again'. (*Hampshire Telegraph*, November 6th 1875)

~ November 7th ~

1829: The naval schooner *Nightingale* commanded by Lt George Wood, ran aground on the Shingles at Yarmouth. Mr Burridge, pilot from Cowes and the coast guard station went to her aid. Everyone was confident that she could be refloated and the ballast was shifted and the hatches secured while the rescue boats anchored in deeper water. At about 8 p.m. the sea became so rough that it appeared dangerous for the boats to come alongside. As every effort was made to refloat her, she drove forward in the heavy seas striking the ground and a breach was made in the vessel, greatly alarming the poor sailors working the pumps. As the *Nightingale* was now struck and every soul washed from one side to the other, she fell on her beam-ends. It now being dark, the sailors waited for death, as the rescue boats still could not reach them. Eventually, when they came in sight, the crew reached the boats however they could and thirty men were rescued. The *Lancaster Gazette* that carried a report confirmed that the wife of the captain, who had shared much of his thirty-year career at sea, was drowned. The ship's surgeon had attached a rope to her and risked his own life but failed to save her while the captain crippled his hands in his attempts to help save her. Her last words to her husband were: 'Ah, my dear children, may the Almighty spare one of our lives for your sakes.' They had three children. A poor, unfortunate and insane Lt Cole who was on board also drowned. (*Lancaster Gazette*, November 7th 1829)

~ November 8th ~

1856: The first burial to take place at the newly opened Northwood Cemetery was that of James Cribb, a shoemaker of Cowes who died on November 5th 1856. James died from typhoid fever at the early age of 32 and his demise was also marked by another unique occurrence. James had married only two years earlier to Mary Ann Clark and understandably his widow was grief-stricken. After the ceremony, however, she became increasingly upset and insisted that James had been buried facing the wrong direction, towards the west rather than the east. The family was informed that there was nothing to be done, it being illegal to exhume a grave once the coffin has touched the ground in the burial plot. Undeterred, Mary Ann's family went by night to the graveyard and, after hanging a lantern on a tree branch to give some light, they proceeded to clear all the earth around the coffin. Once there was sufficient room they manoeuvred the casket 180 degrees without removing it from the grave. In 1865, Mary Ann married again, to local man 58-year-old Samuel Underhill who died in Cowes in 1880. Mary Ann then seems to have left the Island. (Archives, courtesy of Friends of Northwood Cemetery)

~ NOVEMBER 9TH ~

1850: Lady Emily Tennyson recorded in her journal today that her husband Alfred had received a letter from Colonel Phipps, equerry to Queen Victoria and keeper of the privy purse, offering him the post of Poet Laureate. The night before, Alfred had dreamed that the queen and Prince Albert had called on him at his mother's house and been very gracious, the prince kissing him, which made him think 'very kind but very German'. After consideration, he accepted the post, but only on condition that he was not expected to write verse for the royal family or state occasions. Tennyson accepted a payment of £72 a year and refused the traditional 'butt of sack', electing to accept a further £27 instead.

On the same day eight years later, Emily and Alfred visited Sheepwash Farm at Middleton, newly acquired by their gardener Mr Merwood. Emily commented that: 'I am glad to see that the Oreb spring runs through the Green of which "A" is Lord!' The word Oreb is of Hebrew origin and refers to ravens, which seems an appropriate name for the stream at Middleton as ravens were once common on the down from which the spring rises. Much of Middleton and the High Down were then in the ownership of the Tennyson family. The 'Oreb' that runs through Middleton and along the oddly named Spinfish into Freshwater is now simply known as 'the stream'. (Lady Emily Tennyson's journal, 1850 and 1858)

~ NOVEMBER 10TH ~

1914: Today's *Surrey Mirror* thought that the goings-on at the petty sessions at Newport were worthy of report:

> Admiral Algernon de Horsey presiding over the Isle of Wight Bench on Saturday, said to some lads who were playing in the street, that they should be learning to shoot. He added: 'When I see reports of football matches, I say "Good God, what has come to our people playing football when the country is in a life and death struggle!"'

Admiral de Horsey had joined the navy in 1840 and served across the globe. When he died on October 22nd 1922 he was described by *The Times*, to which he was a frequent contributor, as the 'Doyen of the Navy'. He lived at Melcombe House in Cowes. (*Surrey Mirror*, November 10th 1914)

~ November 11th ~

1877: On this day the *John Douse*, a brigantine under sail and travelling from Rouen to Cork, ran into trouble off the eastern coast of the Island. Subsequent events were described as one of the greatest rescues in Isle of Wight history, nearly costing the lives of the Bembridge lifeboat crew. As a force-nine gale blew her towards the shore, the ship anchored in Sandown Bay but the wind increased, the anchor was dragged and she ran ashore at 8 p.m. A messenger was immediately summoned and he rode the 6 miles to Bembridge to get help. The lifeboat *City of Worcester* was taken overland, being pulled by eight horses borrowed from a neighbouring farm, and it took 1½ hours to make the journey. In the bay there was nothing to see, the lights from the ship having been extinguished by the waves. The lifeboat set out and the brigantine's captain, named Sanders, dropped from the rigging into the boat while the mate was plucked from the sea. The rescuers being in danger of drowning stood off until the morning but meanwhile the coastguard rowed a galley out to the wreck and was able rescue the four remaining crewmen who were clinging to the rigging. (*Shipwreck Index of the British Isles*, Lloyds Register)

— NOVEMBER 12TH —

1881: On this day a man who escaped from Chatham Prison in 1879 was arrested on the Island. Giles Hutchings was sentenced to twenty-four years in prison for the manslaughter of Police Constable Nathanial Cox near Yeovil. Along with his father, brother and another, Hutchings had been poaching when they were discovered and the constable was kicked to death. Having been apprehended, Hutchings slipped away from the police on the way to Newport and swam across a stream, but one of the constables followed him through the water and over the fields and eventually succeeded in recapturing him after an exciting chase. Hutchings' identity was confirmed by several persons and by the unique identifying marks on his body published in the official description. For some time past he had been living a strange, mysterious life in a small hut under a down near Niton. The prisoner was finally lodged in the county police station in Newport and the Home Office and Chatham Prison have been communicated with. (*Western Daily Press*, November 16th 1881)

1854: Henry Norris of the Isle of Wight militia was charged with having a pair of boots in his possession, them being part of the military necessaries of Private William Smith of the 4th Regiment. It appeared that he bought them at the Military Arms beer house for 2s 6d and Police Constable Stubbs gave evidence that he found in the possession of the defendant. The chairman said that there could be no excuse, as Norris must have known that a soldier had no right to sell his necessaries. He was fined 21s plus three times the value of the boots (24s) and costs of 5s, amounting to £2 10s. He was committed, in default of payment, to six weeks in prison with hard labour. (*Hampshire Telegraph*, November 13th 1854)

~ November 14th ~

1811: Today both the *Cheltenham Chronicle* and the *Morning Post* advertised this forthcoming event: 'Doherty and Hall of the Isle of Wight are matched to fight on a stage for 200 guineas on Wednesday next on South-sea Common.' Tom Hall was a Newport man, a 'celebrated bruiser' who refused to surrender. In a fight a year earlier the *Oxford Journal* described how he was 'half blind of both eyes, which he got in the first twenty minutes, and although such was his state, his courage led him to victory'. Locally, an impromptu match took place at the Horse Shoe pub at Northwood, the scene being described by the *Hampshire Chronicle* as: 'surrounded by booths and vehicles for the accommodation of the immense crowd which flocked, not only from all parts of the Island, but from Portsmouth, Southampton, the New Forest &c to witness the spectacle.' Unfortunately, at the very moment the combatants were making 'dreadful note of preparation' the magistrates stepped in and stopped them. Bare-knuckle boxing matches were played with very few rules, being simply a fight that continued and sometimes lasted for hours, until one of the competitors could fight no more. Until 1838 the only conditions imposed were that the fighter should not gouge his opponent's eyes or hit him when he was down. Hall later married the landlady of the Five Bells Inn at Shorwell. (*Cheltenham Chronicle*, November 14th 1811; *Morning Post*, November 14th 1811; *Hampshire Chronicle*, April 5th 1822)

— November 15th —

1894: On this day 43-year-old Charles E. Lock, a member of the Newport Corporation, succumbed to typhoid. The day before, his condition had appeared to be improving so his death was a greater shock. A second councillor, Frederick Brading was also suffering an attack but his condition was more reassuring. The *Portsmouth Evening News* announced that Lock's funeral would take place tomorrow, November 16th, and also suggested that the council was 'scared' and had decided to hold its next meeting at Ryde Town Hall instead of Newport. The County Magistrates intended to follow suit and hold their weekly sittings at Ryde. At Cowes the town council met to receive a report from Dr Thompson, the Government Board inspector with regard to the water supply. The report was not of the satisfactory nature that the corporation had anticipated. (*Portsmouth Evening News*, November 15th 1894)

~ November 16th ~

1895: Today's *Hampshire Advertiser* reported events that took place this week in the Westminster County Court. The Honourable William Fitzwilliam was defending two charges brought by Swan and Edgar Limited for failing to pay for his wife's dresses purchased at the store. Although a cheque had been twice presented, it was dishonoured. Brokers were then sent to Sir William's house at East Cliff on the Island and again accepted a cheque from him because 'it would be an insult to people in such a position to doubt it'. Sir William stated that he gave his wife £160 a year for her dresses. Cross-examined, he supposed it was pin money; she paid her maid out of it and did not keep a separate horse and carriage. Prosecuting, Mr Ashton asked: 'Do you move in the best society?' The defendant laughed and when pushed for an answer replied 'I hope I do'. The defendant added that he went to evening parties with his wife and always wished to see her dressed as a lady. It was on his authority that a letter had been written saying that he had paid the amount of his wife's dishonoured cheque into her bank and it would be met on a second presentation. It must have been his fault it was not done. His Honour the judge thought the defendant should have seen that West End tradesmen were not treated like that and added: 'It is not right, you know – even in the best society.' Sir William said that he only wished to show that he was not liable for his wife's dresses. He had come up from Bembridge to show that. This was the fifth case that Mr Ashton had brought against him and a sum of £10 was accepted. (*Hampshire Advertiser*, November 26th 1895)

- NOVEMBER 17TH -

1906: Today the battleship HMS *Ramillies* was reported as still stationary about 4 miles off Sandown Pier. Her anchor was down with 120 fathoms of cable and with a heavy sea running she was unable to recover it. Should a gale arise, her position would be serious. There were eight men on board and the two tugs, *Challenge* and *Vanquisher*, which had been towing her to Swansea had broken adrift but were still in attendance. The *Ramilles* and her class saw service until the introduction of the dreadnoughts. She was one of seven similar ships, including the slightly modified HMS *Hood*. *Ramillies* had seen service with the Mediterranean Fleet until 1903 and in 1906 was part of the naval reserve. In 1911, she was decommissioned and at the time of her sighting at Sandown was being towed to Italy to be scrapped. (*Lichfield Mercury*, November 21st 1906)

~ November 18th ~

1853: 'Testimonial to an unprotected farmer.' A handsome silver Tankard and Salver supplied by Mr Wearn, silversmith, was today presented to Mr Lock late of Rowborough by his brother agriculturalists and friends to mark their opinion of his worth and show their sympathy on his being turned out of a farm, on six months' notice, which he had occupied for nearly forty years. He was approaching his eightieth birthday. The *Telegraph* felt compelled to comment that 'his landlord was a strong Protectionist and opposed to Free Trade as sure to bring ruin on the farmers; but now, having engaged a new steward, the rents are raised on the improvements made by tenants and the law is "either submit to the rise and turn out." Who are now the farmers' friends?' (*Hampshire Telegraph*, November 19th 1853)

~ November 19th ~

1829: Following the arrest of twenty young men in Ryde for 'riotously assembling on the night of November 5th last', today's *Hampshire Chronicle* reported that, having thrown fireworks in the public streets and assaulted the constables, 'through the humanity of the prosecutor they were permitted to plead guilty'. The chairman, addressing the young men, said he was happy the matter had been thus disposed of as it would have been extremely painful for him to be obliged to send such a number of young men to the treadmill for six or seven months. This would have been the case had they been convicted, as he understood there were circumstance of aggravation connected with the charge. They would enter into their recognizances of £20 each to keep the peace towards all his Majesty's subjects, particularly at Ryde, for one year, and severally pay a fine of 40s to the king. He would advise them to be very cautious in their future conduct, for should they again offend then payment of the penalty would be enforced, and in the event of non-compliance a long term of imprisonment would be the consequence. (*Hampshire Chronicle*, November 19th 1829)

— November 20th —

1859: Furner Warren, a Baptist preacher from the Isle of Wight, went to London to hold a service today at the Surrey Music Hall, London's biggest venue for entertainment. The music hall, an ornate cast-iron building on the site of the former Walworth Palace, had seating for an audience of 12,000 and on Sunday mornings, the regular preacher, Charles Spurgeon attracted a congregation of 10,000 to hear his sermons, his own chapel having proved far too small. The *Louth and North Lincolnshire Advertiser* was interested in the brave attempt of Warren to step into Spurgeon's shoes. Their verdict was that although the event had been extensively advertised and a good deal of curiosity was excited to know who and what he was, the enormous hall was not full, and 'it was impossible to avoid contrasting him with the usual occupant of that great auctioneer's rostrum which serves as a pulpit. Mr Warren showed himself wanting in that powerful eloquence which is wont to roll in sonorous periods through the hall, and though he now and then aimed at a semi-dramatic force, he always fell short. Had not this constant comparison, however, forced itself upon the large audience, no one could have denied the earnestness and power of the young preacher.' (*Louth and North Lincolnshire Advertiser*, November 26th 1859)

~ NOVEMBER 21ST ~

1895: After having suffered a stroke, Sir Henry Ponsonby, equerry to Queen Victoria, died today at Osborne Cottage. His funeral was held on the 26th at Whippingham church at 1.30 p.m., his coffin conveyed on a gun carriage pulled by six horses. The coffin, covered by a union flag, was topped by his helmet, sword and epaulettes. Ships in Cowes Roads flew their flags at half mast and the queen, who was at Windsor, was represented by her son the Duke of Connaught. Her daughter Princess Louise and her husband the Marquis of Lorne were also present. A special service was also held at Windsor which the queen attended in person. Apart from family flowers, Queen Victoria's wreath was also placed on the coffin. Ponsonby was buried at Whippingham church, Lady Ponsonby remaining inside during the interment. The queen's frequent quarrels with her nine children often left Ponsonby caught in the crossfire and her later dalliances with John Brown then Abdul Karim tested his diplomacy to the limit.

While the funeral was in progress the house of East Cowes tradesman T.H. Deacon, who was present at the church, was broken into and ransacked. A quantity of watches, gold chains, necklaces and brooches were stolen, valued at £100. Detective Inspector Ayres said that he had the matter in hand. A witness reported that two gentlemen and a lady left Mr Deacon's house at about the time of the funeral and the men had raised their hats. (*London Standard*, November 22nd 1895)

- NOVEMBER 22ND -

1877: On this day Edgar William Tyler Greenshield, Arctic missionary was born in Newport. He grew up in St John's Place near to the church where his parents were devout churchgoers and wished to become a missionary from an early age. Twice refused entry to the Church Missionary Society, he was eventually accepted but postponed his training in order to go to Baffin Island. This started a love affair with the Arctic and during his career as a missionary, Greenshield made ten voyages to Greenland, Blacklead and Baffin Islands. The hazards faced were enormous and his life was frequently in danger. He was shipwrecked on several occasions, ice threatened to crush the ships, and when they were icebound polar bears climbed aboard. In addition, starvation threatened when supplies failed to arrive. Greenshield was in charge of medical supplies and with the aid of medical books he adopted a teach-yourself technique as he tried to treat the local people. The Inuit had their own religious beliefs in keeping with their way of life but Greenshield felt it to be his mission to teach them about Christianity. During his periods of leave he frequently returned to Newport and gave lectures, often dressed in arctic animal skins and displaying Inuit weapons. Leaving the Church Missionary Society, he worked with the Missions to Seamen and travelled to Calcutta. He was briefly a curate at St John's church in Newport and, having married, he ended his days in Redcar. (*Biography of Edgar Greenshield*, privately published by John Matthews, Isle of Wight)

NOVEMBER 23RD

1861: When the Revd Dunbar Isador Heath was presented to the parish of Brading, there was little reason to think that the appointment would end badly. His first act was to personally pay for a new vicarage, the existing building being so unsanitary as to have earned the epithet Kill Parson House. The reverend was known to be rather shy and sensitive but after his arrival he settled into the parish, married and had two sons. As time passed, however, Heath, who was an expert in Egyptology, began to preach and publish more and more controversial sermons until in 1852 the point arrived when he was virtually accused of heresy and steps were taken to deprive him of his living. He did not go quietly. On learning of the forthcoming trial the *North London News* noted that the fact he had been asked to leave did not come as any surprise. In their words, 'we may expect hair splitting, niceties of argument, quips and cranks ecclesiastical, subtleties of legal quibbling and judicial distinction'. It took until 1862 before he was ousted. (*North London News*, November 23rd 1861)

~ November 24th ~

1900: The *Isle of Wight Observer* today reported the following information about the queen's servant Abdul Karim:

> The Queen's Munshi and Indian Secretary has rejoined the Court at Windsor Castle after an absence of about a year, which he spent in the East. The Munshi has Royal cottages both at Windsor and at Balmoral for the accommodation of his wife and her Indian servants, and it is understood that during the winter residence of the court in the Isle of Wight a house will be provided for them in the park at Osborne. The Munshi has the management of the shooting at Osborne, where, however, pheasants are not now preserved on nearly so large a scale as formerly, and he also has charge of the Queen's private drives and walks at and around Balmoral, and he alone is authorised to grant admission to strangers who desire to visit any of the sights in the royal domain.

Perhaps it is not surprising that he engendered so much resentment. (*Isle of Wight Observer*, November 24th 1900)

— NOVEMBER 25TH —

1886: Today's *Huddersfield Chronicle* was pleased to publish a letter from William Patchell, a gunner serving at Golden Hill Fort in praise of Warner's Safe Cure. He informed the readers that:

> Before I began to take Warner's Safe Cure, I suffered from a pain on the right side of the stomach, which at night would get worse, extending round the back, making the parts very tender. I had also shooting pains up the right shoulder, being very sick and feverish, and would have to go to bed, the next day I would be just as bad again. I greatly suffered from constipation and a constant noise in my ears. Since taking Warner's Safe Cure, I have been relieved of all this, and am now able to go about my work without pain, the entire day.

This, along with other letters from grateful customers was declared Indisputable Evidence of the efficacy of the pills. (*Huddersfield Chronicle*, November 25th 1886)

– November 26th –

1898: With six columns of newspaper coverage, the *County Press* today reported a 'Disastrous Wreck at the Needles' that had occurred two days earlier. In a force-eight gale, a three-masted wooden-built schooner *Ernst*, bound from Liverpool to Danzig, ran aground on the infamous ledge some 3 miles distant from Totland. The lifeboat *Charles Luckombe* was immediately launched but in the furious storm it could not approach the stricken ship. A message was sent to call for a tug and Mr Marfleet of the Supply Stores called the Southampton police 'with his own instrument'. Meanwhile, the *Charles Luckombe* stood by as near to the *Ernst* as possible, waiting for the tug – that did not come. At about six o'clock the *Ernst* foundered and they heard the cry of the poor fellows struggling in the water. They managed to locate the captain, bringing him aboard, followed by the mate and one other crewmember. These they took to the Alum Bay hotel where they were provided with dry clothes, food and a bed. A report then reached the lifeboat men that a raft had been seen in the area with several people on board. They immediately went in search but after 5 hours had found nothing and it was concluded that the watcher had seen a piece of driftwood. The following morning, five men were picked up on a raft just off Christchurch Point. They had been adrift for 12 hours. The *Ernst* had been carrying a cargo of 420 tons of salt. (*County Press*, November 26th 1898)

NOVEMBER 27TH

1959: The Isle of Wight awoke to the news that Albert Ketèlbey, once rated as the most celebrated composer of the age, had died yesterday at his home of Rookstone on Egypt Hill at Cowes. He was 84 years old. Born in Birmingham, as a student he beat Gustav Holst for a musical scholarship. Ketèlbey's musical talents saw him become musical director of the Vaudeville Theatre, his work being admired by, among others, Edward Elgar. Such was the popularity of his work that when King George V arrived late for a concert, he asked him to play one of his favourite compositions again as the king had missed it. Among his many familiar works were *In a Monastery Garden*, *Bells Across the Meadow* and *In a Persian Market* and 1 million copies of sheet music for *In a Monastery Garden* was sold in 1926. His music was frequently used as an accompaniment to silent films. Albert Ketèlbey had twice married but had no children. His funeral was at Golders Green Crematorium. (www.albertketelbey.org.uk)

~ NOVEMBER 28TH ~

1840: It was announced on the Island that 'Our much loved Queen, by the recommendation of her Medical Gentleman, has selected from our Town the infant Princess's Wet Nurse, in the person of Mrs Ratsey, wife of Mr Restall Ratsey of the firm Ratsey and Sons, merchants and ship owners of this Town. A special Messenger arrived from Buckingham Palace on Saturday morning and conveyed her and her infant, then at the breast, to Southampton and thence to London, where on arrival she had the honour of succouring the Offspring of Her Majesty.' The infant in question was the queen's first child, Princess Victoria, born November 21st 1840. In adulthood she married the Emperor Frederic of Germany and her first child was Kaiser Wilhelm II. The queen was later to name a cow at Barton Farm 'Alice' after her second daughter, who broke with tradition and decided to breastfeed her own children. (*The Era*, December 6th 1840)

~ November 29th ~

1830: Today's *Hampshire Chronicle* reported on the disturbing events at the House of Industry in Parkhurst Forest and that the paupers cultivating the land were in a 'state of revolt and intended to march in a body to the town, for the purpose of demanding an increase of pay. Henry Sewell, Esq, of the Firm of Sewell, Hearn, and Sewell, mounted his horse with the praiseworthy intention of meeting the men, but unfortunately, in hastily turning the corner of the street, by the Free Grammar School, the horse fell, and was very much injured, and Mr Sewell was so severely bruised as to prevent his proceeding.' Fortunately two other men took up the challenge and on meeting the paupers they promised to increase their wages. At the same time, the magistrates called a meeting at the town hall and swore in 100 respectable tradesmen as special constables. A general meeting of the inhabitants was also called to consider 'the best means to effectually check the spirit of insubordination which so extensively prevails; and as large rewards are offered for the discovery of ill disposed persons, it is hoped that further mischief and outrage will be prevented'. (*Hampshire Chronicle*, November 29th 1830)

— November 30th —

1901: At the invitation of Mr H.C. Damant of Cowes, representatives of the Island cricket clubs were called together to discuss forming an Isle of Wight Cricket Club. The proposal met with hearty approval and a subcommittee was appointed to draft the rules, fix the subscriptions, arrange fixtures and any other business prior to calling a public meeting to obtain approval. As time progressed, the Isle of Wight Cricket Ground was settled at Newport. An annual general meeting on February 14th 1903 held at Warburton's Hotel, Newport reported on some recommended changes to the running of the club. There was currently a deficiency of £4 4s and outstanding subscriptions of £5 needed to be got in. It was recommended that no professionals be engaged by the club, although they could be called upon to play in some matches, and a collector of subscriptions should be appointed to received 5 per cent of the monies raised. Some fixtures had already been arranged for the coming season with the Hampshire Hogs and the Trojans. (*Portsmouth Evening News*, November 30th 1901)

− December 1st −

1829: On December 1st of this year:

> A widow woman named Williams, between 80 and 90 years of age
> who possesses some property and resides alone in Adgestone, was
> aroused from sleep, and observed a man standing by the bedside,
> with a lantern in his hand. Being of a courageous disposition she
> immediately sprang from the bed and aimed a blow at the intruder
> with a sword that lay near, but the villain made his escape through the
> window against which a ladder had been placed to effect an entrance.
> Looking out to give alarm she perceived two other men at the foot of
> the ladder, who retreated precipitately and still remain undiscovered.

The *Hampshire Chronicle* of December 7th listed other crimes that
had happened during the course of the week, including a break in
at Gotten Farm, the theft of money at a butcher's shop in Newport
and a quantity of timber stolen at Brixton. Four boys had been
apprehended for the theft at the butcher's shop. The culprits had
had the audacity to write the amount of money taken on the
shop's shutters. (*Hampshire Chronicle*, December 7th 1829)

⁓ December 2nd ⁓

1793: Today's *Hampshire Chronicle* reported that on November 30th the gravediggers excavating a burial place in St Thomas's church at Newport Isle of Wight unearthed another coffin. It contained the remains of Princess Elizabeth, the 15-year-old second daughter of King Charles I who, having died at Carisbrooke Castle on September 8th 1650, had been buried in a lead coffin.

Two weeks before her death, Elizabeth and her younger brother Henry had been moved to Carisbrooke Castle, an insensitive choice as it was their father's last refuge/prison before being he was whisked to London for trial and execution. Elizabeth's death was embarrassing to her carers and she was discreetly buried in St Thomas's church and promptly forgotten. The rediscovered remains were reburied in a vault.

This was not the end of the story, however, for in 1854, as the church was being rebuilt, the princess's coffin was removed and locked in a shed to await completion of the work. During this time her body was kidnapped and local surgeon E.P. Wilkins took it upon himself to carry out a port-mortem on the remains. He described the princess as showing marked signs of the condition rickets, with deformities of the spine and the front of the skull. The coffin was returned supposedly intact and Queen Victoria arranged for her reburial and commissioned a romantic likeness carved in marble by her favourite sculptor, Carlo Marochetti. (*Hampshire Chronicle*, December 2nd 1793)

~ DECEMBER 3RD ~

1629: During the seventeenth century, Sir John Oglander of Nunwell House at Brading kept a diary recording both important events and personal thoughts about the people around him. On the death of Sir John Meux of Kingston, he observed: 'Sir John Meux departed this life; he wase the veriest clown tbat evor the Isle of Wight bredd. As he wase destitute of learninge, soe of humanitie and civillitie. Although his clownish humour, a good honest man … more of his lyfe I cannot wryght, being of no great worth …' The Meux family was long established on the Isle of Wight and Sir John Meux, followed by his sons, owned the manor of Kingston, sandwiched between Chale and Shorwell. (*Sir John Oglander's Memoirs*, December 3rd 1629)

– DECEMBER 4TH –

1768: A letter from Plymouth dated December 4th conveyed the following news to the press:

> On Friday [4th] morning between 3 and 4 o'clock, it blew a hurricane, the wind at SE. The storm was attended with the heaviest fall of hail that has been known for many years, accompanied by large claps of thunder and very intense lightning. We hear the same morning, a French vessel was lost on the back of the Wight and every soul perished; the particulars of this accident we have not yet learned. The ships are yet detained at Spithead and the Motherbank by contrary winds. On board His Majesty's ship Dorsetshire, there are with the 25th Regiment and the ship's company upward of 1400 persons, and we learn that they begin to contract sickness by so long confinement.

(*Kentish Gazette*, December 7th 1768)

— December 5th —

1914: As the first casualties of the First World War returned home, they were nursed in various large houses across the Island. Overseen by local committees under the auspices of the Red Cross, much was left to the voluntary sector to provide accommodation, nurses and to raise funds. The best intentions often went awry. Mrs Rachel Vernon Harcourt of St Clare at Puckpool wrote to John Oglander bemoaning the 'curt rebuffs' received following some suggestions she had put forward to the committee:

> I am told that if an offer is made to take them for a drive, the offer is refused on the grounds that they might misconduct themselves! Surely a few drives would freshen the invalids up? My daughter Isabel, who has a genius for managing men and boys, would like much to arrange for some of the friends to bring (in their cars) half a dozen or a dozen men, to this place, give them a time in the garden, tea in the racquet court (which can be heated) or perhaps a little music and a recitation …

Mrs Harcourt was particularly miffed that patients at Northwood House were receiving these treats while those at Hazelwood in Ryde were being denied. Among other complaints was the failure of promised funds to materialise. (Oglander Correspondence, Isle of Wight Public Record Office)

~ December 6th ~

1830: As agricultural unrest flared up across the south, resulting in the transportation of the Tolpuddle Martyrs of Dorset, so the Island had its own riots. Today's *Hampshire Chronicle* reported how:

> The island has been for some days in a state of excitement, rather from the apprehension of riots amongst the labouring classes, than from any overt acts of violence. Threatening letters have been received by several farmers, in consequences of which thrashing machines have been generally disused. Symptoms of discontent made their appearance during the last week amongst the paupers employed on the Forest Farm, and at one time an actual strike took place, and they left their work for the purpose of visiting some neighbouring farmers. They, however, took wit in their anger, and after a little confusion returned to their work. The statement that they were pacified by a promised advance of wages is erroneous. No concession has taken place to any violent demands, but an addition to their wages was made last week by the Guardians of the Poor, in consequence of an advance in the price of bread. A hay rick belonging to Mr Tucker (of Newport) was set fire to on Saturday and totally destroyed ... A hay stack, belonging to the very Rev the Dean of Ely, at Freshwater, and a thrashing machine, belonging to Mr Rich. Harvey at Rookley were wilfully destroyed by fire on Sunday night, and an attempt was made, without success, the same night, to set fire to a corn stack at Gatehouse Farm. It is not doubted that the guilty parties will be brought to justice.

(*Hampshire Chronicle*, December 6th 1830)

DECEMBER 7TH

1859: Overnight, in a raging storm, two ships came to grief along the Brook coast with the loss of at least twelve lives. In a force-eight gale, the *Mirabita*, a small Maltese sailing barque carrying a cargo of oats and en route from Marseilles to London, was blown into Grange Chine. From the shore, local men could hear the screaming but they could do nothing to help. Next morning the bodies of the captain, 54-year-old Salvatori Miribita, Carlo, Vincenzo, Luigi, James, Antonio and Andrea were picked up. Further along the coast the body of Francisco Tanli was discovered. He turned out to be the captain's brother-in-law.

That same night, the *Sentinel* with a cargo of slate also came to grief. After two attempts the lifeboat managed to reach four seamen, but bodies continued to wash ashore over the ensuing days and were buried in Brighstone churchyard. The incident determined the local vicar, Revd John Pellew Gaze to campaign for lifeboats but it was ten years before the first lifeboat appeared. She was appropriately named the *Rescue*. Exactly a year after the shipwreck, the Mirabita's crew were disinterred and shipped home to be buried in Malta. (Jan Toms, 'A Humble Sailing Ship Lost in a Storm', www.suite101.com)

— December 8th —

1898: The *Pall Mall Gazette* today revealed more facts relating to the burial of Princess Elizabeth Stuart in 1650. The last time the princess and her brother Henry saw their father King Charles I, he gave Elizabeth a Bible, took young Henry on his knee and announced 'Sweetheart, now they will cut off thy father's head.' It was with these memories that the two children were moved to Carisbrooke Castle. Following the removal of her coffin and subsequent kidnap during the rebuilding of the church, it was supposedly returned intact for reburial, but William Ledicott, owner of the Old Curiosity Shop in Crocker Street, managed to obtain a piece of bone and a lock of the princess's hair. He displayed them in his shop window to the chagrin of Queen Victoria. Following threats from Whitehall, Ledicott reluctantly removed the display and returned it to the queen's daughter and island governess, Princess Beatrice, for burial with the rest of Elizabeth's remains. After Elizabeth's death in 1650, Prince Henry remained on the Island for two years. He died aged 21. (*Pall Mall Gazette*, December 8th 1898)

DECEMBER 9TH

1904: Under the heading 'Sea Encroachments', today's *Lichfield Mercury* reported on grave anxieties felt by residents of Freshwater on the Isle of Wight on account of the serious encroachment made by the sea:

> The tides have been unusually high and strong winds have carried in huge waves, causing much damage to the esplanade. An enormous slab of concrete has been carried away from the sea-wall causing some anxiety as to the security of the foundations of various properties. On Friday last the committee of the Isle of Wight Rural Council visited the spot and it is feared that unless prompt steps are taken the sea may break through the low lands and thus create two islands.

(*Lichfield Mercury*, December 9th 1904)

December 10th

1943: The *Catholic Herald* today reported the death of Revd Dom Jacques Kerrsemakers, a Dutch priest who had been serving at Quarr Abbey for some years before the war. Having returned to his original abbey of St Paul's at Oosterhout in Holland, he was arrested by the Gestapo as he was having breakfast. For some months he was held in a concentration camp and eventually put on trial and found guilty. The original report suggested that he had merely said something not to the Nazis' liking, but the charge against him seems to have been espionage and helping the Jews; he was an alleged leader of a local resistance group. Following his trial, Dom Kerrsemakers was executed, allegedly by being shot. He was born in December 1896, making him in his late 40s. While he was at Quarr Abbey he was the Master of Ceremonies and during that time he translated several works by Abbot Vonier of Buckfast Abbey into Dutch. His war grave is at St Paul's Abbey and bears his name, date of birth and the date of his shooting: 'May 7 1943 at the Fortress de Bilt, used as a site of execution. Here, 140 Dutch people were killed.' (*Catholic Herald*, December 10th 1943)

― DECEMBER 11TH ―

1866: A community of nuns arrived today to take possession of the Dominican Priory built by the Countess of Clare at Carisbrooke. The nuns, eighteen in number, had arrived from Whalley in Lancashire and theirs was a closed community. Among their numbers was a nun aged 84 and a second, described as 'aged and blind'. The report contained the rather ambiguous statement that 'At Cowes the nuns were mobbed owing to some defective police arrangements.' The founder of the priory, Elizabeth Julia Georgina, Countess of Clare, had already donated a church and a school to Ryde where she took up residence in Brigstocke Terrace. She also had a suite of rooms for her use in the priory. On her death, on April 30th 1879, the countess lay in state at her home before a huge funeral procession to Mountjoy Cemetery. Here, nuns from the priory chanted *De Profundis* at the graveside. A grave was reserved next to her for her priest, and on the northern side her long-term companion Miss Charlotte Elliot, who had died in 1861, was separated from her only by a glass panel. (*Dublin Evening Mail*, December 11th 1866; *Hampshire Chronicle*, December 15th 1866)

— December 12th —

1917: Today Florence Beatrice Astbury, matron second class, received a Red Cross decoration from King George V. Astbury was working at Afton Lodge Auxiliary Hospital in Freshwater as part of the Southern Command set up by the Red Cross in response to the need for medical aid for the returning soldiers. On the Island, the main military hospitals were at Parkhurst (eighty-one beds), Golden Hill (twenty-one beds) and Sandown Fort (twelve beds). They were augmented by eight other buildings: Afton Lodge, Brooke Hill House, Northwood House, Gatcombe House, Hazlewood (at Ryde), Quarr Abbey, the Castle (Ryde) and Underwath (Ventnor). Brigadier the Right Hon. J.E.B. Seely presented Book Hill as a convalescent house for the Royal Flying Corps. He paid most of the costs himself while other locations were busily fundraising to cover the expenses. A medal was later presented to Miss Isabel Mary Watson, nurse at Afton Lodge. ('Guidelines for Awarding the Decoration', *Aberdeen Journal*, November 17th 1915)

— December 13th —

1891: Newport boys James Riley and William Shepherd were charged under the Town Police Clauses Act with playing football in South Street on the afternoon of Sunday 13th December. Police Constable Attrill stated that the two defendants were playing with a lot of other boys and when approached, Shepherd said that they didn't have a football, it was only a penny ball. The other players seem to have been dismissed but James and William were each fined 1s or one day in prison. In a similar incident a few days later, 'Troublesome Juvenile Footballers' William White and Albert Downer were charged with playing football on Hunny Hill 'to the annoyance and obstruction of the public'. The boys were said to have been kicking the ball to each other, one at the bottom and other further up Hunny Hill. The lads declared that they had merely been throwing the ball to a younger child but Police Constable Jeremiah Murphy had previously cautioned White and his mother about it. As a result, White was fined 1s without costs and Downer cautioned then dismissed. (*Isle of Wight Observer*, January 9th 1862)

— DECEMBER 14TH —

1878: Today, Queen Victoria's second daughter Princess Alice died of diphtheria. Her death occurred on the seventeenth anniversary of her father's demise, since which the queen had largely remained at Osborne in mourning. In the words of the *Pall Mall Gazette*:

> We must say that Princess Alice is dead, the news must be told: but except to recall the time when she, seventeen years ago, nursed her dying father with the skill of a woman as well as the tenderness of a child … and when she was seen again, the most steady and untiring nurse at the bedside of her brother, the Prince of Wales, we shall say no more. None of the Queen's children held a higher affection in the place of the country than the lady whose death we now deplore … [and] millions of truly grieving people give their sincerest sympathies to the grieving mother, their Queen.

Alice had married only a few months after her father's death and the queen insisted that the ceremony should be held in the dining room at Osborne House, where she sat and sobbed throughout the occasion beneath the portrait of her dead husband. Alice and her new husband, Prince Louis of Hesse, escaped the gloom to spend a brief honeymoon at St Claire at Ryde. When the queen called on them Alice allegedly tried not to look too happy. (*Pall Mall Gazette*, December 14th 1878)

~ December 15th ~

1840: Perhaps the Island's most notorious daughter died on this day. Sophie Dawes was born at St Helens, the child of smuggler Richard 'Dickie' Dawes. Her mother was driven to go with her brood into the workhouse and Sophie was found work as a domestic. She soon escaped to London and came to the notice of French émigré Louis Henry, Prince of Conde. Pursuing him to France, with a mixture of threats and bribery she took charge of his household in the process making herself extremely rich. When she had taken everything that she could, she possibly murdered him. Her desire to enter French society, however, failed and she eventually returned to England, bearing the title Baronne de Feucheres, having conned a French army officer into marrying her. Sophie set herself up in a house in Hampshire and a second property in London and converted to Catholicism, giving much of her money to charity. Here she died from a heart attack. (Marjorie Bowen, *The Scandal of Sophie Dawes*, John Lane, 1934)

~ DECEMBER 16TH ~

1878: The *Aldershot Military Gazette* today carried a report, headed 'Fired on by a Revenue Cutter':

> An inquest has been opened at Haslar Hospital on the body of George Grainger, one of the crew of a fishing lugger called The Dewdrop, who was shot in July last at the back of the Isle of Wight by the revenue men employed on the cutter Spy. The mate of the vessel alleged that he called upon the cutter to heave to and she refused and that shots were fired. Grainger received a wound in the back and was removed to Haslar Hospital where he died. The Times of London also reported the case in which Captain Johns, skipper of the Dewdrop said that they were 7 miles NW by N off the Needles when they saw a vessel that looked like a pilot's cutter. Suddenly Grainger, who was bending forward, toppled to the ground. Moments later 3 shots were fired. The captain of the Spy asserted that the Dewdrop had ignored instructions to stop. Johns insisted that no such warning had been given. The Dewdrop was held until a replacement could be found for the wounded man.

(*Aldershot Military Gazette*, December 16th 1878)

— December 17th —

1940: After undergoing a refit, the destroyer *Acheron*, was sent for speed trials off St Catherine's Point. Aboard was a crew of 6 officers, 184 ratings and 25 dockyard workers charged with monitoring the engine's performance. In the early morning of the 17th, as the *Acheron* was turning, a massive explosion broke her in two. The forward bow sank immediately and the stern remained afloat only for a short while. Those surviving the blast, including fifteen wounded men, managed to cling to Carley floats but by the time they were discovered the following morning, only sixty had survived the cold. The wreck still lies on the seabed, at some 48 metres' depth. (*Shipwreck Index of the British Isles*, Lloyds Register)

~ DECEMBER 18TH ~

1794: Today the *Caledonian Mercury* carried the unhappy news of a death occurring at Newport on the 10th:

> Early this morning the body of a female was discovered in a water-course which leads out of the forest and passes through some meadows down to the Medina River. A great number of people soon assembled at the spot; but no one could form any idea who the person was, till a poor woman, not half a mile distant, was sent for, who, in all the agonies of grief, soon recognised her own daughter, a fine handsome young woman, about 18 years of age! The mother was almost frantic at the sight of the lifeless remains of her dear child, who, on the Friday, she accompanied to Cowes, to see her safe on board the packet to Portsmouth, in order to obtain of her father, who works there, a few shillings to defray the rent &etc. She accomplished this, and the next day returned to the island, and on her way home re-crossed the forest; when, from the darkness of the night, occasioned by the excessive heavy rains, which had deluged the levels of the forest, and ran in torrents to the river from every quarter, it is supposed, she mistook her way, or was unexpectedly borne down by the current, and perished. No mark of violence appeared on her body, and the money she had received was, with other things, found in her pockets. The jury brought it in accidental death.

(*Caledonian Mercury*, December 18th 1794)

— December 19th —

1824: On this day the pilot vessel *Favorite*, belonging to Nettlestone and carrying fifteen passengers from the East India ship *Cambridge*, ran aground in fog near Brook and shortly afterwards went to pieces. Happily a small boat got alongside and the ladies were immediately put ashore while the crew and passengers made every possible exertion to get the vessel off. Unfortunately their efforts failed, the vessel bilged and filled with water. For upwards of an hour, Mr Reynell the purser, Captains Prissick, Bret and Anthony, and Lieut Warlow preserved themselves by clinging to the mast and boom, when at length boats arrived from the shore and rescued them. They were hospitably received at the house of M. Howe who generously supplied them with every comfort. Four boxes, containing about 1,700 packets and letters, were got on shore – and fisherman have since picked up two other boxes, containing despatches for the company. Some boxes and luggage were washed ashore which were broken open, and their contents carried off by a few heartless marauders. (*Hampshire Chronicle*, December 27th 1824)

~ DECEMBER 20TH ~

1884: *The Penny Illustrated Paper* today featured an article on a local hero, Brake the Collecting Dog. When the dog had been accused of biting a child, in spite of widespread disbelief, his owner handed him over to be destroyed. Brake was taken instead by a furniture dealer to the Isle of Wight, where he quickly discovered that the dog was both docile and intelligent. The dealer, who had premises in both Ryde and Portsmouth, decided to provide Brake with a collar and collecting box and persuaded his wife to travel on the steamboat plying between the ports in order to collect money for charity. The aim was to support various charities including widows, children, the bereaved and disabled who had worked for the Railway Company. Money was also to be distributed to injured and sick seamen, the Shipwrecked Mariners' Society, The Isle of Wight Infirmary and Portsmouth Hospital. In thirty-one weeks ending in July 1883, Brake raised £31 7s 6d. He was photographed for posterity by F. Broderick Junior at Ryde. (*The Penny Illustrated Paper*, December 20th 1884)

~ December 21st ~

1886: In November the steamer *Cormorant* had left New Orleans carrying a cargo of 1,200 tons of cotton. She had on board a crew of thirty-three and no passengers. All went well until December 21st when she was just off the Isle of Wight and travelling in thick fog. When it cleared the captain found that they were just 30 yards from the shore and although the engines were immediately reversed full speed astern the steamer was grounded at Whale Chine. Happily the crew was saved and the cargo salvaged, but the *Cormorant* was a loss. At an enquiry questions were asked as to whether sufficient care had been taken to verify their position. The captain had not taken soundings believing that they were at a sufficient distance from the land. He reported that the ship's compass had been adjusted about a year previously. A bearing had been taken by the North Star and showed them to be 11 degrees at the time of the stranding. In delivering his judgement the Wreck Commissioner said that the responsibility for the accident rested solely with the master, James Lowe. He had had a long and meritorious service but they could not shut their eyes to his reckless conduct on this occasion. The verdict: to lose his licence for six months, a mate's certificate being granted in the meantime. (*Isle of Wight Observer*, January 22nd 1887)

~ DECEMBER 22ND ~

1838: Today's *Hampshire Telegraph* reported how, having taken lunch with Joseph Jolliffe Esq. at Bowcombe last Monday, the Crockford Harriers 'were informed by him that a fine hare had taken up her quarters under one of the beehives in the garden'. Having unearthed the hare, the gathering set off in pursuit during which chase Mr John Harvey of Marvel Lane 'took one of the finest leaps ever witnessed in the Island ... over a heather hedge on a high bank at which none of the other horses would show'. After about half an hour, the 'honourable gentlemen' who had taken a considerable circuit including Bowcombe Down were able to witness the kill. Fortunately for these 'honourable gentlemen', being winter, the bees did not take exception to having their beehive being disturbed or the outcome might have been different.

According to Sir John Oglander, in order to increase the number of hares available to kill, in 1574 the Island's Governor Sir Edward Horsey approached his mainland friends announcing that 'whosoever should bring in a live hare should have a lamb for him' thus increasing the number to be pursued. Harvey's Crockford Harriers was founded in 1820 making a third pack on the Island. (*Hampshire Telegraph*, December 22nd 1838)

– December 23rd –

1883: An extraordinary scene took place at St Catherine's church at Ventnor this Sunday evening, when the vicar in charge, the Revd Willan, demanded the keys to the vestry and tried to lock the door to prevent more members of the congregation from entering. He then went to the vestry, gesticulating in an extraordinary manner and accused the curate, the Revd James Jones of having sold his soul for thirty pieces of silver for the sake of popularity. The incident arose because the Revd Jones, who had been appointed to a curacy in Birmingham, was leaving Ventnor and a very large number of people had turned out to hear his last sermon; Revd Willan was apparently driven by jealousy. Revd Jones left the church as did most of the congregation and Revd Willan then announced that because he had not prepared a sermon there would not be one. Revd Jones had promised to lead off the psalms but in his absence, Mr Petherick the organist started but Revd Willan immediately shouted down the church 'Shut up Petherick!' When the vicar left the church he was greeted by groans and hisses by the congregation who followed him to the vicarage. He was escorted by three policemen. Reaching the safety of his garden he turned and shouted 'such is religion' to which the congregation responded 'such is hypocrisy'. The matter was brought to the notice of the Bishop of Winchester. (*Portsmouth Evening News*, December 24th 1883)

~ December 24th ~

1871: The *London Daily News* reported that ten of the crew of the ship *Iron Duke*, out of Liverpool, were charged before the county magistrates on Christmas Eve with unlawfully refusing to work the ship which had been chartered by government to carry emigrants from London to Australia. The *Iron Duke* had had to contend with headwinds from the time she was cast off by the tug, and the sea washed away one of the hatchways. When off Portland it was found necessary to run to the Motherbank for repairs and, when ordered to get ready for sea, the prisoners had refused to work, pleading that the ship was unseaworthy and alleging that at one time there was so much water on the deck that for 2 hours they were compelled to remain in the rigging to avoid drowning. The bench, after a long hearing, decided that the plea was not sustained, and recommended the men to return to work. They declined, remarking they would prefer to go to prison, and were accordingly removed in custody. (*London Daily News*, December 25th 1871)

~ December 25th ~

1654: The romance between Dorothy Osborne and William Temple was of Romeo and Juliet proportions. Dorothy's father was the Royalist lieutenant governor of Guernsey and two of her brothers died in the Civil War. Travelling in 1648 with a younger brother to St Malo, she called at Carisbrooke Castle and there met William Temple, a cousin to the castle's Parliamentarian Governor Robert Hammond. There was an instant and mutual attraction between them. Dorothy's father objected to the match both on the grounds of Temple's politics and also because he wanted a more lucrative groom for his daughter. Defying her father, Dorothy kept up a secret correspondence with William, the pair meeting briefly only once. In 1654, Dorothy suffered smallpox and nearly died but survived, although badly scarred. Temple finally married her on Christmas Day. In her letter of May 25th 1654, she wrote:

> This world is composed of nothing but contrarities [*sic*] and sudden accidents, only the proportions are not at all equal; for to a great measure of trouble it allows so small a quantity of joy that one may see 'tis merely intended to keep us alive withal ... I took a coach and went to see whether there was ever a letter for me, and was this once lucky to find one ...With reference to her brother with whom Temple was on bad terms, she wrote ... you will at the same time remember his sister loves you passionately and nobly ... and could love you as much a beggar as she could do a prince.

In the end, their mutual constancy paid off. (Letters of Dorothy Osborne)

— December 26th —

1951: The good folk of Seaview had long felt that they were 'deprived of the advantage possessed by other Watering Places of a pier for Promenading'. As a result, the Sea View Pier Committee, with a capital of £6,000 raised in £10 shares, set out to rectify the situation. The intention was to attract steamers bringing day visitors and also those planning to stay longer. The design was drawn up by local man Francis Caws who ultimately took charge of the project when the first contractors failed to complete the work on time. They had reason to be pleased with themselves for the new structure was exceptional, being one of only two in the country to be a suspension pier, the other one being at Brighton. The pier opened on June 11th 1881 and to the company's delight, the Prince and Princess of Wales patronised it by landing there.

By 1901 it had been widened and lengthened. Business was not quite as brisk as hoped for, however, depending on the whims of the steamer companies as to when and if they decided to call. As a result, the company decided to purchase its own vessel. Unhappily, the service was only in operation for a few months before the pier was closed by war. Although it reopened after the conflict it was dogged by expensive repairs and over the next two decades it continued to decline until in 1939 it was once more out of bounds to the public. After the war it was sold and although the new owner intended to repair it, he came to the conclusion that it was just too costly and decided to knock it down. What then seemed like a miracle occurred. Because of its rare design, it was declared a listed building, the only pier to be so designated. Plans were in hand to renovate it when, on Boxing Day 1951, a storm of violent proportions virtually destroyed the entire structure overnight. The beautiful Seaview Pier was no more. (*Piers of the Isle of Wight*, Marian Lane)

— December 27th —

1932: The funeral was held today at Carisbrooke, Isle of Wight of Captain Joseph Woodhouse of the Church Army who was assistant chaplain at Parkhurst Convict Prison for twenty years. He died suddenly in his office at the prison on Friday 23rd. The floral tributes included a wreath from the prisoners at Parkhurst bearing the inscription: 'With respect and affection from the inmates of His Majesty's Prison, Parkhurst. For all of us he did his best, we hope in heaven he'll find sweet rest.' The governor acceded to the prisoners' request that they might be allowed to send the wreath and it consisted of one chrysanthemum and eight carnations. The card was written by one of the inmates. (*Western Morning News*, December 28th 1932)

~ December 28th ~

1892: Whilst out with a hunting party at Osborne, Prince Christian of Scheswig Holstein was accidentally shot in the eye which, according to the *County Press*, evoked universal sympathy for him as well as for the royal family generally, whose Christmas rejoicings were clouded. In 1846, Prince Christian had married Helena, the third daughter of Queen Victoria. The marriage had been permitted only if the couple agreed to reside in England and according to the *County Press* 'After 26 years, Prince Christian has so identified himself with English life that he is now regarded as an Englishman.' The stray bullet penetrated his eye destroying the sight and the following morning Mr George Lawson FRCS, assisted by the queen's personal physician Dr Reid, carried out an operation to remove it. While the operation was underway, Queen Victoria, the Duke and Duchess of Connaught (Queen Victoria's son Arthur and his wife) the Prince and Princess of Battenberg (the queen's youngest daughter Beatrice and her husband) plus other members of the royal household, attended divine service in the queen's private chapel at Osborne. Prince Christian recovered from the operation, living until 1917. (*Isle of Wight Observer*, January 2nd 1893)

~ December 29th ~

1840: The *Hampshire Telegraph* printed a letter from a correspondent dated December 29th with the message 'don't panic':

> The landslip near Mr B. Wild's hotel increased so on Friday as to render it necessary to stop carriages from proceeding to Ventnor by new Steephill Shoot. The chasm in that part is not above a foot in width but it appears to be very deep. Great fears are entertained for the inn and the houses in the immediate neighbourhood, which the passage of heavy carriages so near, are likely to heighten … This must not be construed as to the village of Ventnor being about to take its departure on a sea voyage: it is a mere crack in the cliff occasioned by the heavy rains, and which, in the opinion of many well informed, will extend very little farther; and that of all, it can only affect the two or three houses residing beneath it. We are thus particular to remove any fears from the minds of the numerous strangers residing here for the benefit of their health. There is a similar cleft in the road near Black-chine, and several in other parts. The land has slipped also, we hear, at Cowes; and Oak-Hill House, lately occupied by Lords A Fitzclarence and Delaware, is considered unsafe.

(*Hampshire Telegraph*, January 2nd 1841)

～ December 30th ～

1833: Whilst praising the local nobility and gentlemen of the Isle of Wight for making their usual donations of beef and clothing to the poor, the *Salisbury and Winchester Journal* added a rather sour note, 'we regret to hear that the blankets given in the neighbourhood of Calbourn [*sic*] were purchased in London: not that the small amount of profit which would have been obtained is of any great importance to the respectable drapers of Newport, but purchasing these goods in London is likely to raise a prejudice against the tradesmen of Newport and to materially injure the trade and prosperity of the town.' (*Salisbury and Winchester Journal*, December 30th 1833)

~ December 31st ~

1947: This year ended on a positive note with a report that the Peoples' Dispensary for Sick Animals had awarded a special silver medal to a retriever dog named Laddie for his part in rescuing two young boys adrift off the Island in a dinghy. Laddie belonged to Mr A. Player who lived at Ashlake, Fishbourne, near Ryde. As the two boys were swept out to sea, Laddie jumped in and swam some 50 yards to reach the boat. One of the boys grabbed him by his collar and the dog turned and swam towards the shore, pulling the dinghy with him. The PDSA medal was instituted in 1943 to acknowledge acts of bravery during the war and became known as the animals' Victoria Cross. The largest number of awards went to carrier pigeons. (*Derby Daily Telegraph*, December 31st 1947)